BURNBANKS VILLAGE

JOE McLEOD

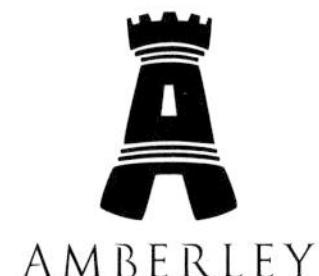

AMBERLEY

First published 2021

Amberley Publishing
The Hill, Stroud
Gloucestershire, GL5 4EP

www.amberley-books.com

British Library Cataloguing in Publication Data.

A catalogue record for this book is available from the British Library.

ISBN 978 1 3981 1091 5 (print)
ISBN 978 1 3981 1092 2 (ebook)

Typesetting by SJmagic DESIGN SERVICES, India.
Printed in the UK.

Contents

Introduction

I live in Burnbanks Village, Aberdeenshire, Scotland. It is a small hamlet situated near the North Sea coast, 4 miles south of Aberdeen. The village has been here for over 200 years and there are currently twenty-two houses in a small circle.

From the 1960s to the 1980s it lay in various stages of dereliction and abandonment came gradually: elderly residents died, people moved out, families moved on and the houses were not re-let, so from the 1980s onwards it was uninhabited and derelict. A plan by a local builder, Scotia Homes, brought it back to life, rebuilding the shattered ruins.

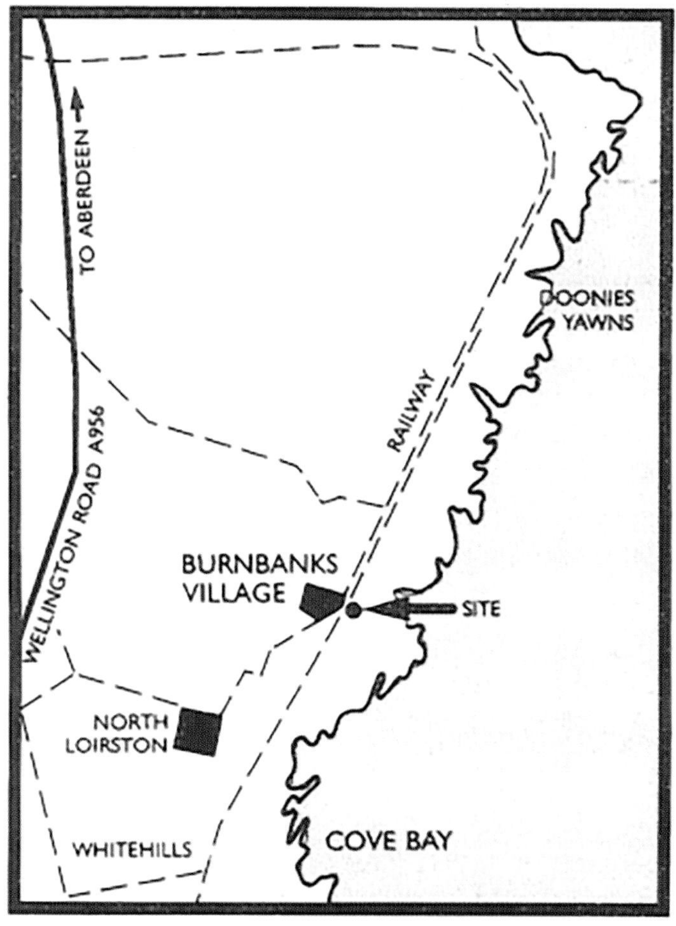

LOCATION PLAN

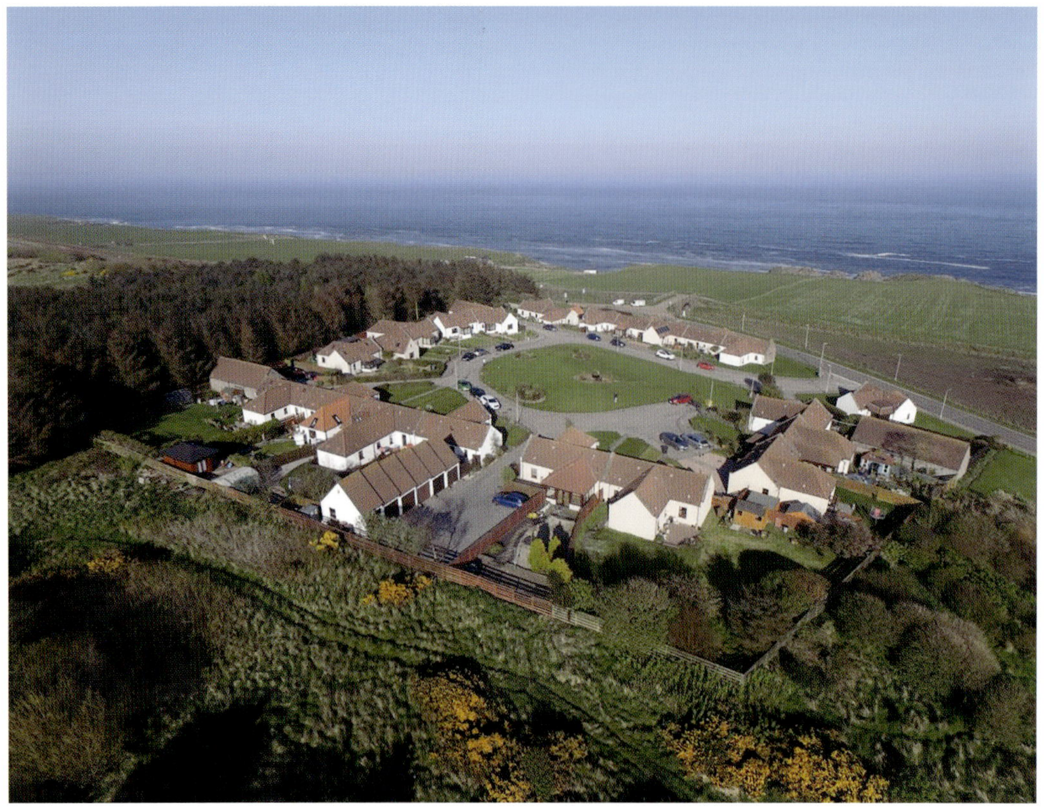

The early history of the village often came up in conversation with my neighbours, so we started trading stories and collecting historical photographs. My first photograph shows the children of the village in 1921. This photograph is discussed in detail in a different chapter. As my research deepened, I was surprised at the amount of times Burnbanks Village appeared in the news. For such a small place, it has a wealth of stories and many are covered in this book.

Hundreds of people have been born, lived and died in our small area and the stories happened right here, not in some remote location around the world. Stories about the hard day-to-day struggles in the old village, shipwrecks, sudden and accidental deaths, an alarming amount of suicides, a heartbreaking incidence of cholera, casualties of war. Births, marriages and deaths. Villainy, thefts, assaults, fights and bigamy. More stories and photographs were collected and then I had an article printed in the local paper, Aberdeen's *Evening Express*, in 2011.

My telephone was ringing red hot for a few days with ex-residents bursting to tell their stories of their upbringing and how much they loved living here. So many photographs and information was collected that I was determined that it would not be consigned to a dusty drawer only for my family to throw it out once I died, so I decided to publish a book on Burnbanks Village. Those that I have contacted would concede that it was indeed a hard existence, but they are fiercely proud of their community and I hope I can do them justice by telling the story of their village, and now our village.

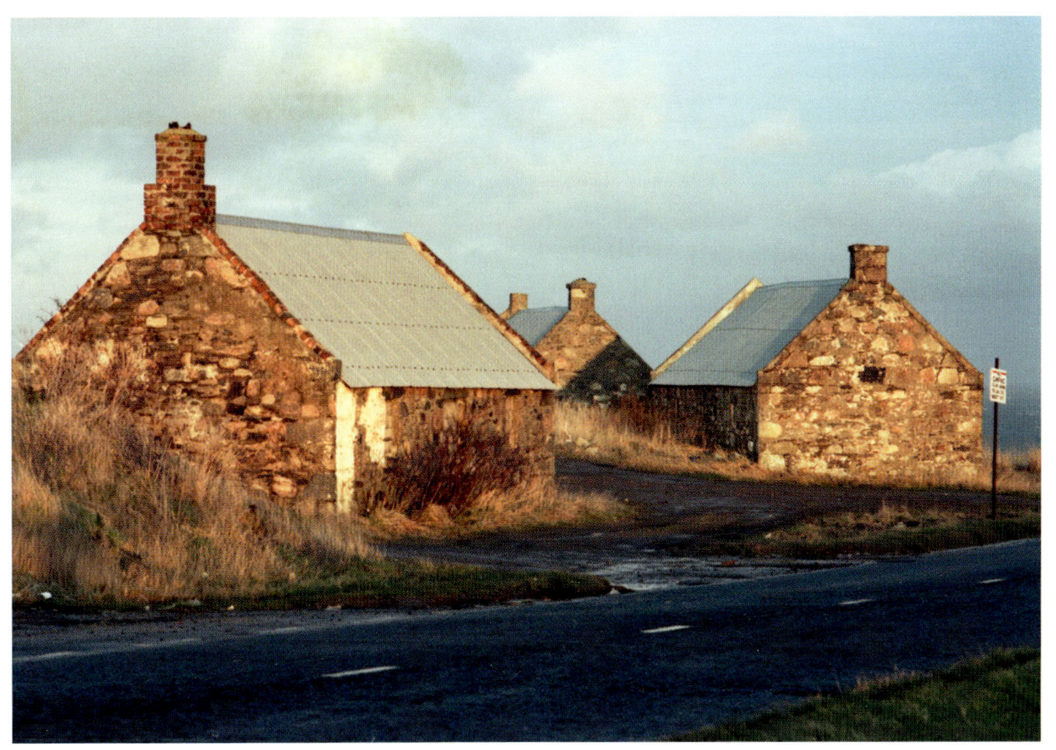

(Photo by Aberdeen Journals Ltd. Used by kind permission of DC Thomson & Co. Ltd)

The 1921 Postcard

I moved into Burnbanks Village in 1992 as it was being refurbished. Although the last of the villagers left in the 1980s, some of the houses had not been occupied for over seventy-five years.

There was a sense of excitement from a lot of the new villagers and we knew we had something unusual. We collected photographs and information over the years and it was receiving this postcard below that sparked my interest in the history of the village.

In 2011, we decided to recreate the photograph with the current children. The houses in the background are the same except the one on the left, which was demolished before the refurbishment.

Unfortunately, the photographer we hired just didn't have control of the situation. He was struggling to have the children lined up or all looking the same way, and smiling at the same time just seemed impossible. At the point this shot was taken, all the kids were bored, fidgeting and frustrated and fights were breaking out, but here we have a great shot because of this. The last photograph of the day.

Both photographs were used in the local paper in an article reproduced below and that was when the floodgates opened and ex-villagers contacted me to tell their stories about their time in the village.

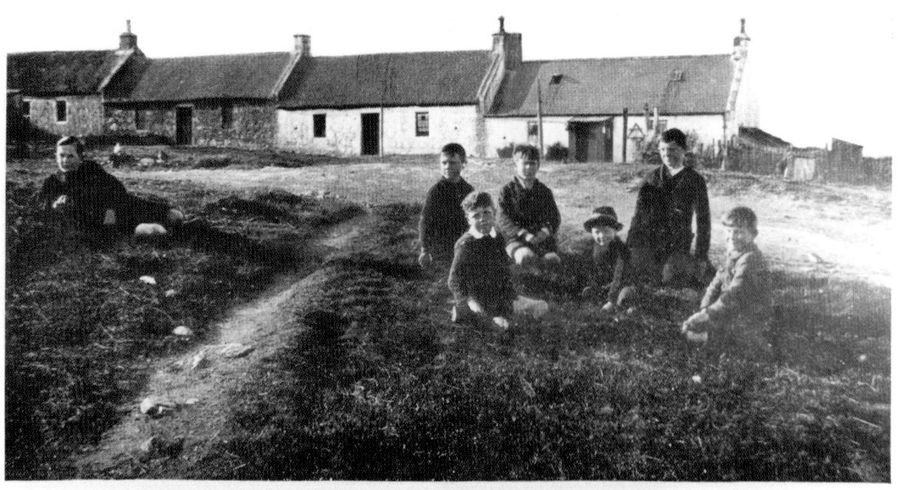

(Courtesy of Aberdeen City Archives from an article in the *Deeside Field* 1929 publication)

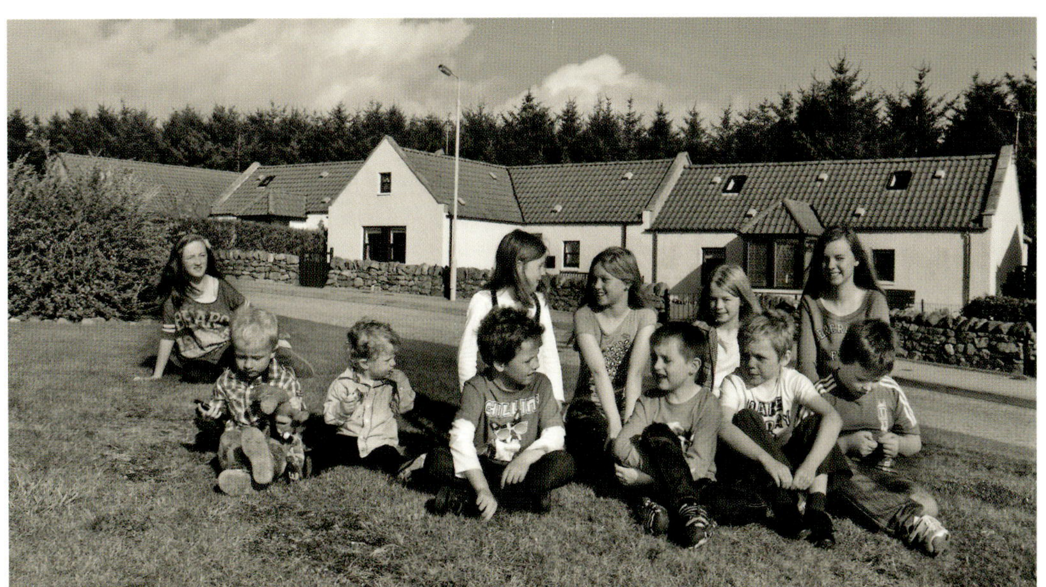

Above: The 2011 Recreation. L to R: *Back row*: Iris, Axel, Marco, Christina, Chiaran, Molly, and Jessica. *Front row*: Struan, Liam, Aiden, Murdo.

Right: (Courtesy of Aberdeen Journals)

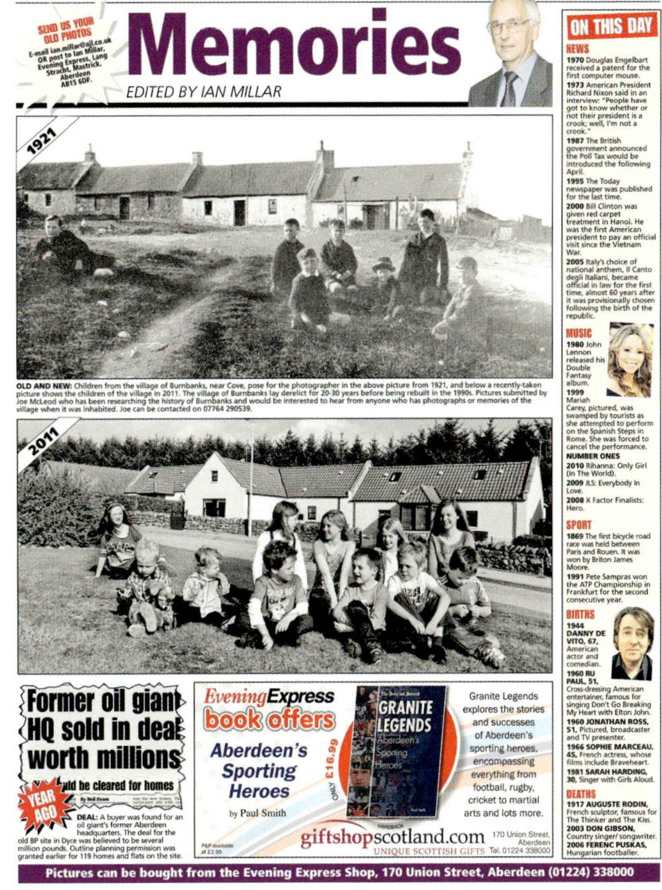

Thursday, November 17, 2011

SEND US YOUR OLD PHOTOS
E-mail ian.millar@ajl.co.uk OR post to Ian Millar, Evening Express, Lang Stracht, Mastrick, Aberdeen AB15 6DF.

Memories

EDITED BY IAN MILLAR

OLD AND NEW: Children from the village of Burnbanks, near Cove, pose for the photographer in the above picture from 1921, and below a recently-taken picture shows the children of the village in 2011. The village of Burnbanks lay derelict for 20-30 years before being rebuilt in the 1990s. Pictures submitted by Joe McLeod who has been researching the history of Burnbanks and would be interested to hear from anyone who has photographs or memories of the village when it was inhabited. Joe can be contacted on 07764 290539.

ON THIS DAY

NEWS
1970 Douglas Engelbart received a patent for the first computer mouse.
1973 American President Richard Nixon said in an interview: "People have got to know whether or not their president is a crook; well, I'm not a crook."
1987 The British government announced the Poll Tax would be introduced the following April.
1995 The Today newspaper was published for the last time.
2000 Bill Clinton was given red carpet treatment in Hanoi. He was the first American president to pay an official visit since the Vietnam War.
2005 Italy's choice of national anthem, Il Canto degli Italiani, became official in law for the first time, almost 60 years after it was provisionally chosen following the birth of the republic.

MUSIC
1980 John Lennon released his Double Fantasy album.
1999 Mariah Carey, pictured, was swamped by tourists as she attempted to perform on the Spanish Steps in Rome. She was forced to cancel the performance.

NUMBER ONES
2010 Rihanna: Only Girl (In The World).
2009 JLS: Everybody In Love.
2008 X Factor Finalists: Hero.

SPORT
1869 The first bicycle road race was held between Paris and Rouen. It was won by Briton James Moore.
1991 Pete Sampras won the ATP Championship in Frankfurt for the second consecutive year.

BIRTHS
1944 DANNY DE VITO, 67, American actor and comedian.
1960 RU PAUL, 51, Cross-dressing American entertainer, famous for singing Don't Go Breaking My Heart with Elton John.
1960 JONATHAN ROSS, 51, Pictured, broadcaster and TV presenter.
1966 SOPHIE MARCEAU, 45, French actress, whose films include Braveheart.
1981 SARAH HARDING, 30, Singer with Girls Aloud.

DEATHS
1917 AUGUSTE RODIN, French sculptor, famous for The Thinker and The Kiss.
2003 DON GIBSON, Country singer/ songwriter.
2006 FERENC PUSKAS, Hungarian footballer.

2

Early Days

It is difficult to find Burnbanks in early maps, statistical accounts or gazettes. The accuracy of early maps can vary and this one from 1833 shows only four dots and the scale doesn't allow any detailing.

The earliest mention I can find is a newspaper article printed in the *Caledonian Mercury* on 15 June 1805.

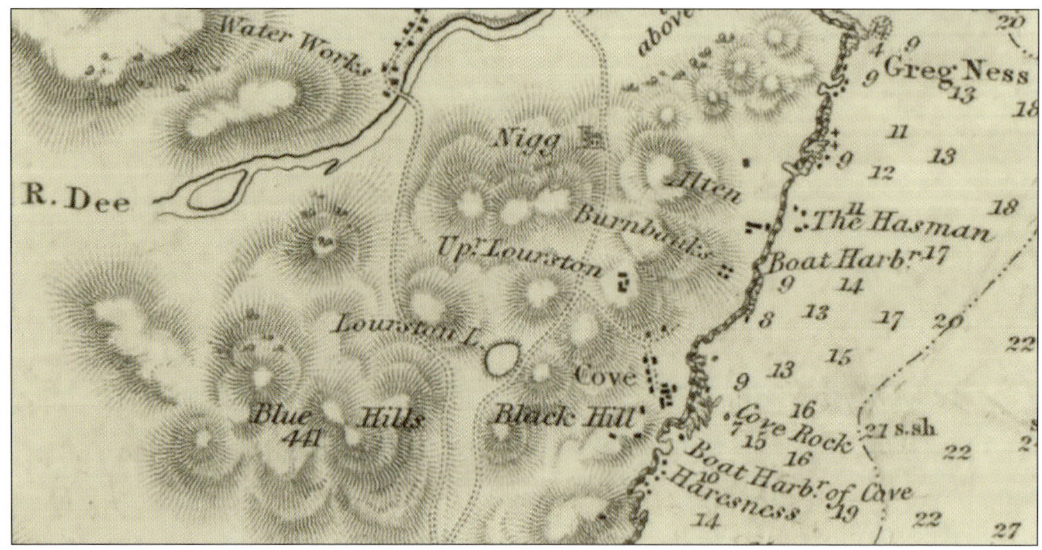

(From National Library of Scotland Map Collection)

> A boat from Burnbanks, near Aberdeen, which, in the gale of Saturday Morning, was in hazard and whole crew were entirely exhausted by fatigue, was taken in tow by the Margaret of Leith, bound for the Orkneys, and with great humanity brought into Aberdeen Bay.

It always seems to be referred to as an old fishing village but over the years, it has been home to agriculture workers, white-fish and herring fishermen, salmon fishers, railway workers, a blacksmith's workshop and a haulage business.

Birth certificates and old parish records show that many families came from Portlethen, Durris or Downies.

By 1867, the village has taken the familiar shape that still exists today. The long-gone houses across the railway line may have been the earliest dwellings and are present at this time. Due to the muddy field and constant water logging, this area and the families in it were known as 'The Boggers'. It's now a field for cows and the hardy beasts are often knee deep in watery mud.

The population fluctuated depending on the local prosperity, ranging from fifty-three people at the first reliable census in 1841 to a maximum of 120 people at its peak in the 1880s and down to only one family with one solitary occupant in 1979–80.

At this peak, there were not many different surnames and the families called Craig, Main or Leiper accounted for ninety-nine out of 120 persons. There were fifty-two Mains, thirty-three Craigs and fourteen Leipers. Eight people were called George Main, ranging in age from one-month to forty-eight years old. There were six Jane Mains, eleven Janes and eight Marys in total. Because of this, finding these family lines has been very difficult, so if there is a lesson to be learned from history: give your children unusual and unique names.

The population started to decline after the 1880s as families migrated into nearby Torry and Aberdeen to work on steam trawlers during the fishing boom years. The works were better paid and were a much safer option.

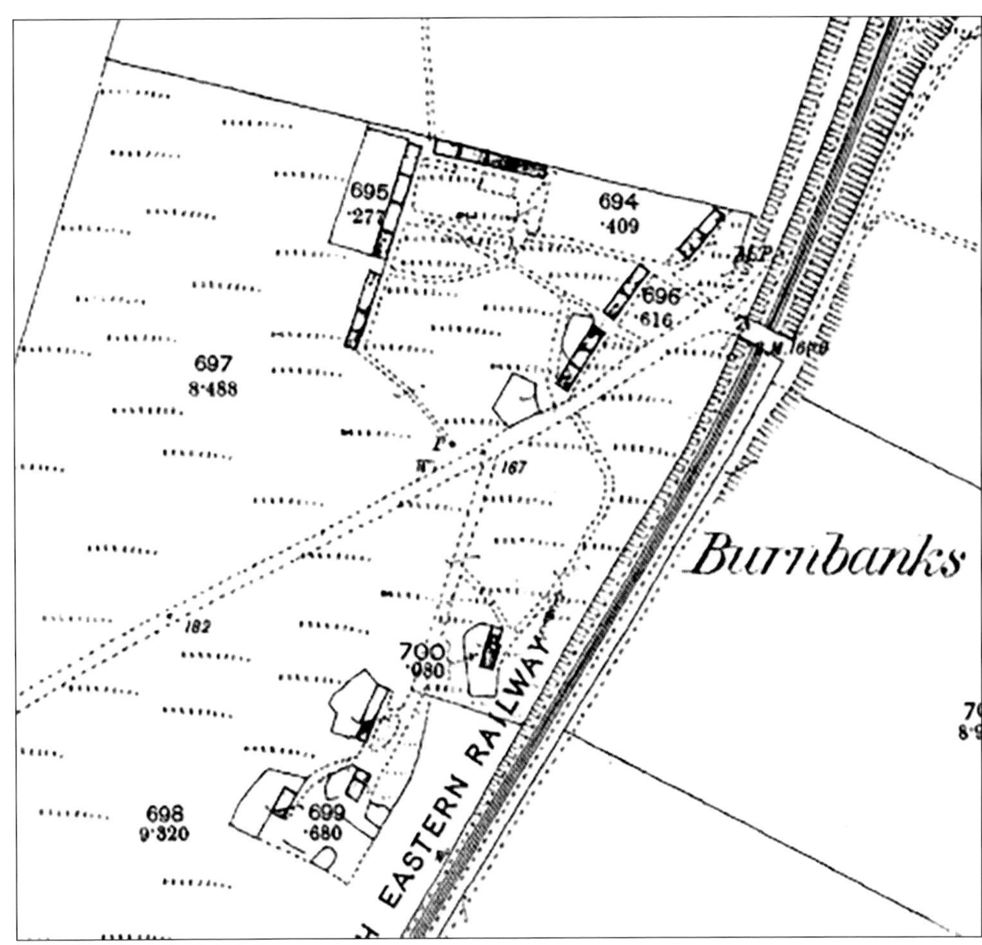

1867 excerpt from Ordinance Survey. The sea is 200 metres to the east.

In the 1929 edition of the *Deeside Field* publication, an article was written by fisherman William Leiper who was born in Burnbanks in 1865. The article was titled 'The Fishing Industry at Aberdeen Fifty Years Ago'. His descriptions of village life in the 1870s–80s are a fine historical record.

He describes the interiors of the houses as being only two rooms for eight people and a windowless closet that had a bunk bed. Lines and fishing gear were prepared in the loft.

The diet consisted of fresh fish in the summer months and preserved herring in barrels for winter months. Oats and milk were purchased from local farmers and a baker visited the village once a week. Potatoes were grown on the landowner's neighbouring fields and turnips, carrots and leeks were grown in vegetable gardens.

Fish were smoked inside the houses and he describes how they would bury their heads in blankets, so sore were their eyes from the smoke from their home kiln.

Heating was from peat fires and lighting was from fish oil lamps.

3

Burnbanks Haven

Burnbanks Village is only 200 metres from the sea and the reason the settlement developed here is because of Burnbanks Haven, which is a rocky inlet where the fishers operated their boats from. A narrow path zig-zags its way down very steep grassy cliffs.

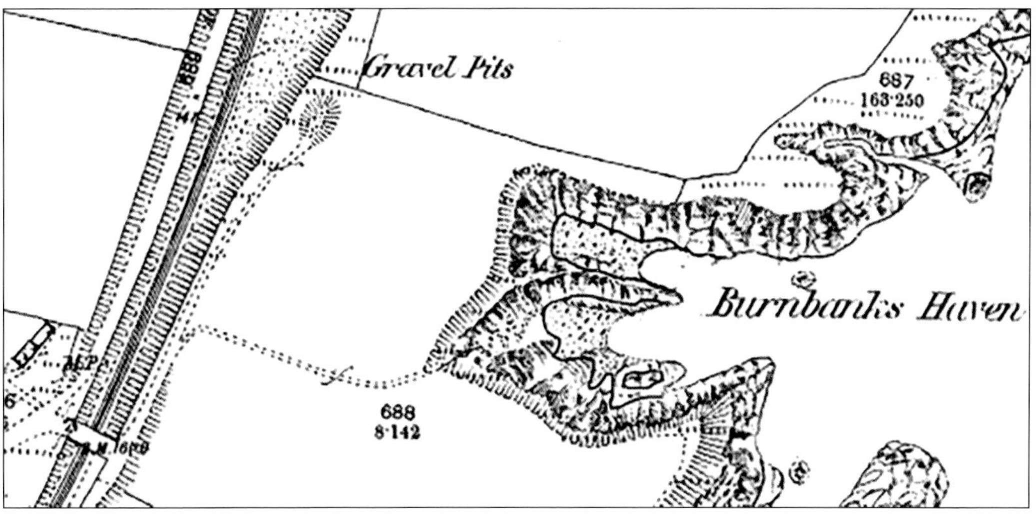

The path down to Burnbanks Haven shows on maps from the 1860s onwards but was here much earlier. (Excerpt from Ordinance Survey)

The Haven could only take four yawls at a time and they had to be hauled up the shore after each trip. The women of the village would be at the Haven to assist pulling the boats ashore, then take the lines, nets and the catch up to the houses. They would clean the fish and smoke them and then carry them into the city to be sold. They would then bait the lines for the next trip.

In later days, hand winches were used to pull the boats up the slipway. A Blondin rope and winch was installed to carry the catch to the top of the cliffs. William Leiper's 1929 article notes that it was first tested by hoisting an elderly portly fisherman up the cliff to much hilarity.

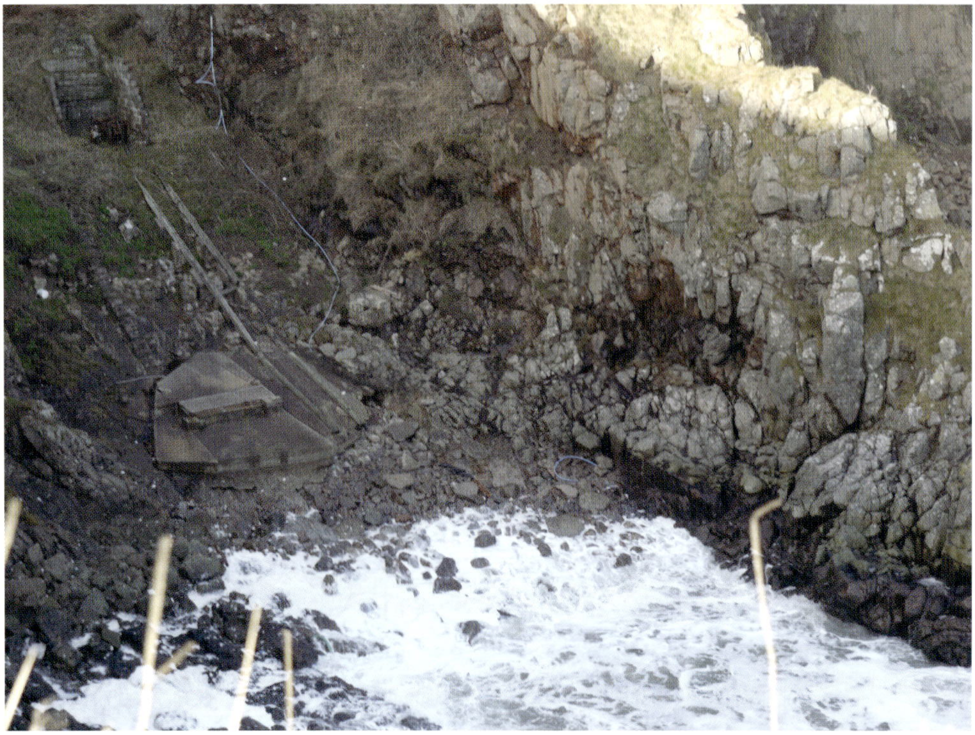

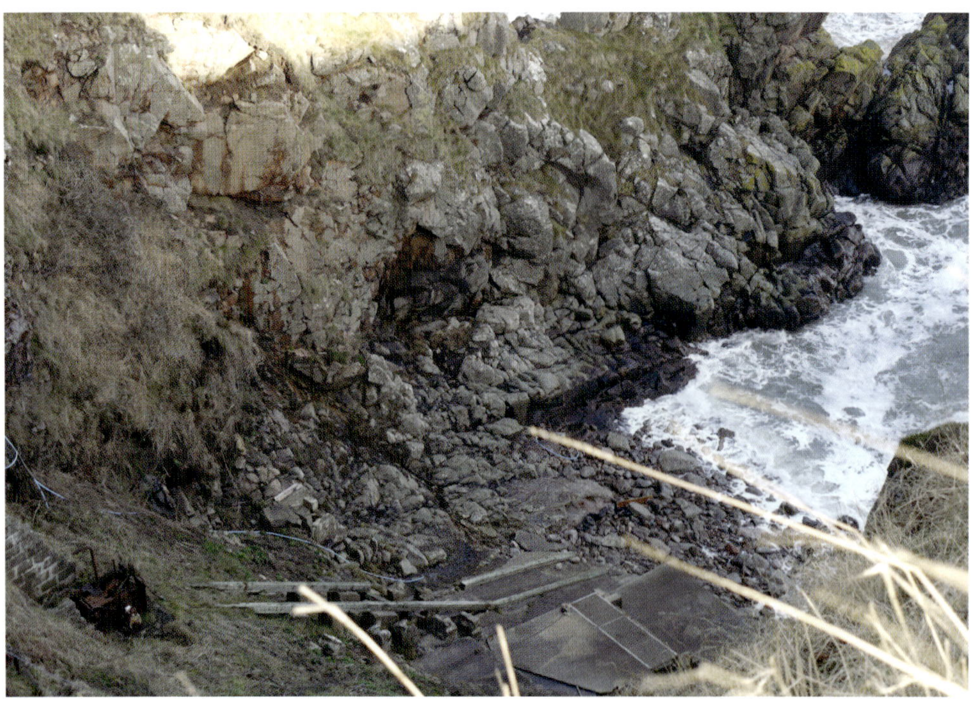

The remnants of the landing area and slipway can be seen in this photograph from 2016.

When the weather is even slightly rough, the approaches from the sea are very dangerous.

Right: Boys had to leave school and go to sea as early as they could to help crew the vessels and local school records show many being withdrawn to go to the fishing. The page from Cove School from July 1876 is a very common entry in the registers. (From Aberdeen City Archives)

Below: My Grandmother, Lizzie Ritchie, and my Mother, Mary McLeod. Not from Burnbanks but doing a very similar job 'sheeling and baiting' mussels onto fishing lines in Fraserburgh in the early 1960s.

37

1876.

9th July. A number of the Children absent from the village owing to the boats leaving for the Herring fishing.

15th " George Craig withdrawn from school to engage in the herring fishing.

15th Registers examined H. McLennan Clerk.

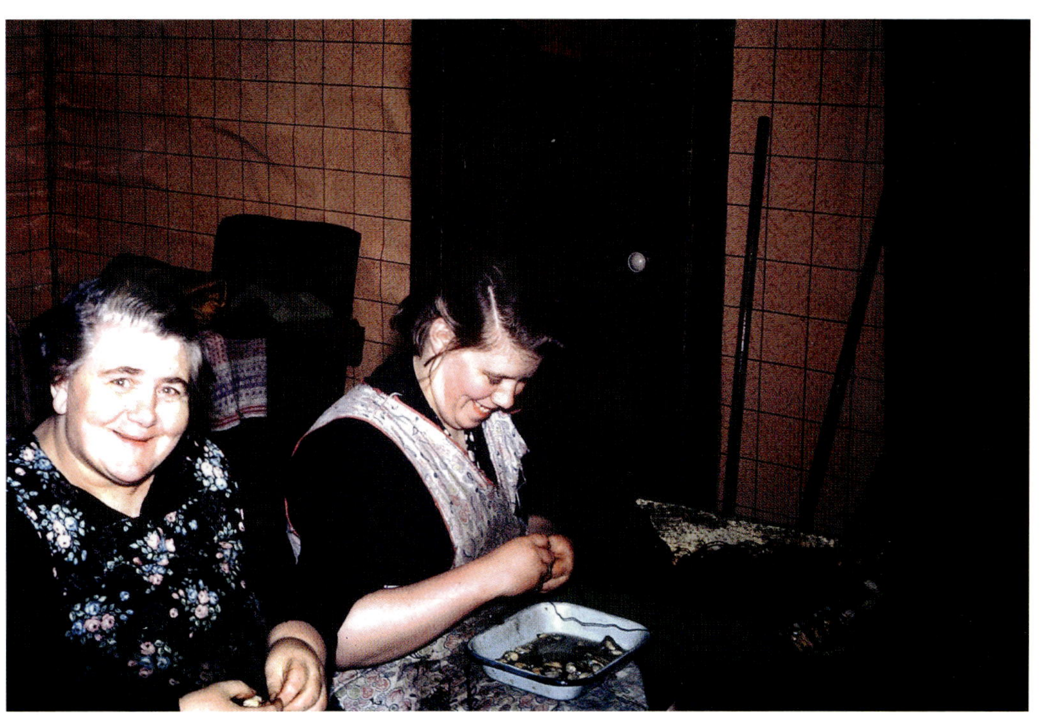

The Altens Haven is only 300 metres to the north and the access on the land side is so much easier. The photographs below show the Altens Haven and salmon boats being offloaded in the 1930s. Burnbanks would have had similar arrangements. Both photos are from the Aberdeen Maritime Museum Collection of MF Bailey's works.

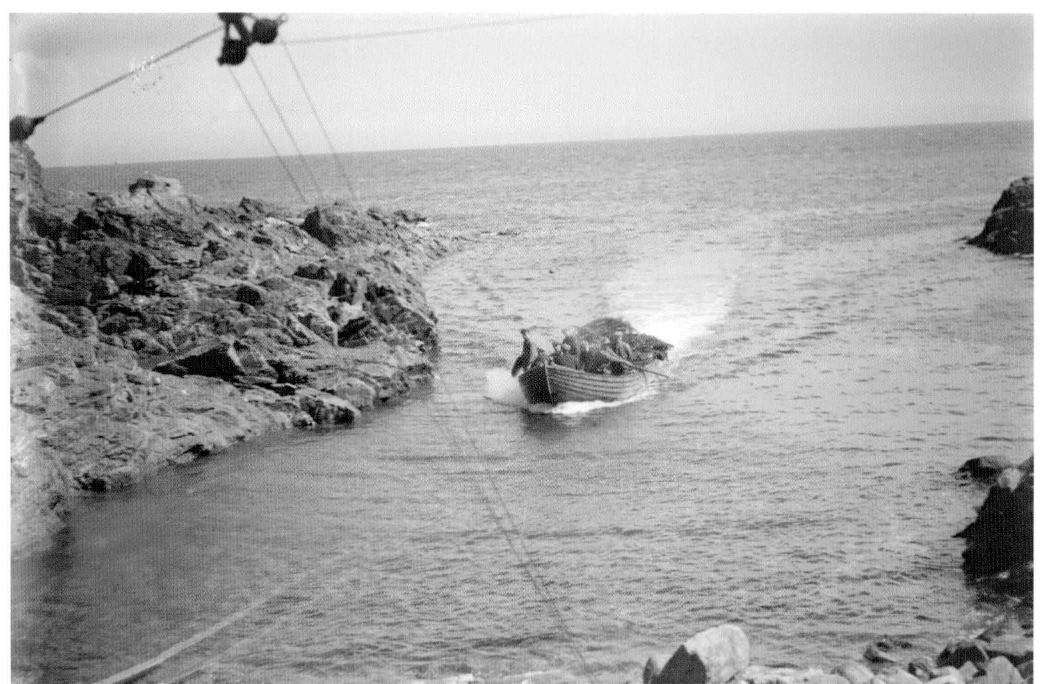

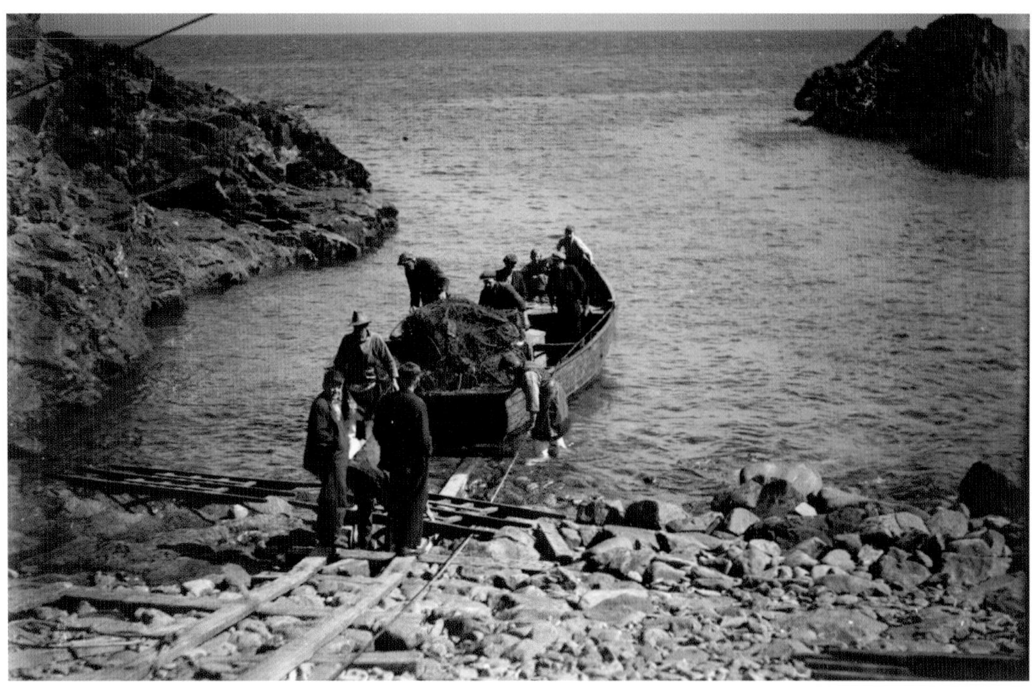

Burnbanks Monster

An early report from 1843 that received nationwide coverage was when a Burnbanks boat captured a shark in their nets. They encountered the 'Monster of the Deep' and with sword in hand they disabled it and brought it to shore. The boat measured 15 feet long and the beast measured 15 feet too – 3 feet across the tail and 9 feet circumference around the body. That's a big fish!

The contents of the stomach included two large turbots and two large salmon, all whole. The liver from the shark filled a herring barrel and produced 30–40 pints of oil.

An Easy Day's Fishing in 1872

The fishing was at its peak and stocks were so abundant. A Burnbanks boat was at sea and came across another vessel that couldn't cope with the huge amount of fish it had caught. Faced with the option of cutting the remaining nets and losing them as well as their catch, they handed six full nets to the Burnbanks men because they couldn't haul them in. Free fish! All they were expected to do was take the nets ashore safely.

January 1875

A fatal accident occurred at the Haven when one of the boats being winched up broke its moorings and immediately slid down towards the sea and crushed Joseph Craig, to his severe injury. He was rescued but died within two hours.

The Wreck of the SS *Kenilworth*, 1906

The photograph below shows the SS *Kenilworth* that was wrecked at Burnbanks in 1906. The Haven was unsuitable for berthing or even sheltering a vessel like this but it broke down and drifted onto the rocks. Sightseeing trips were organised by Hall Russell Ltd Shipyard on a vessel undergoing sea trials in the following days.

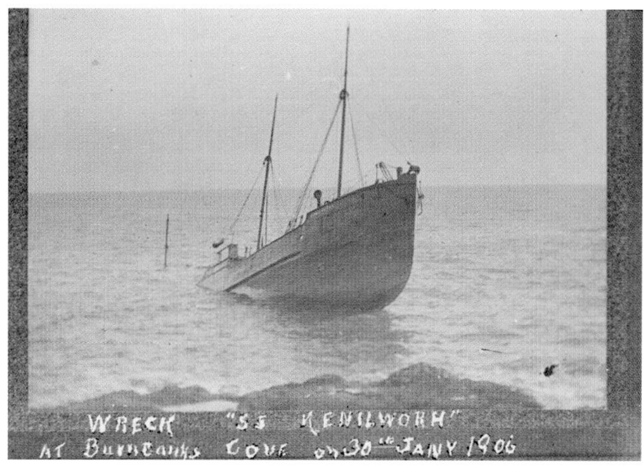

(From Aberdeen City Library Collection)

The steps leading down to the Haven are even more treacherous these days. Erosion, landslides and general lack of use and maintenance make it a very dangerous descent. There are locked gates to deter any explorers.

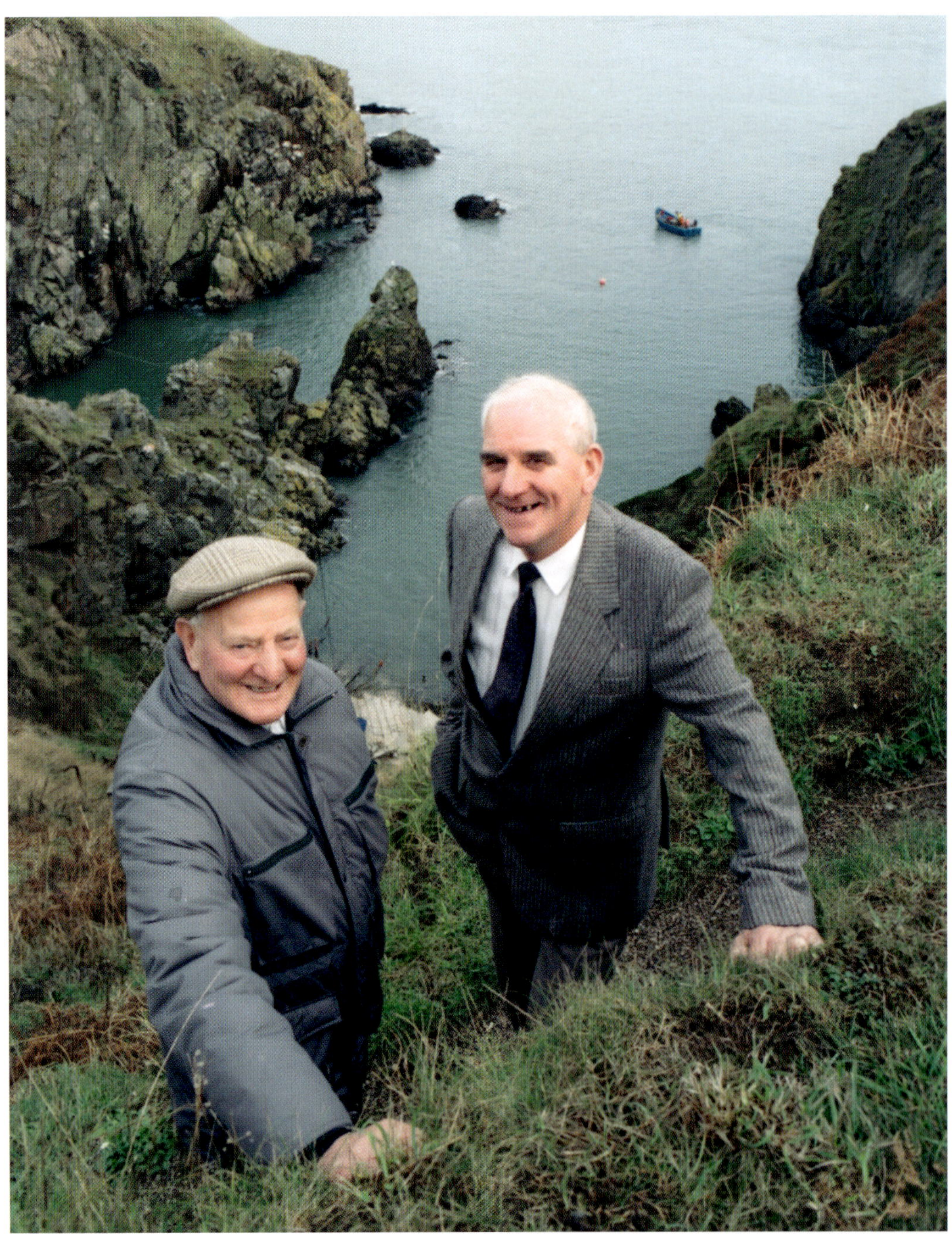

Ex-residents Stuart Davidson and Harry Morrison above Burnbanks Haven in 1991. (Photograph courtesy of Aberdeen Journals Ltd. Used by kind permission of DC Thomson & Co. Ltd)

4

Buildings Now and Then

The house numbers of the village before abandonment are very different to the modern numbering system. Linking people and stories to the correct buildings has been very difficult and at the time of writing, still incomplete.

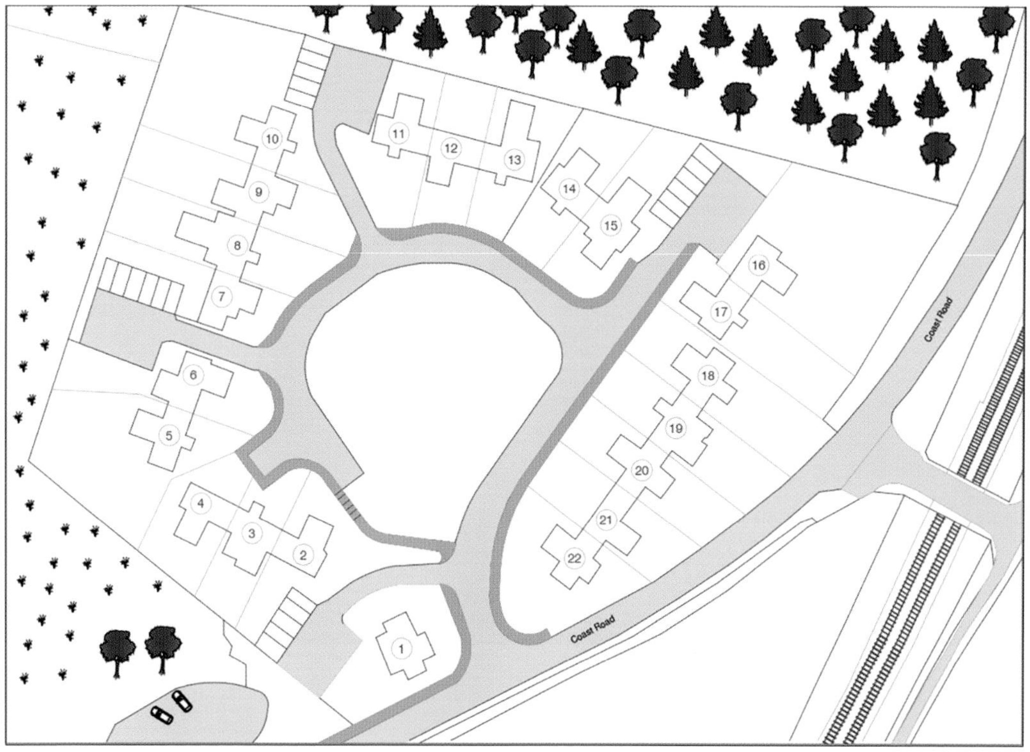

This drawing shows the modern layout and house numbers of the village. (Redrawn from various map sources by Andy Hamilton)

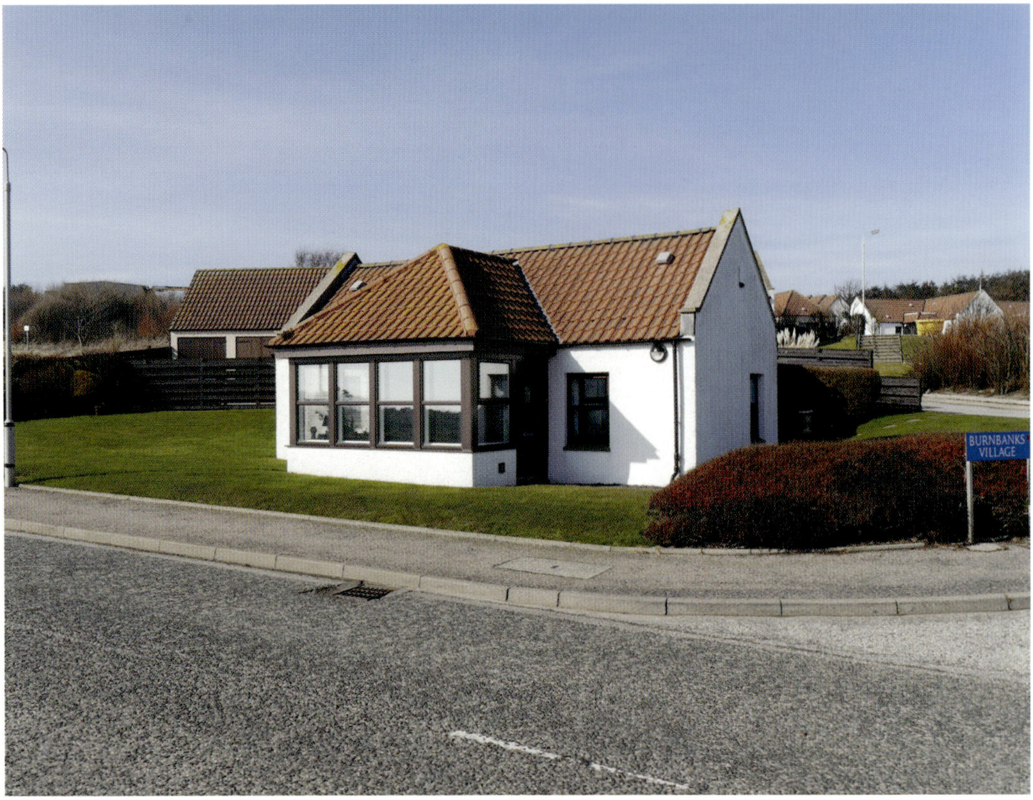

No. 1 in 2016.

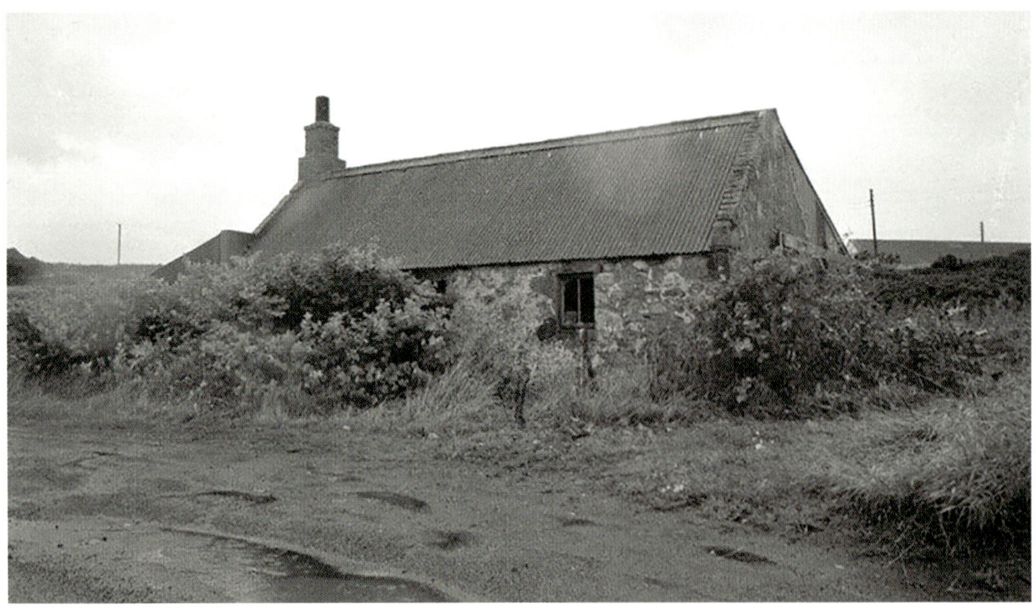

The same building in 1975. (From the Royal Commission for Ancient and Historic Monuments
Scotland – RCAHMS)

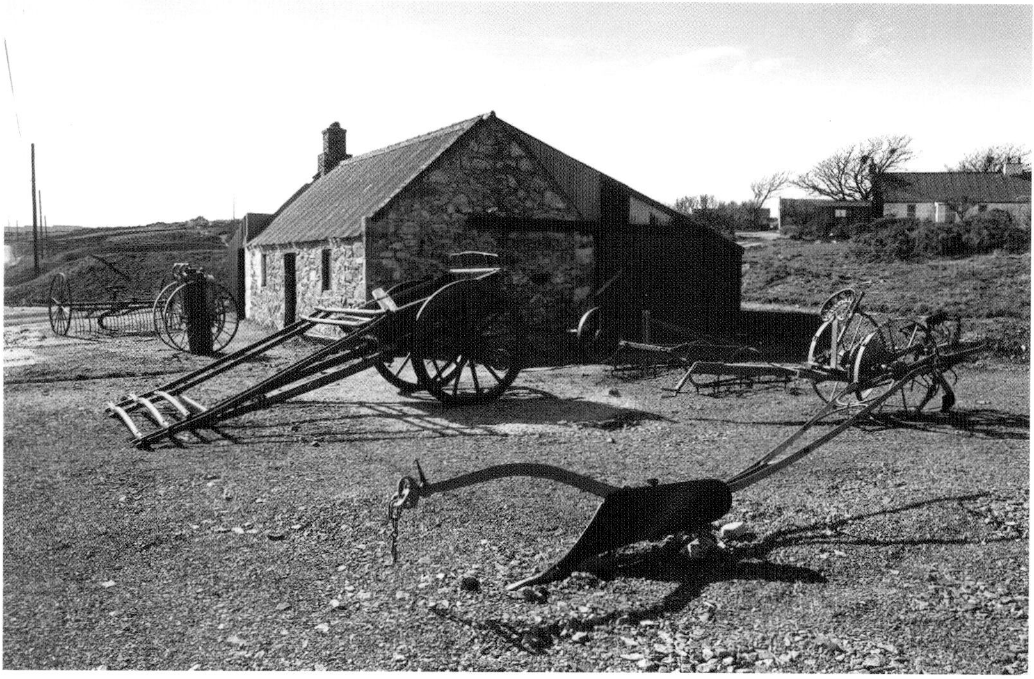

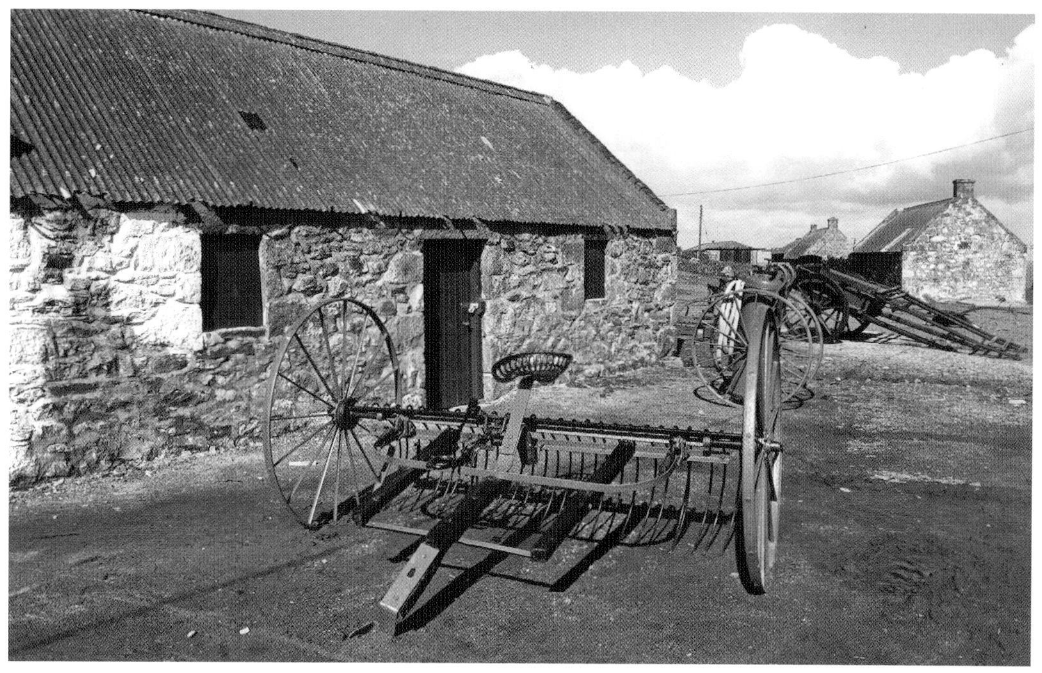

This is a similar shot of the same house looking towards Cove in the distance. It was taken in 1979 when the building had been refurbished to act as an agricultural museum and store for the local council. The lean-to extension to the right of the house was used as a blacksmith's workshop, operated by the Wood family.

Another view looking north.

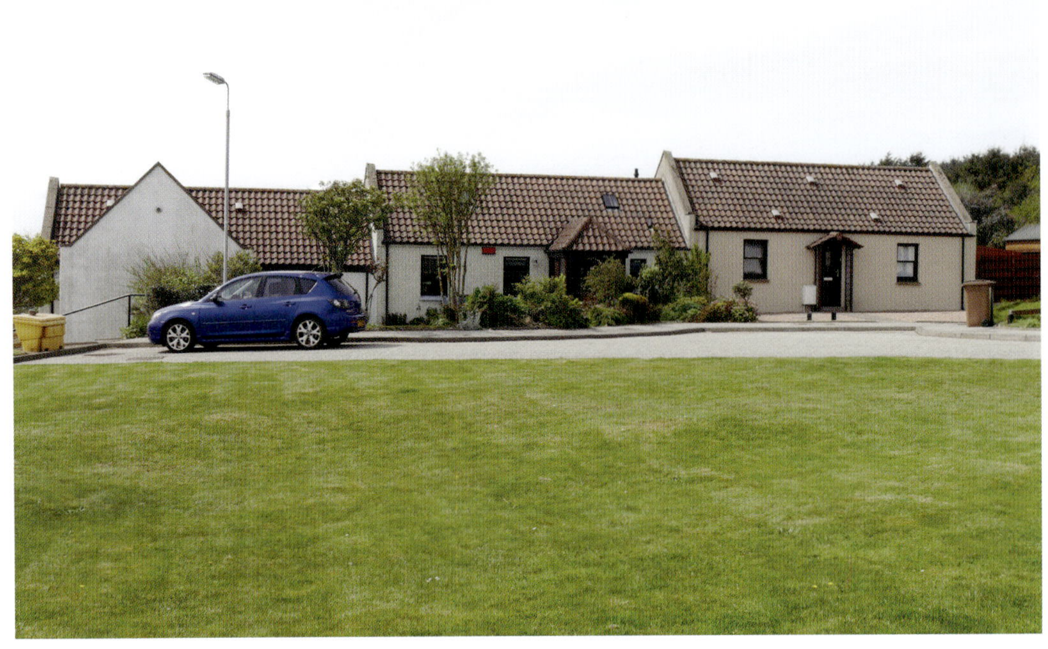

Nos 2–4. These were not present in the original village and were new-builds in 1992.

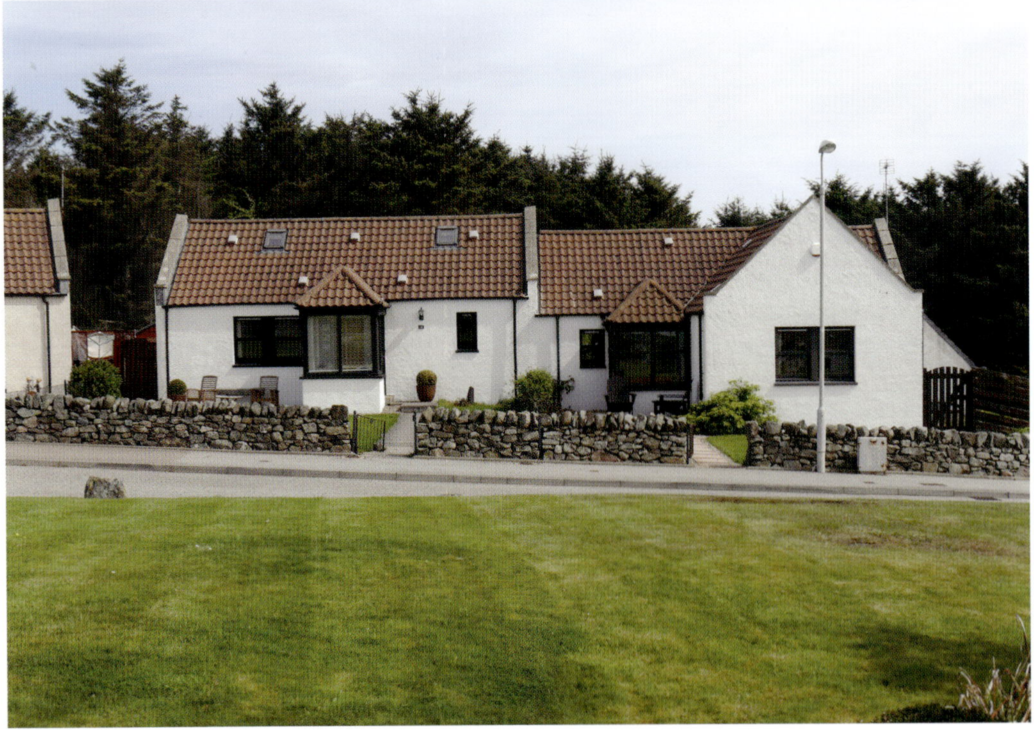

Nos 14 and 15. These were not present in the original village and were new-builds in 1992.

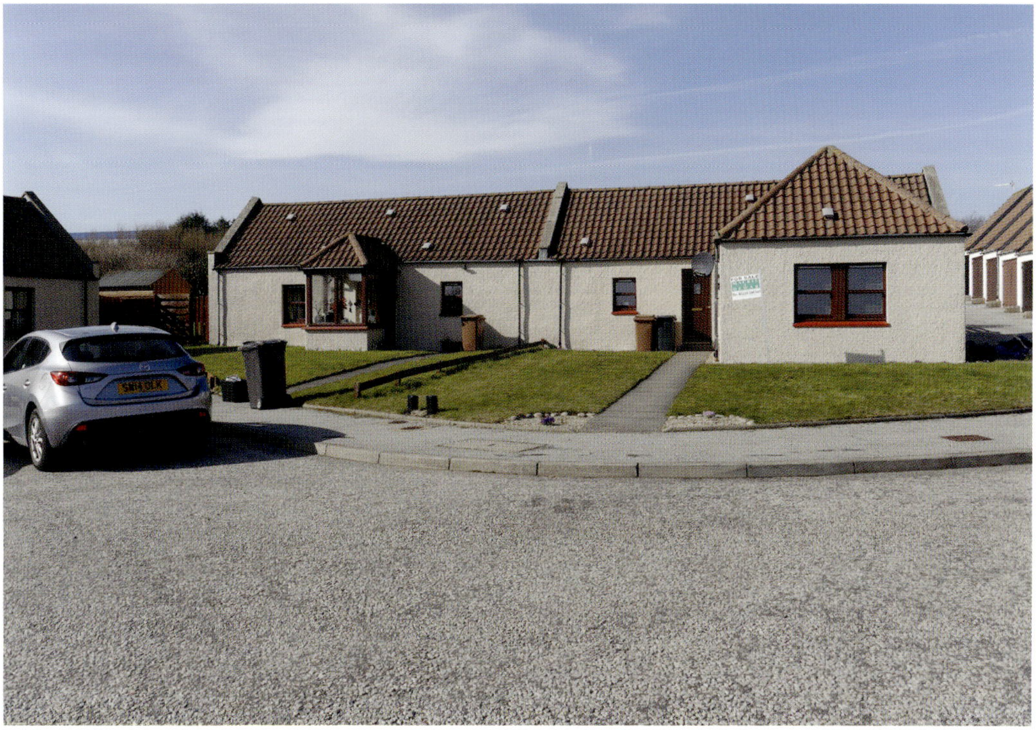

Nos 5 and 6 in 2016.

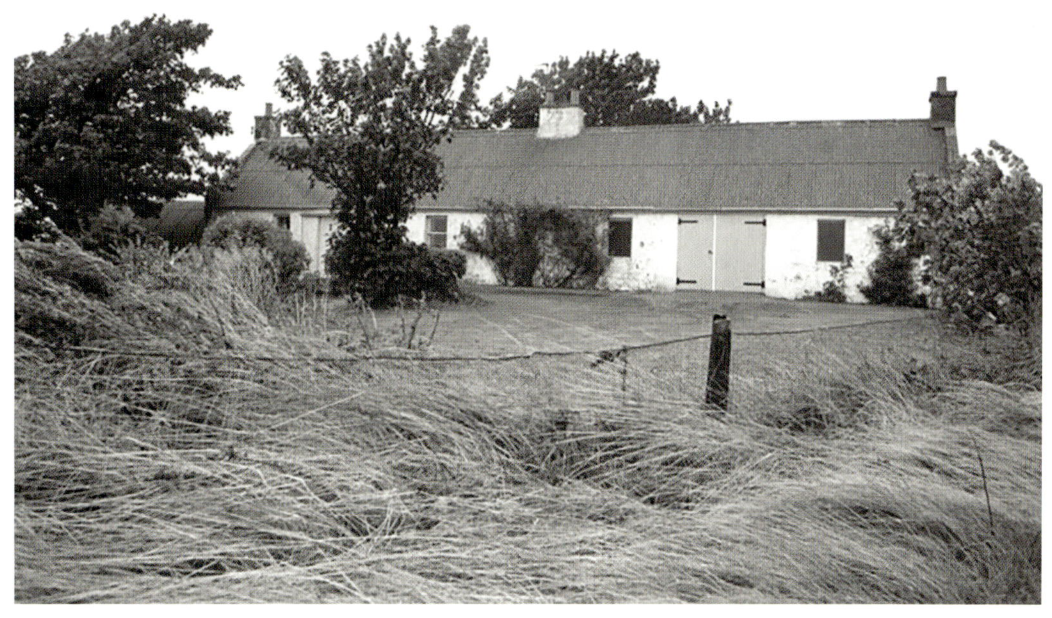

These were No. 7 on the left and No. 15 on the right, the home of Dorothy Beattie's family. (RCAHMS)

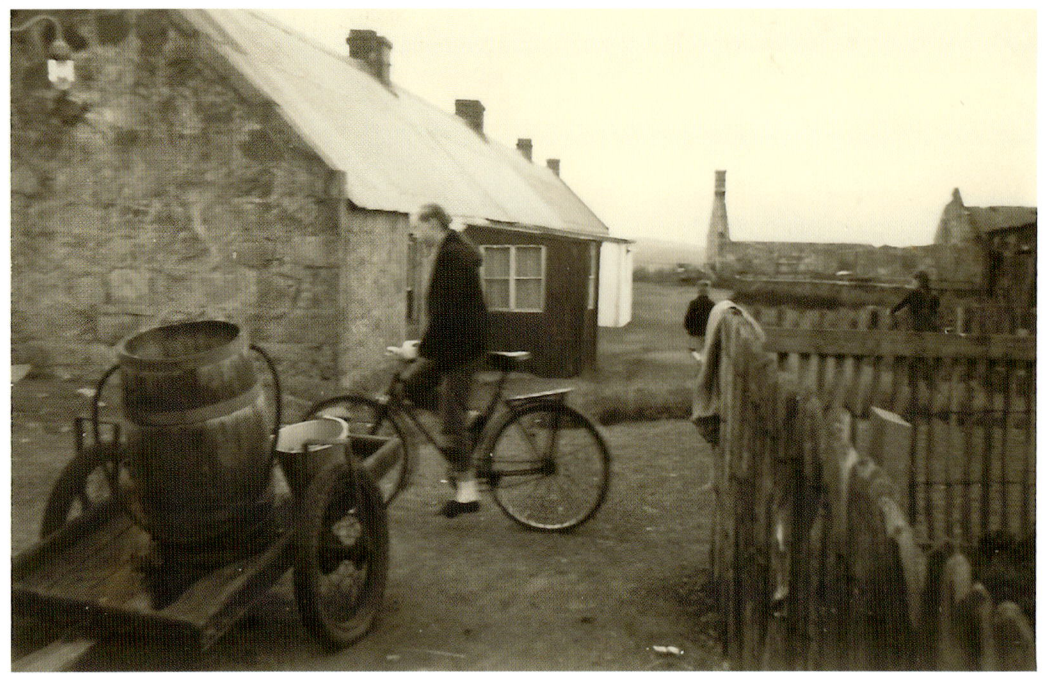

Looking along the row that is now Nos 7–10. The derelict shell of a house in the background is no longer there. The access to one of the parking bays is in its place. (Photograph courtesy of Jake Beattie)

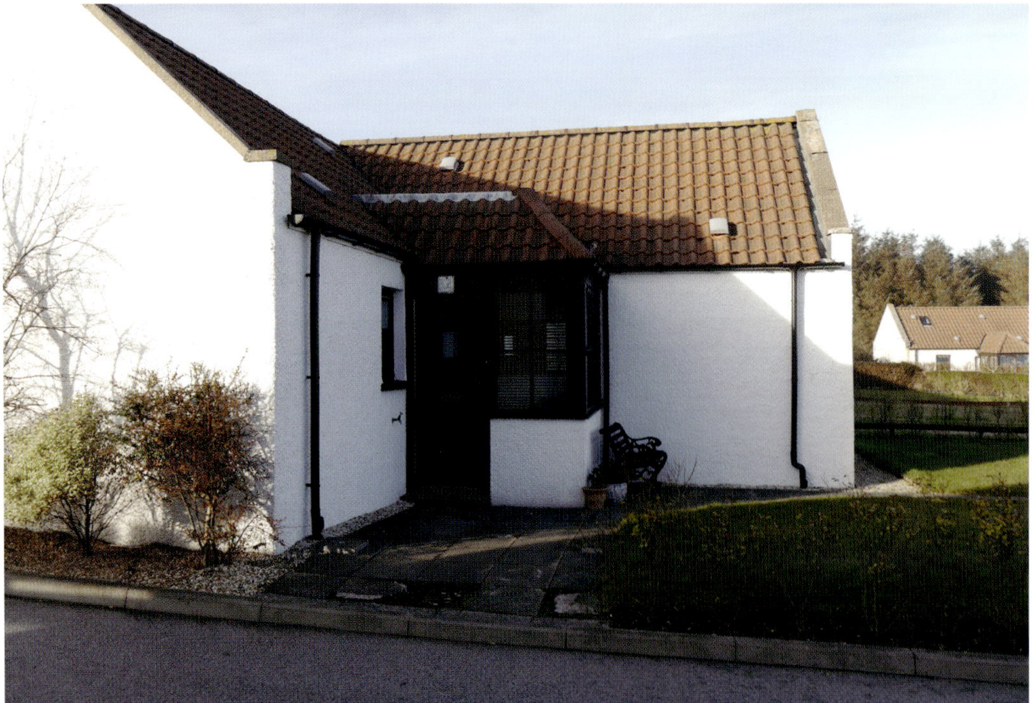

This is modern No. 7.

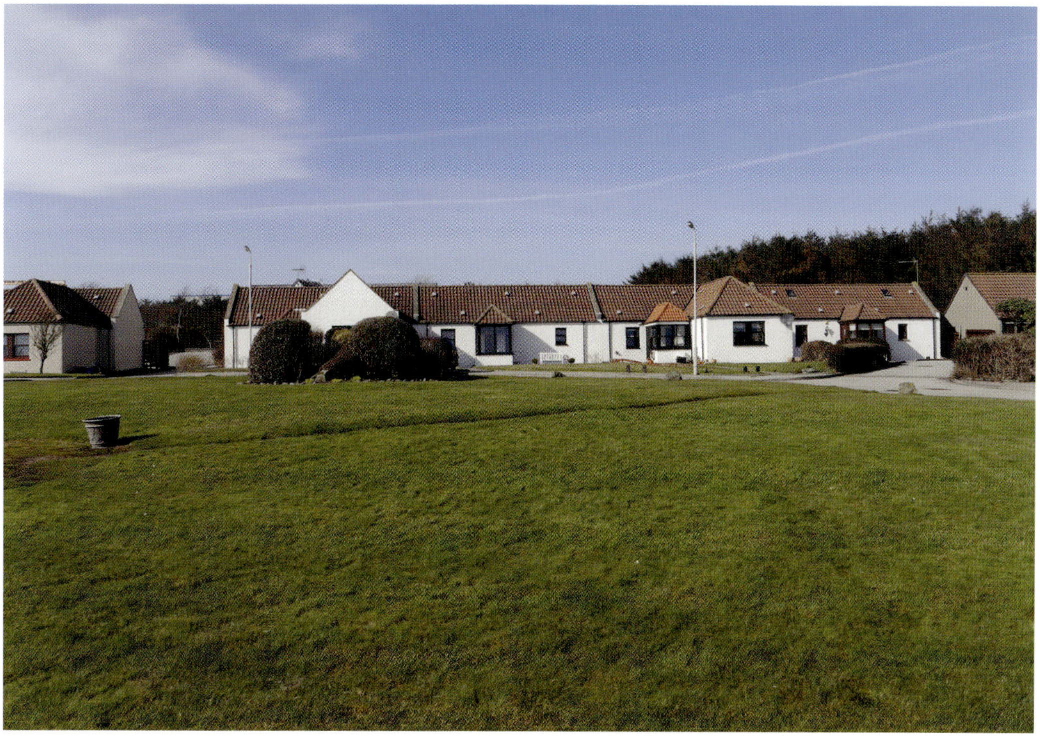

Nos 7–10 in 2016.

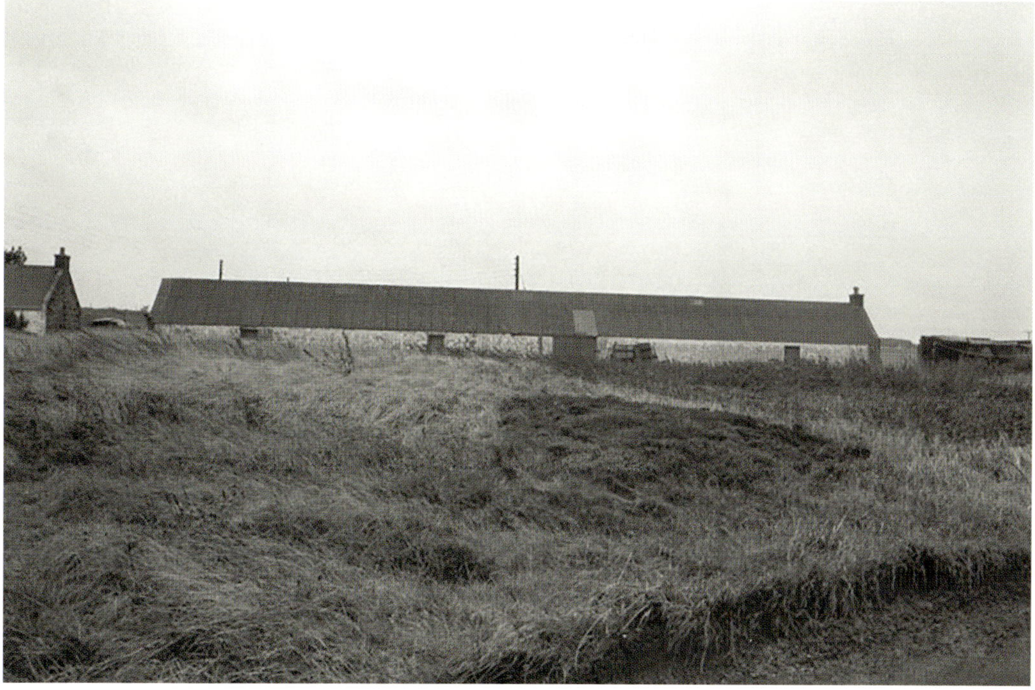

The same row of four houses in 1975. (RCAHMS)

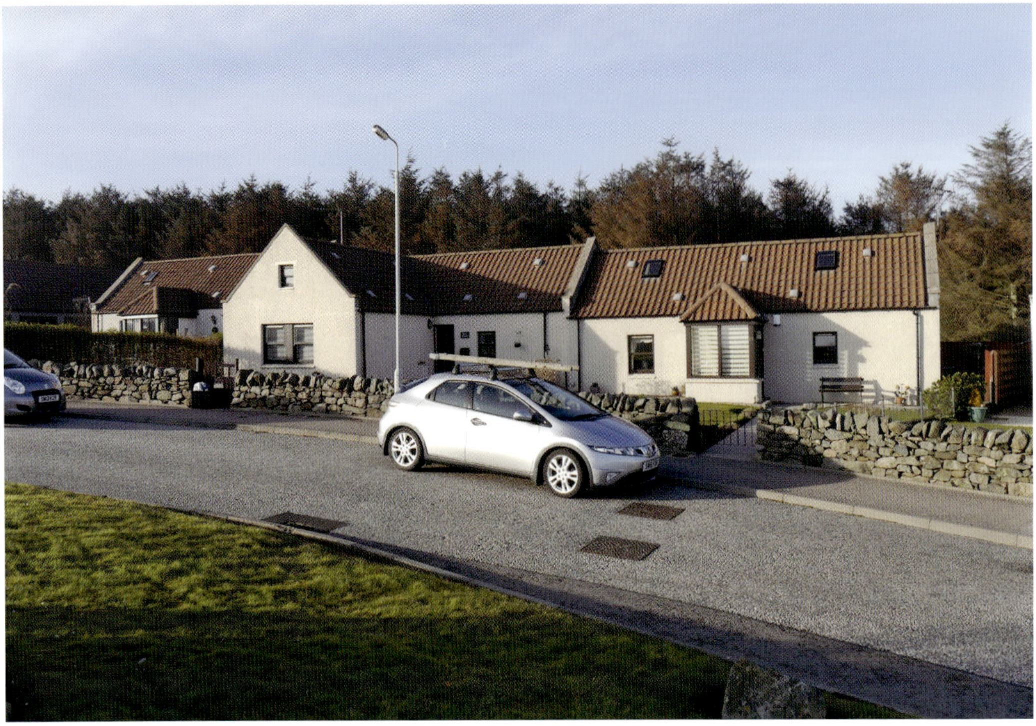

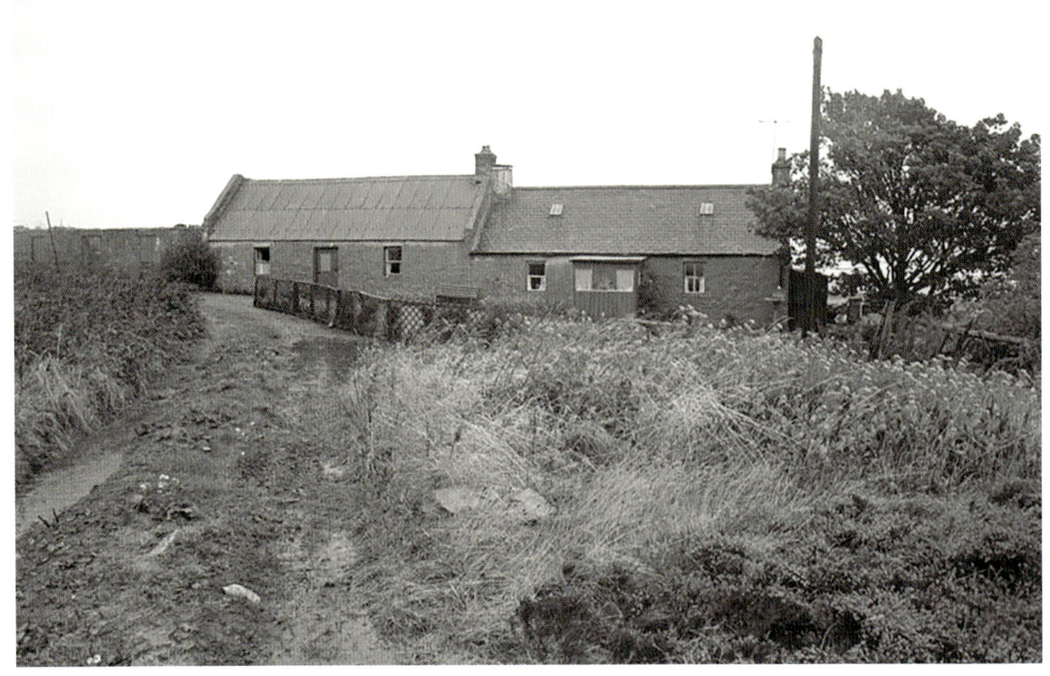

Nos 11–13 in 2016. The house on the right is the one that used to have the slate roof.

The house with the slate roof's old number was No. 10 and was occupied by the Sim family. (RCAHMS)

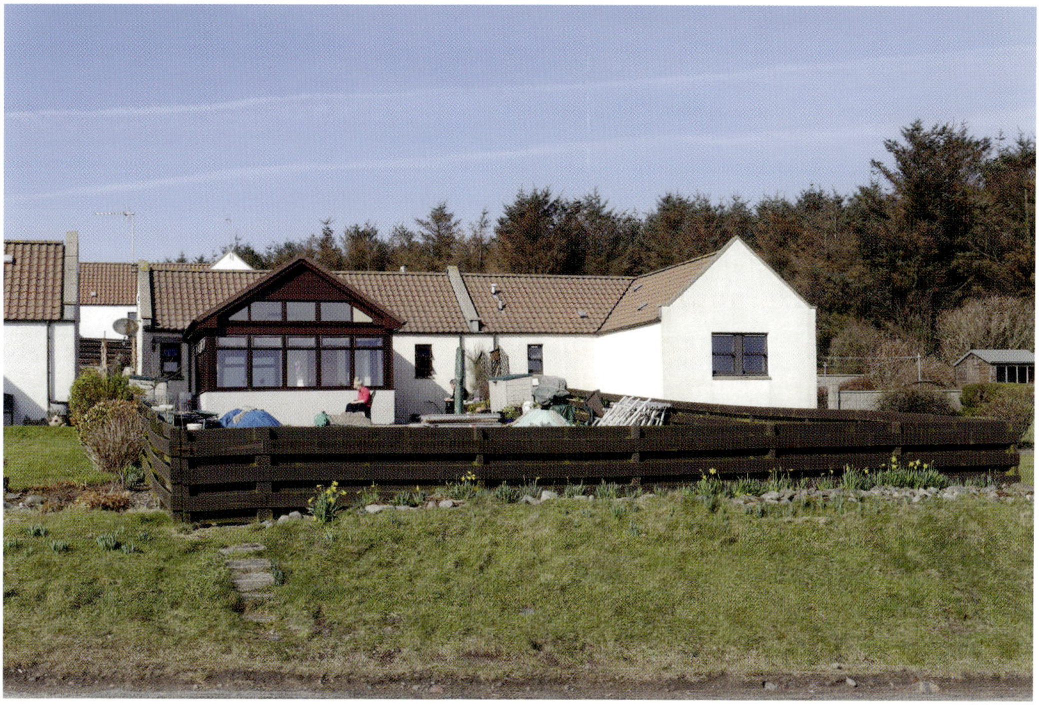

No. 17 on the left and No. 16 on the right in 2016.

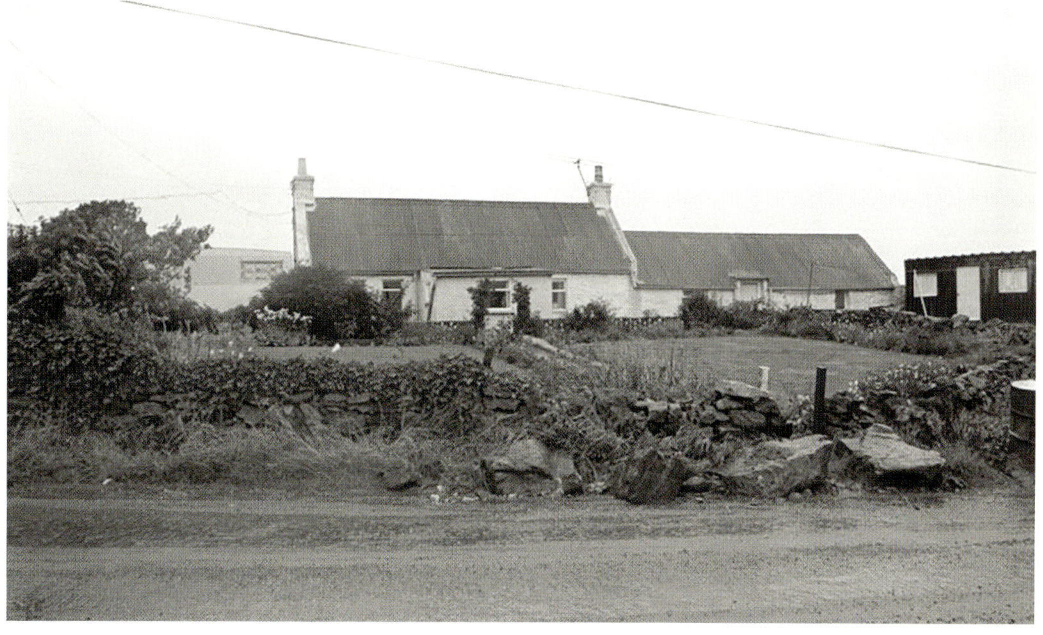

Although this is in the same location, nothing remains of these houses and the position is slightly different from the modern Nos 16 & 17. These were the houses occupied by Henry Duncan's family, then Jim Maharey who married Jessie Duncan. This was one of the last houses to be occupied before the village was abandoned. (RCAHMS)

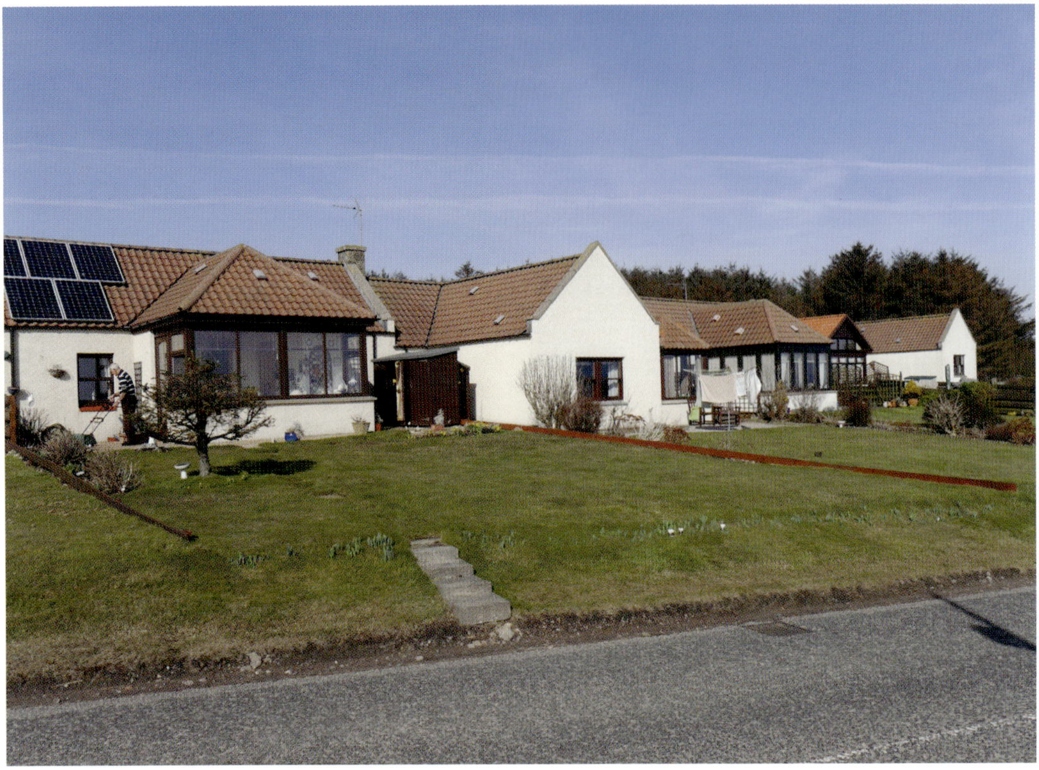

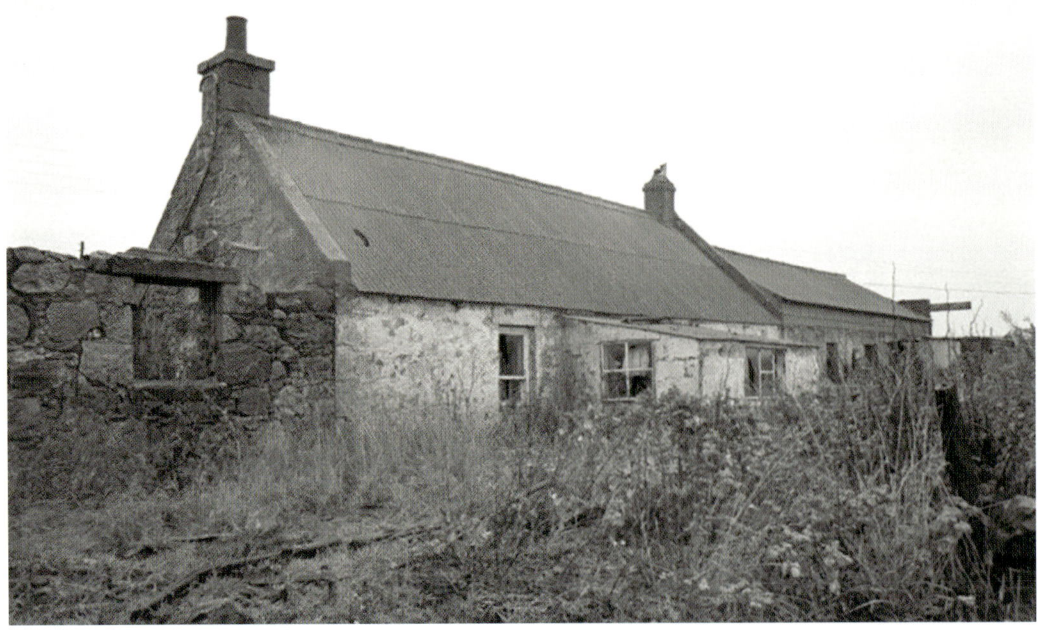

From the left: Nos 20, 19 and 18.

(RCAHMS, 1975)

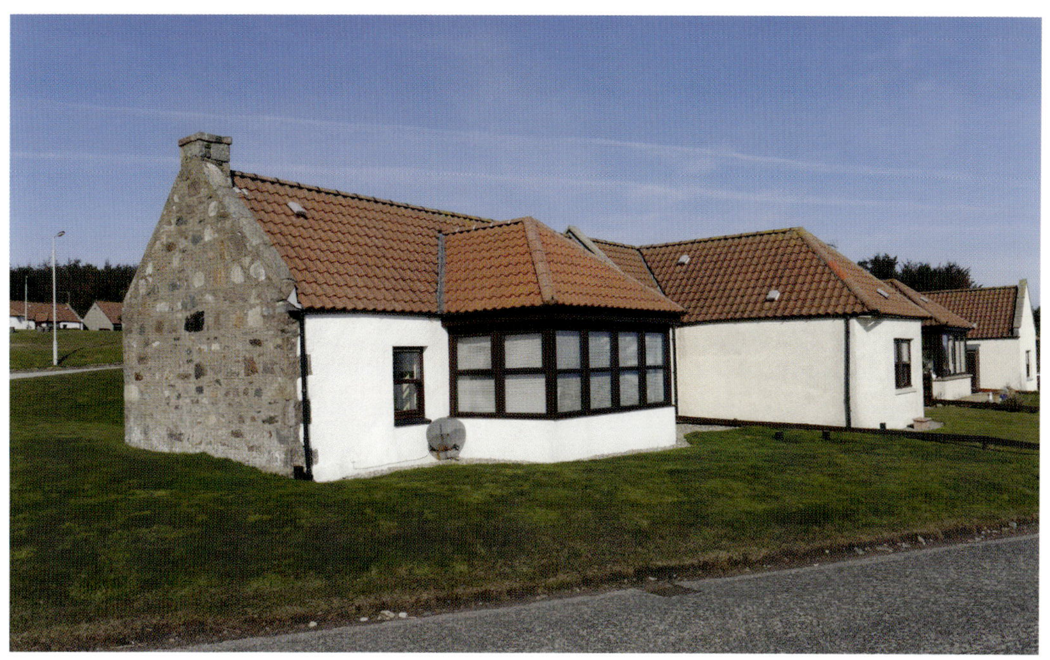

Nos 22 & 21. This gable wall is the only one not painted or harled in the whole village which assisted with the identification of the houses in the older photographs. Note the black granite block in the centre of the wall.

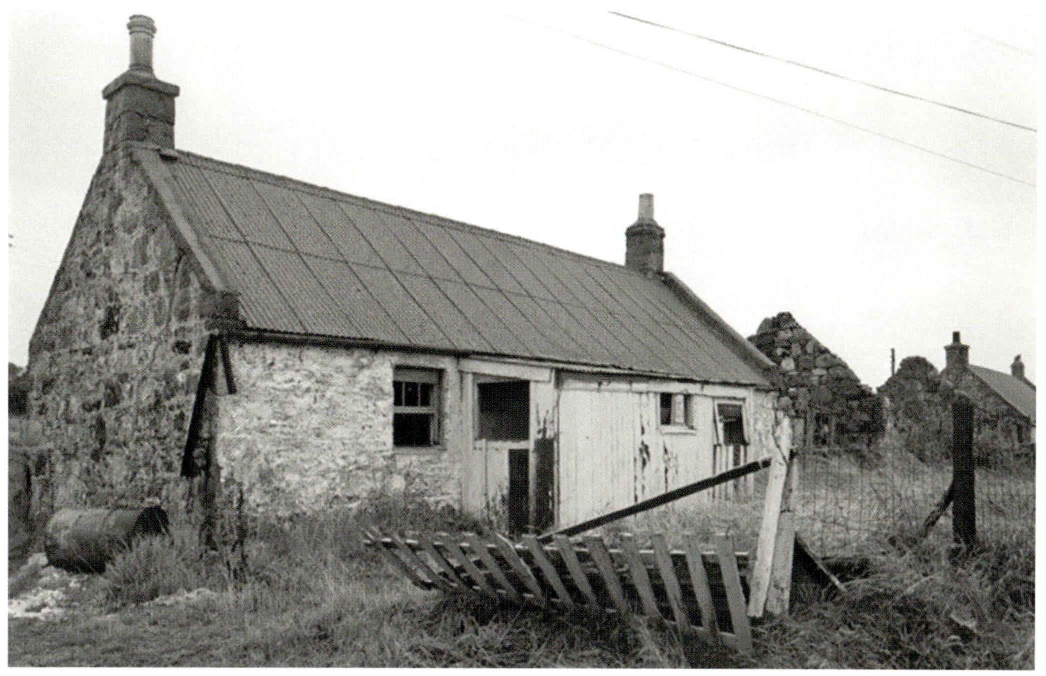

This was old No. 17 in 1975. This was the house of Frederick Beattie's family then latterly the Munro family who ran a small shop from here. This house was also occupied by Stuart Davidson and his family. (RCAHMS)

5

George Washington Wilson

George Washington Wilson was a photography pioneer from the Victorian era based in Aberdeen. He specialised in portraits, landscapes and early stereoscopic photography and had a hugely successful international business. A fascinating book to see more of his work is called *George Washington Wilson: Artist and Photographer (1823–93)* by Professor Roger Taylor.

Aberdeen University holds many thousands of glass plate negatives. This photograph below is looking north towards Cove. Zooming in produces a view of Burnbanks Village

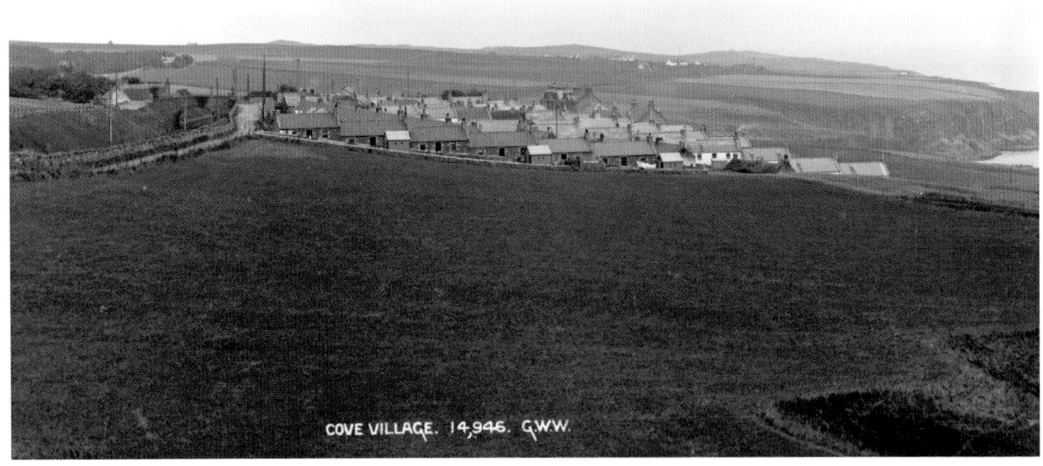

Above and opposite above: (Photographs courtesy of Aberdeen University George Washington Wilson Collection)

and I think this may be the earliest existing image from around 1907. Although George Washington Wilson had passed on by this time, the company continued after his death.

There we are on the horizon and features of the village are not much changed today. The railway bridge is quite clear on the right-hand side and individual houses can be made out. Once again, I tried to recreate the image but the difference in talent from my efforts to a professional photographer are pretty obvious.

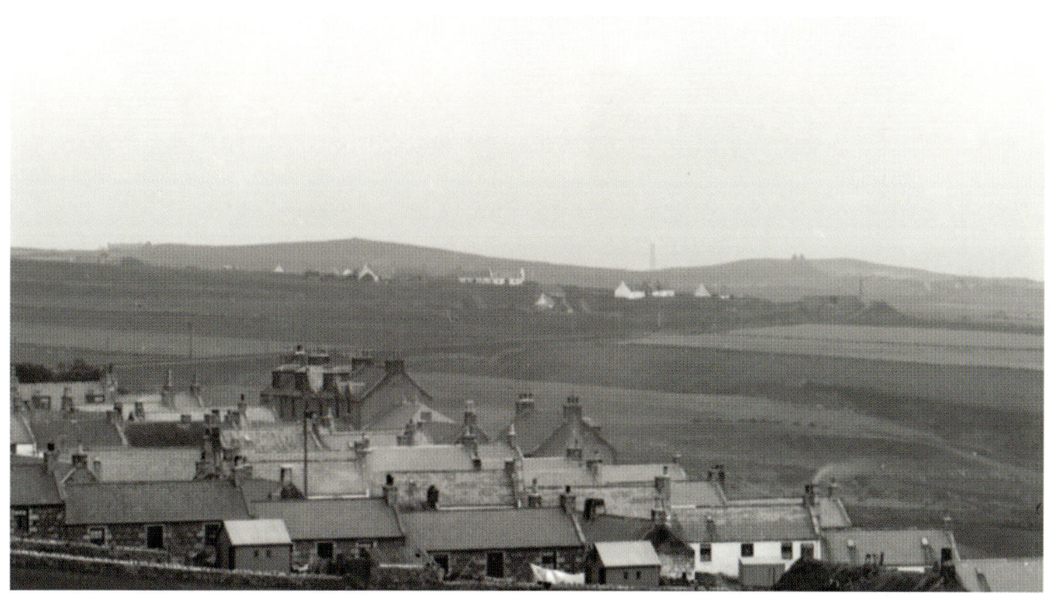

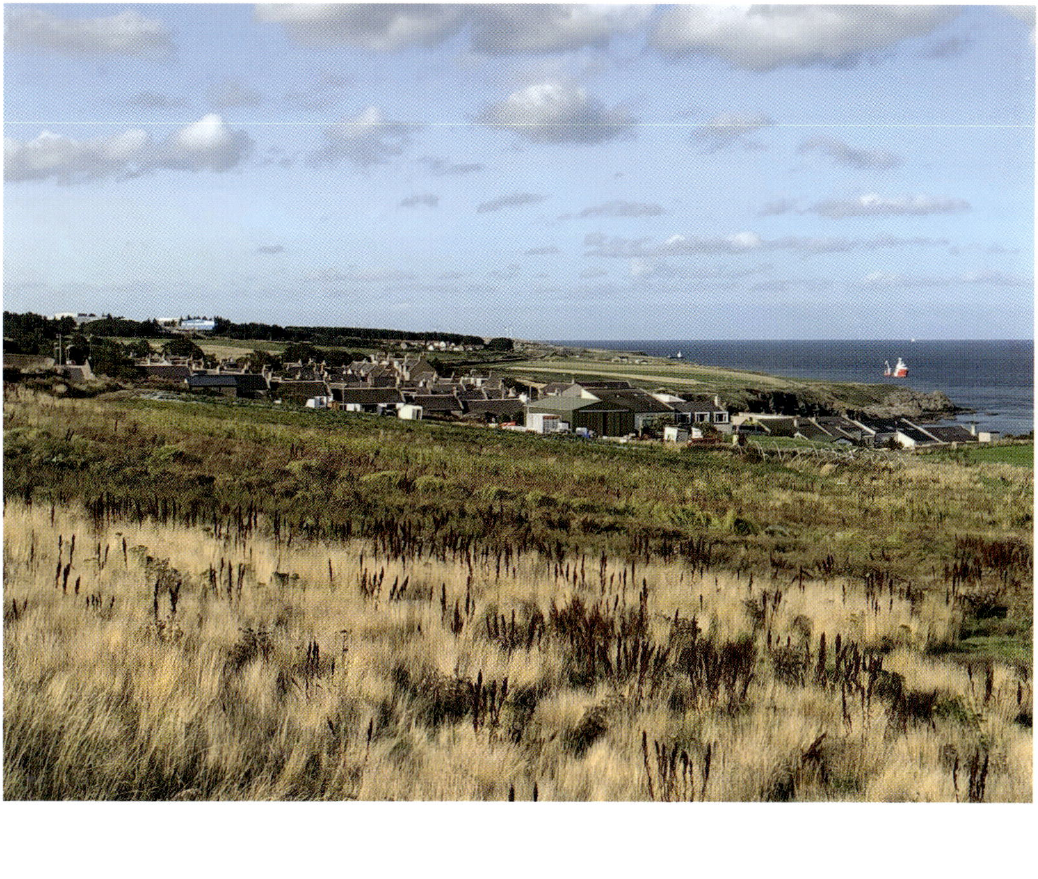

6

Aerial Photography

Aerial photography has been a great asset whilst researching for the book. In the modern day of Google Earth, we forget how special it can be.

I've been able to find a great deal of photographs in the National Collection of Aerial Photography (NCAP). The resolution and detail contained is stunning.

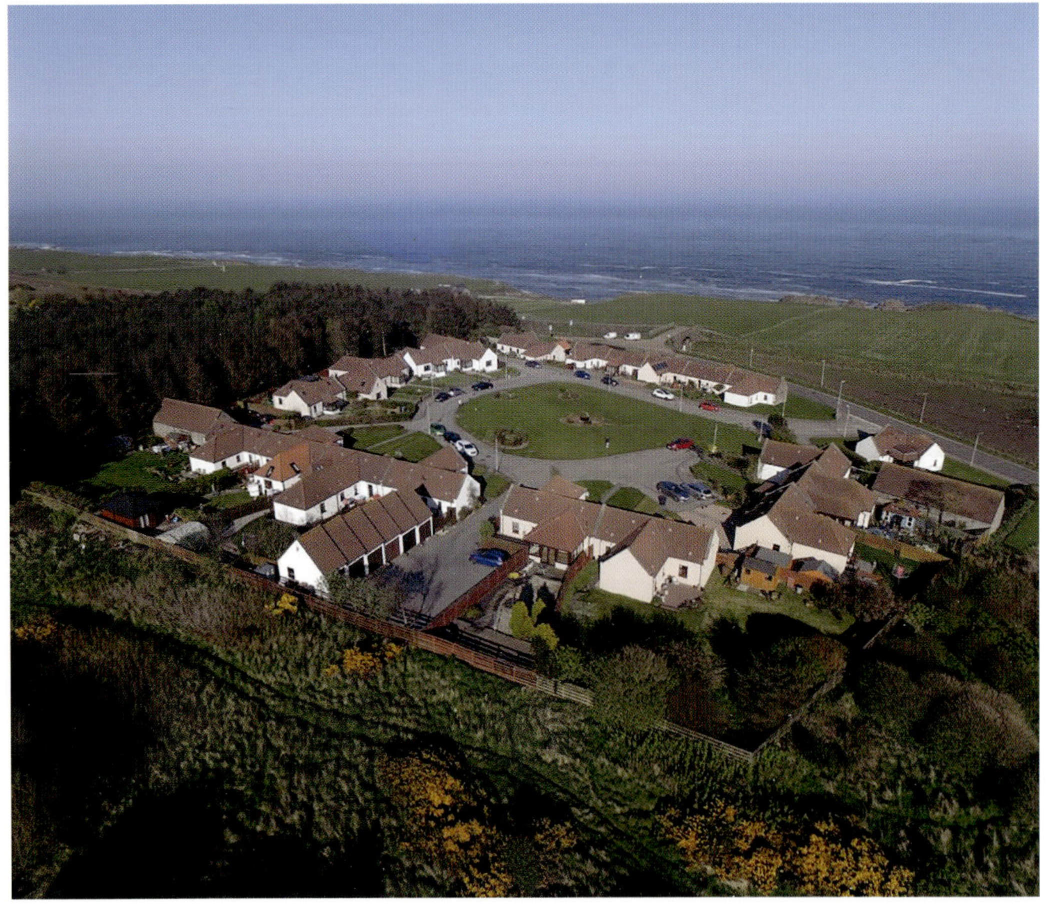

This photograph was taken with a drone in 2016 by ex-resident Barry Craig and was used for selling his house. A great shot on a sunny evening showing the sea in the distance.

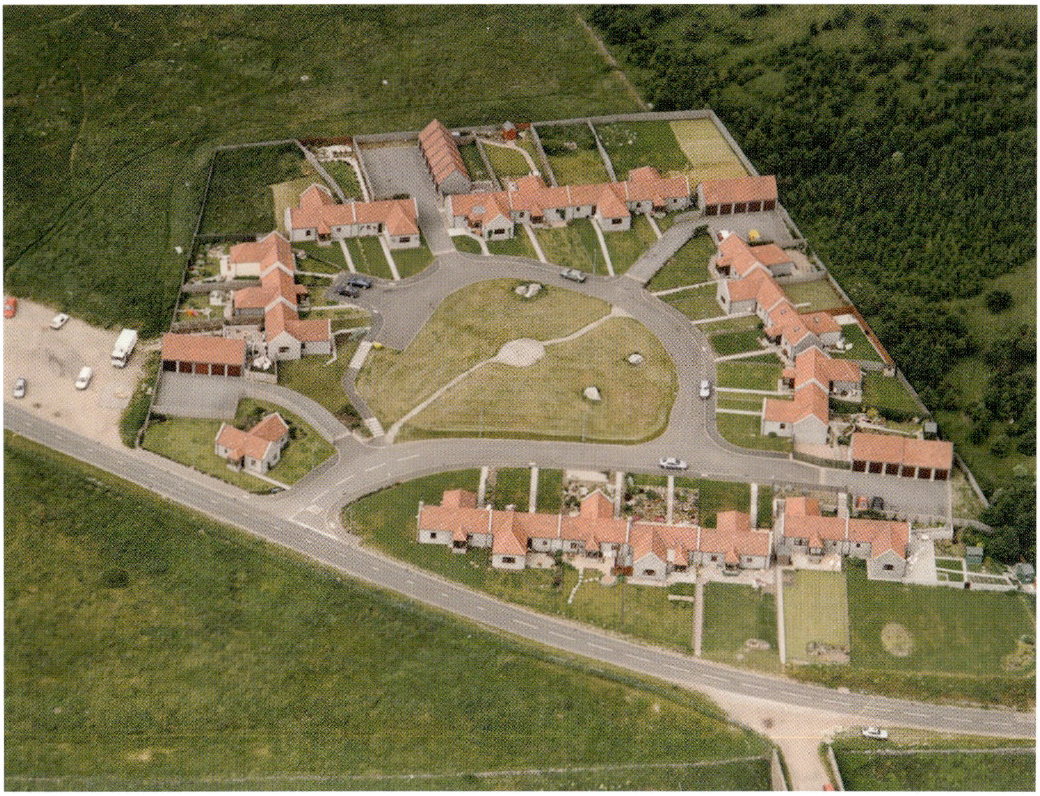

This one from my own collection was taken in 1995 looking West, before any of the extensions were built. I worked away from home a lot during this time and my neighbours were always reminding me that my grass needed cutting.

This shot from the National Collection of Aerial Photography in 1946 shows the path from the village heading north to Sinclair's farm. Residents would walk to the farm weekly, to pay their rent. At the top-right, there is a circular indentation to the left of the road and the railway line.

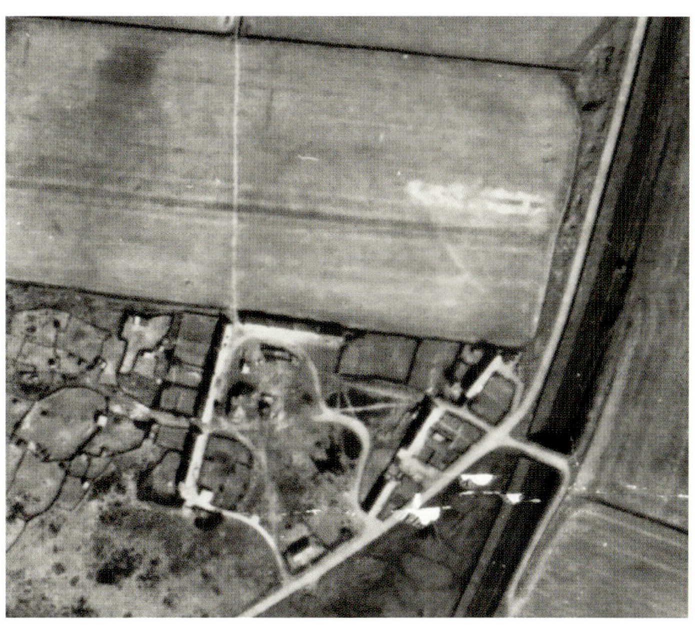

Jake Beattie told me that as a child, he was outside during the Second World War and a German plane was flying very low overhead. The Burnbanks kids were excited about this but adults were shouting at them – Get down! Take cover! This is not a game!

The plane was attacking a train travelling north and unleashed machine-gun fire and dropped a bomb. The railway line took a slight bend and this caused the bomb to miss the line. It took out a section of the dry stane dyke along the railway track and this gap can still be seen today where wooden fencing has replaced the bombed wall.

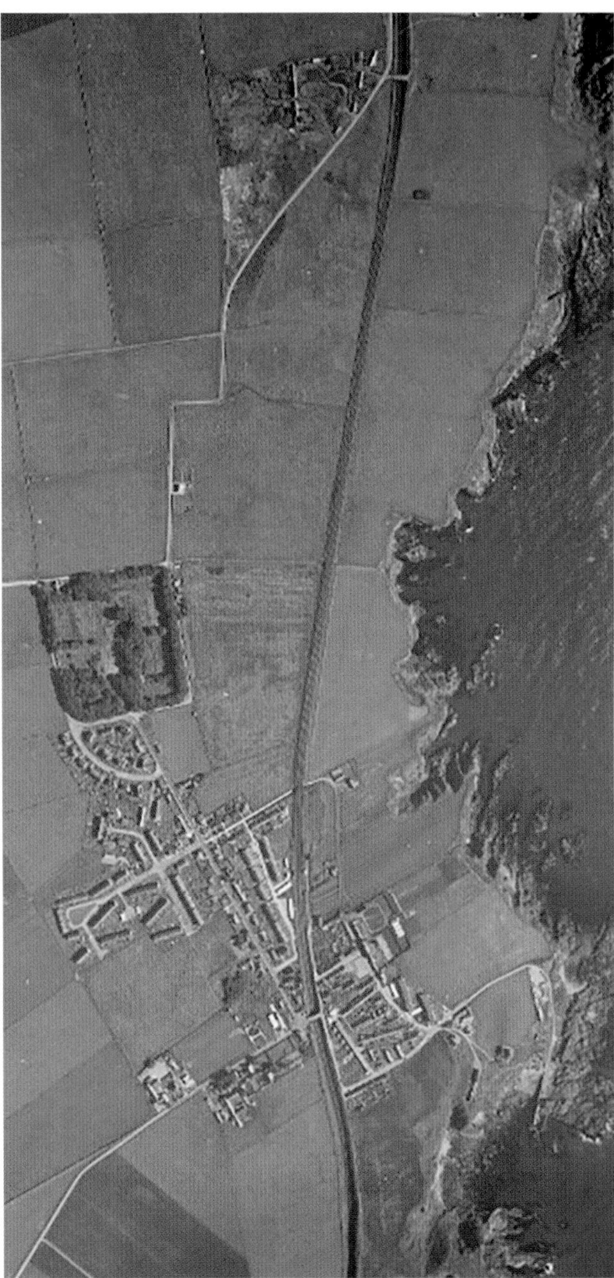

This photo from the National Collection of Aerial Photography was taken in 1973 and shows Burnbanks in the top and centre of the shot. Other notable landmarks are Catto Crescent in Cove just south of the square area of trees which used to be Loirston House, and Cove Harbour is on the bottom right.

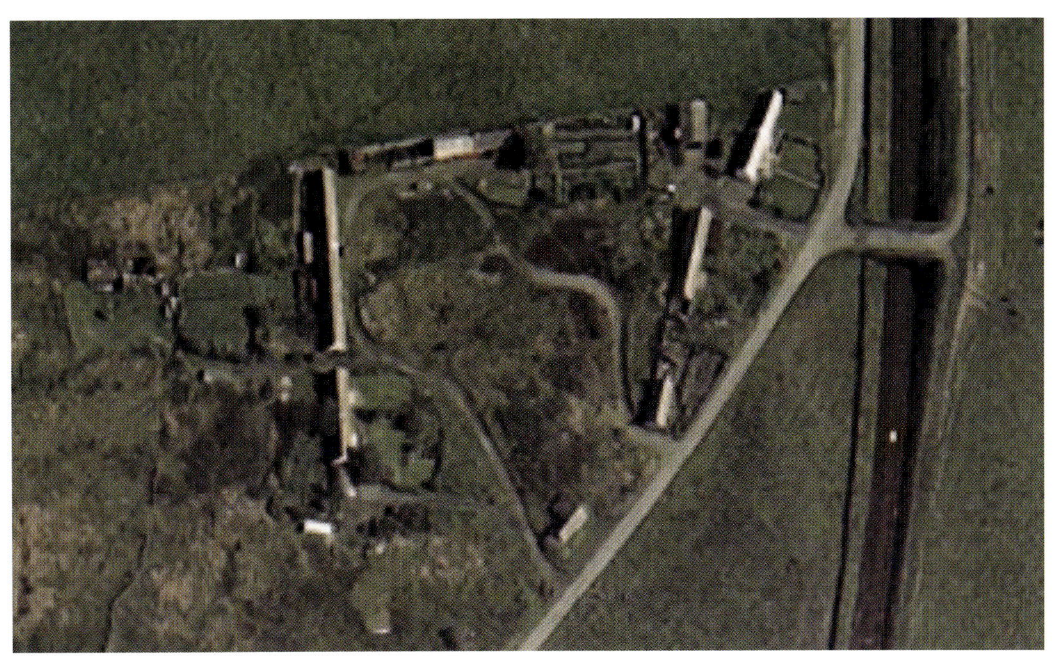

This enlargement from the same photo shows that some of the buildings are now derelict shells and the land to the west does not seem so well tended. My grass needs cutting again.

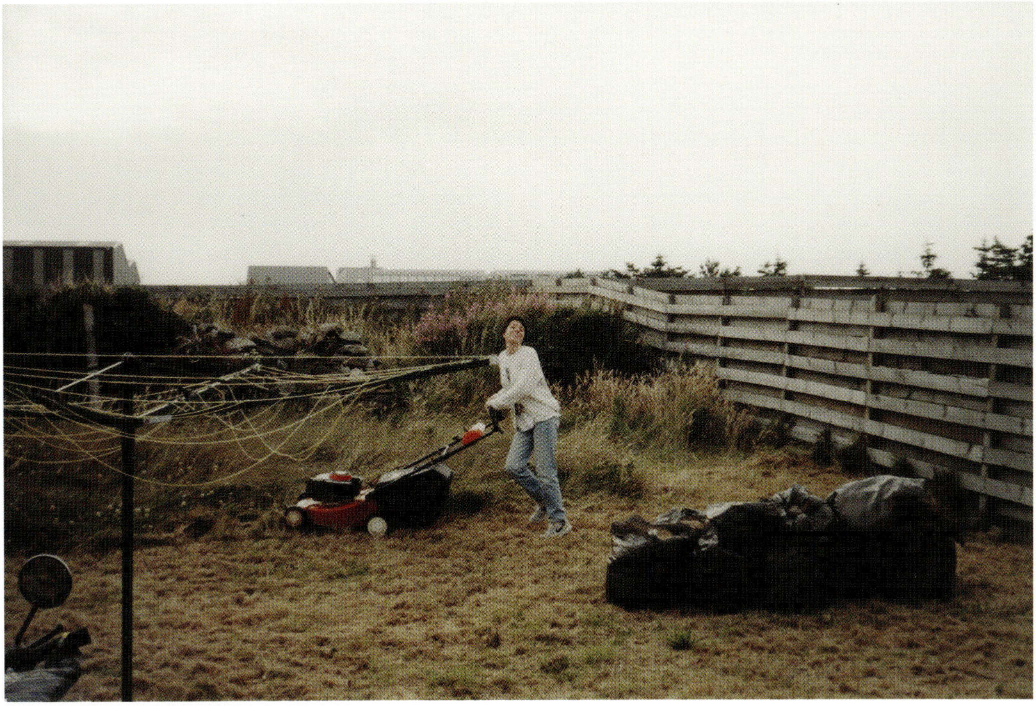

Move forward to 1996 and here's my wife Rosa cutting the grass. At last, the neighbours stop moaning at me!

7

Dorothy and Jake Beattie

When the article appeared in the local paper, I had several calls from ex-residents and one of the first to get in touch was Dorothy Kirton (née Beattie) who had a walk around the village and spoke to one of my neighbours. Contact was made and Dorothy and her brother Jake came around for a chat. They brought some fascinating photographs of life in the village up to the 1960s.

John and Christina Beattie moved into the village in the mid-1930s and lived in what is now No 6. The family grew to include four boys – George, Jake, Robbie, Billy – and then the only girl – Dorothy.

We talked for quite a few hours and the time just flew past. It was fascinating to hear them both and this meeting was the one that really got me going with this project.

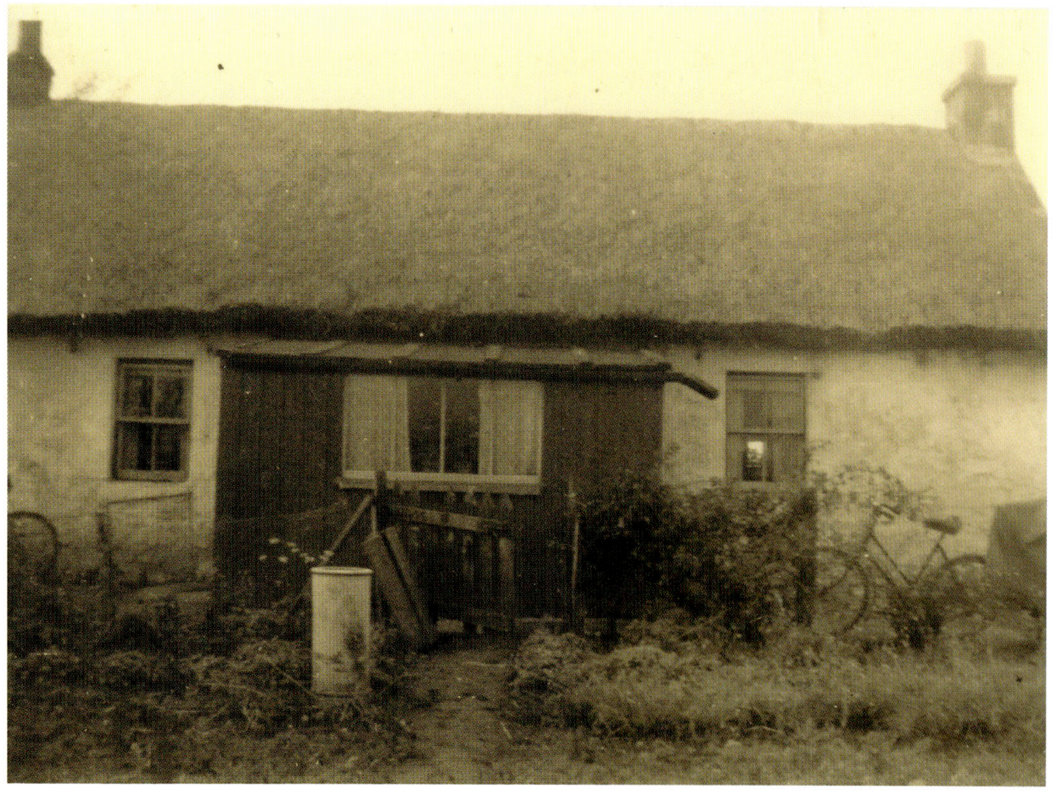

Sadly, Jake passed away before I finished the book but it was obvious when we met that one time that he was so enthusiastic telling stories about Burnbanks. I'm sorry I didn't get the project finished in time for him to see it.

They told me stories of what life was like: a happy, healthy existence which would be considered basic by today's standards. No electricity, no running water, no sewerage.

Light was from paraffin Tilley lamps, and heating was from peat or coal fires. There were two rooms in the house. Dorothy was the only girl so she had the luxury of a separate bedroom, which was actually a box room or cupboard – small luxury, but if you have four brothers, you need that space.

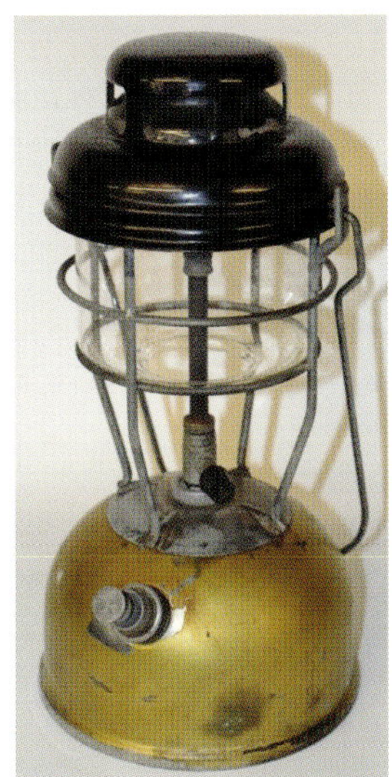

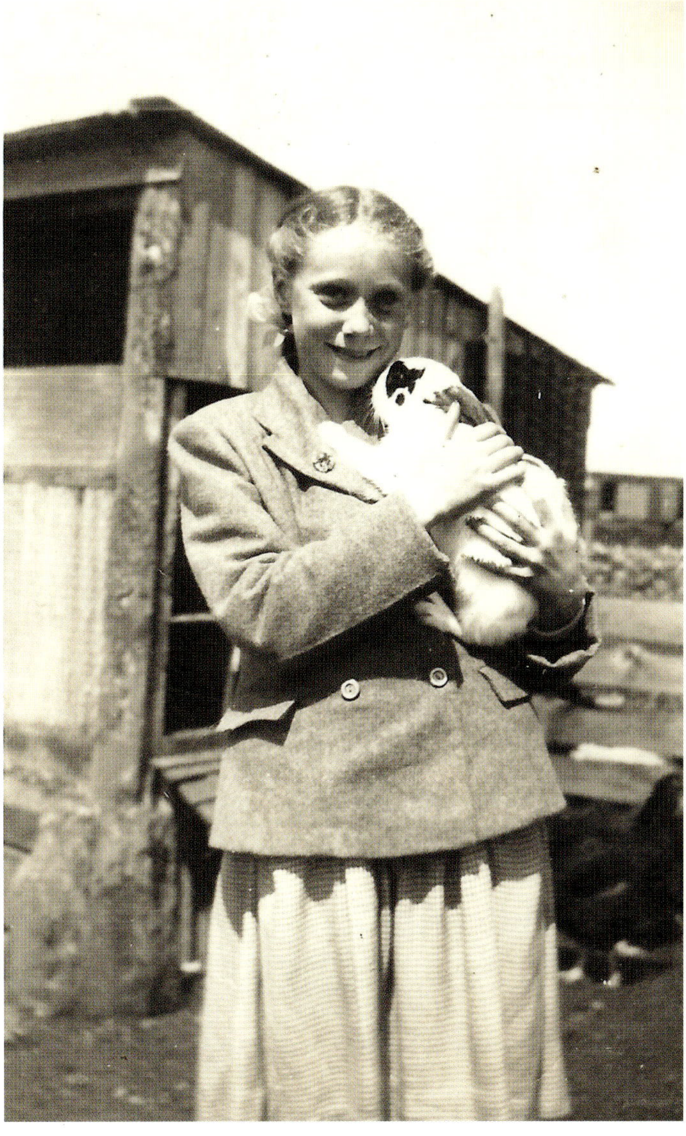

Right: When Dorothy showed us this photograph, my daughter Christina said, 'Ooh, did you have a pet rabbit?'. 'No dear, that was lunch!'

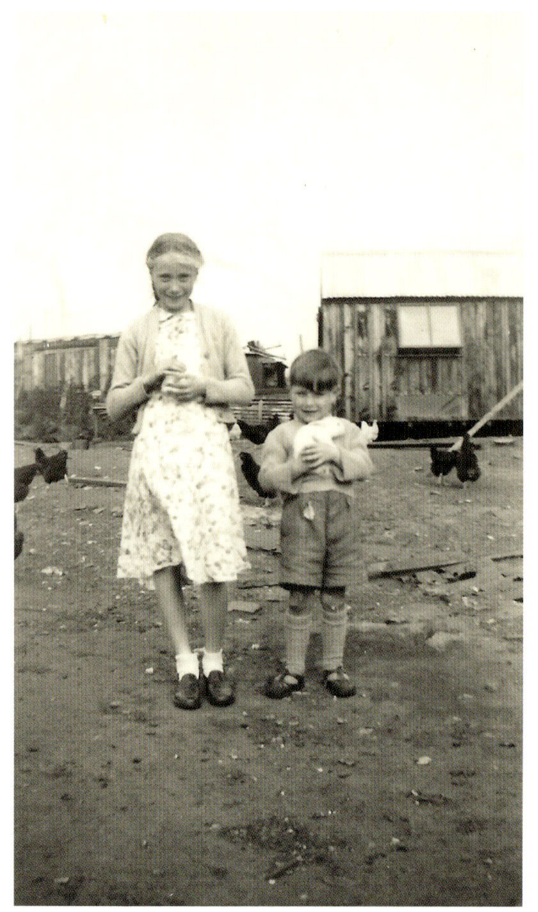

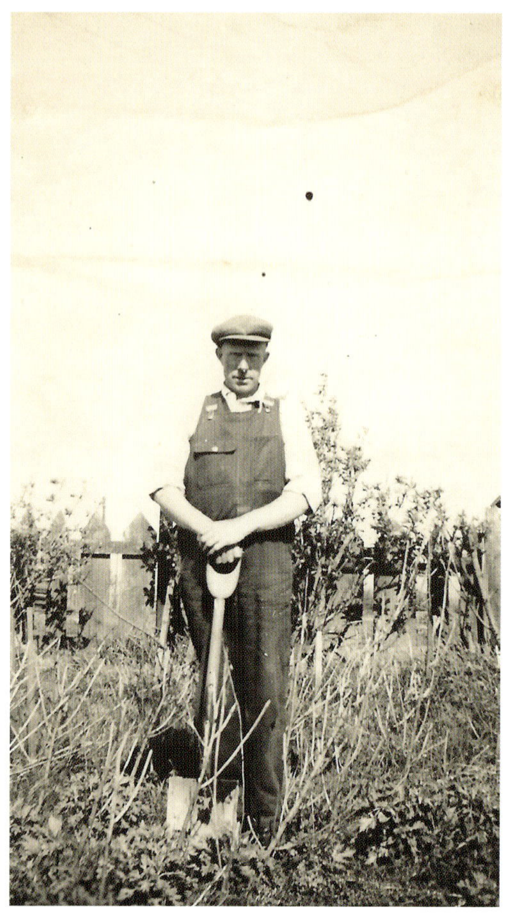

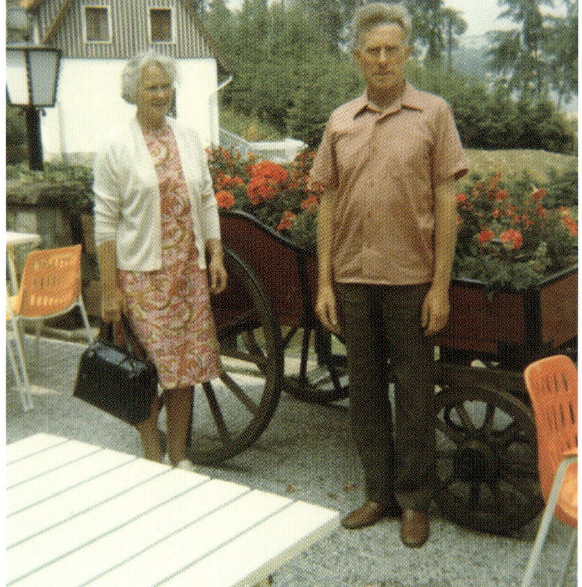

Above left: Dorothy with neighbour John Riddler.

Above right: Dorothy and Jake's father, John Beattie. He worked as a cattleman at Loirston farm and was a market gardener.

Left: John and Christina Beattie sometime after leaving the village.

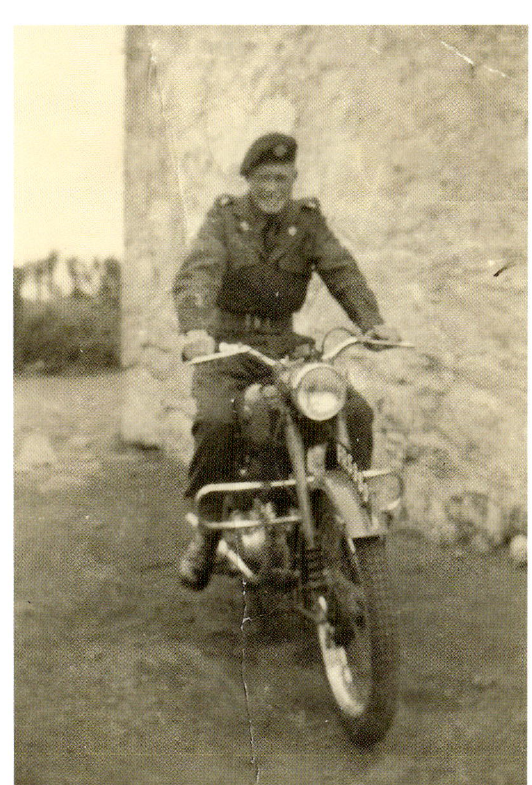

Right: Jake Beattie on a BSA Bantam at the gable end of their house.

Below: Jake's daughter Dorothy-Ann on the right.

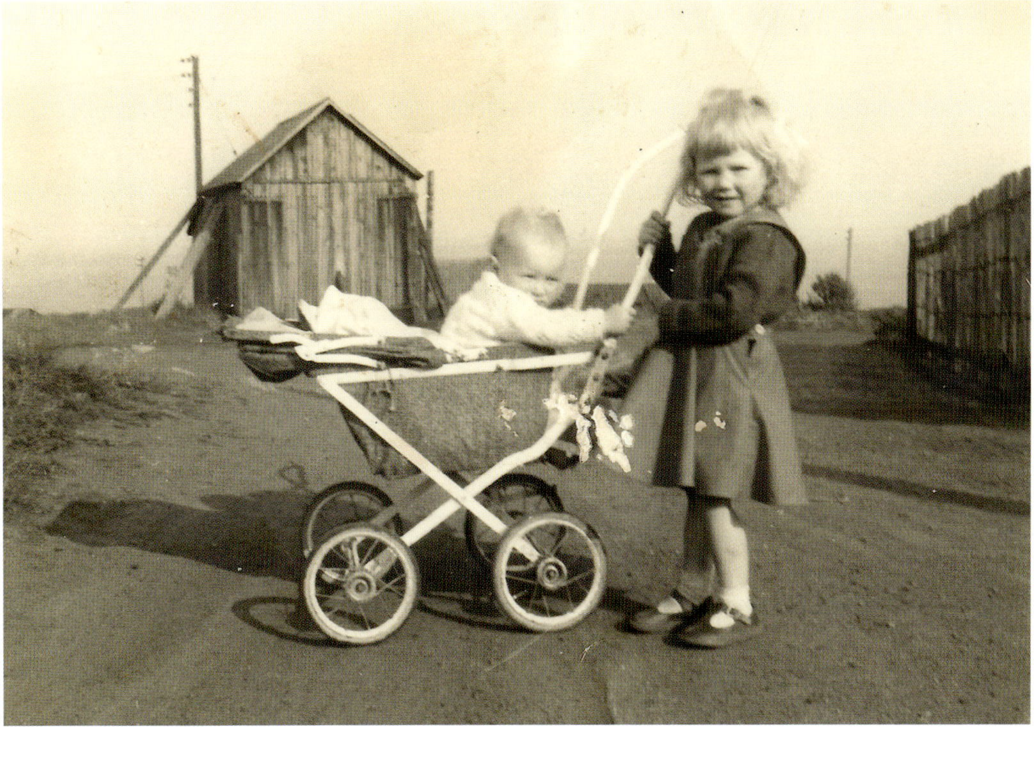

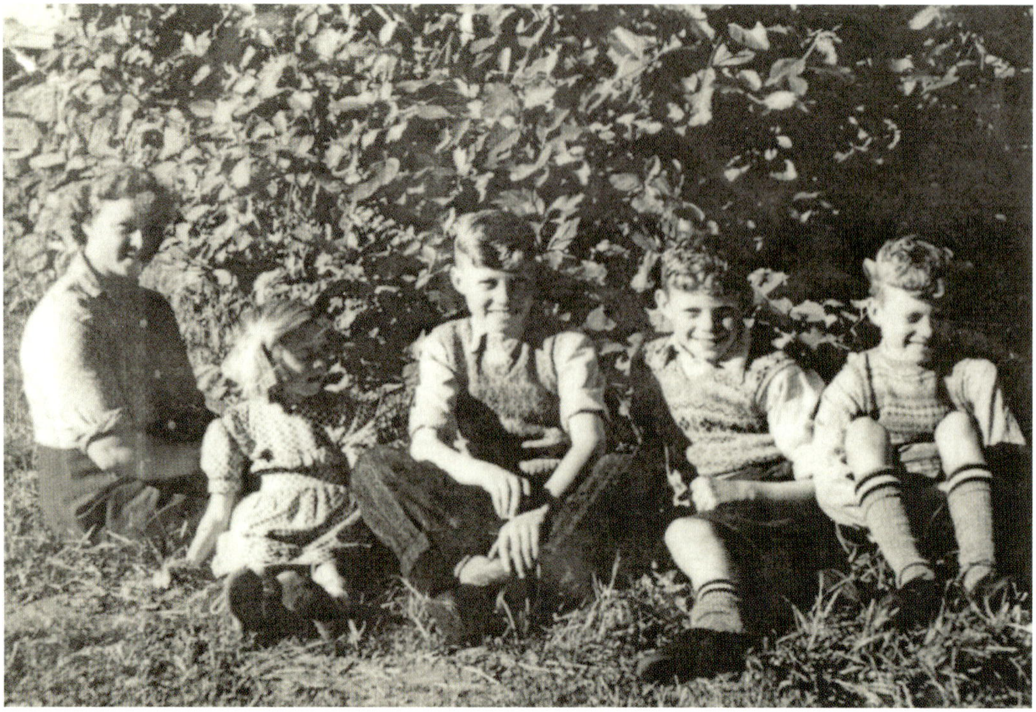

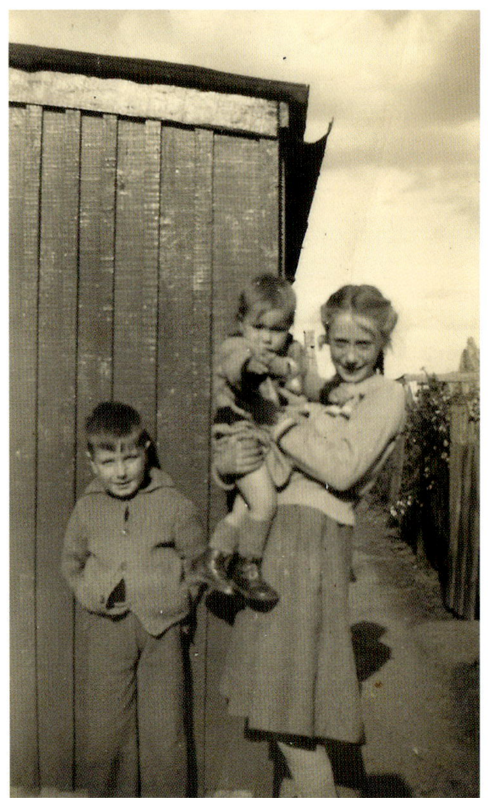

Above: Christina Beattie with her children: Dorothy, Jake, Robbie and Billy.

Left: Dorothy holding Moira Riddler. John Riddler is on the left.

As the family grew up and the boys left one by one, it was time for the Beattie's to move on and they left the village in the early 1960s.

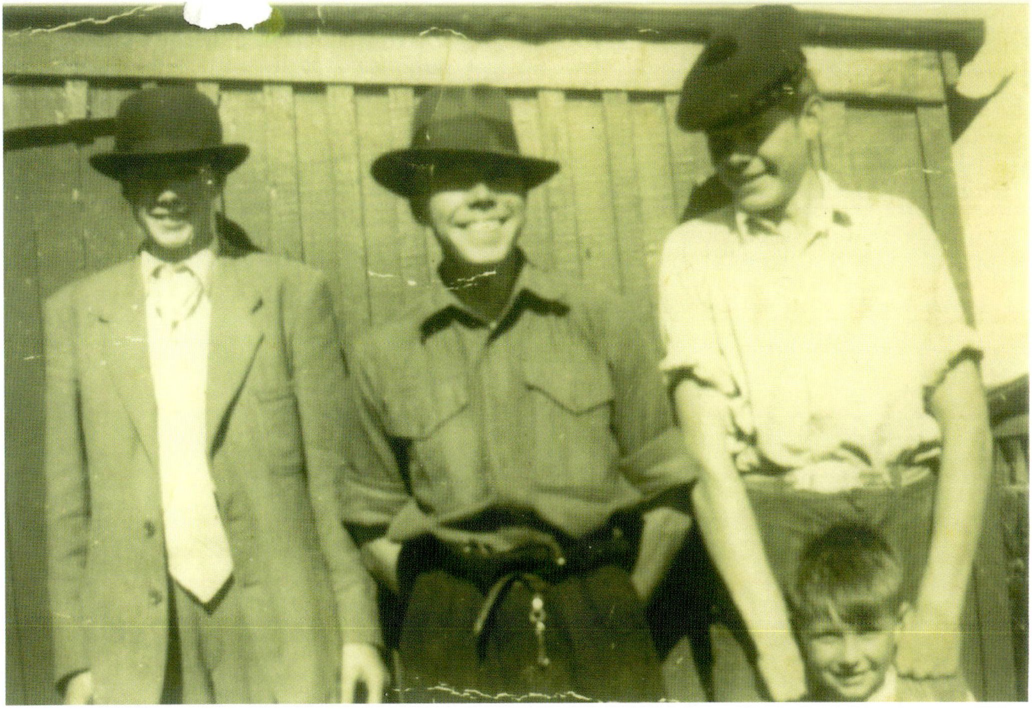

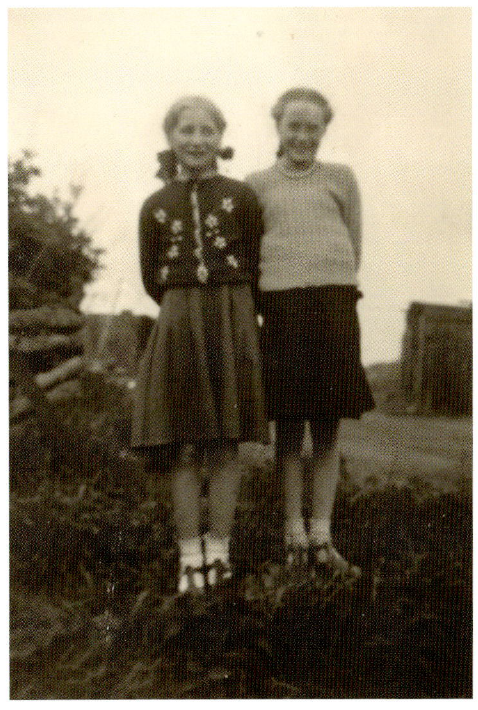

Above: Fun with hats. From the left, John, George and Robbie.

Right: Kathleen Davidson from old No. 17 (modern No. 22) and Dorothy. Still friends after all these years.

8

Moira Riddler

Moira Ritchie (née Riddler) lived in old No. 11 with her parents John and Isabella Riddler, her older brother John and sister Iris. This is now modern No. 7.

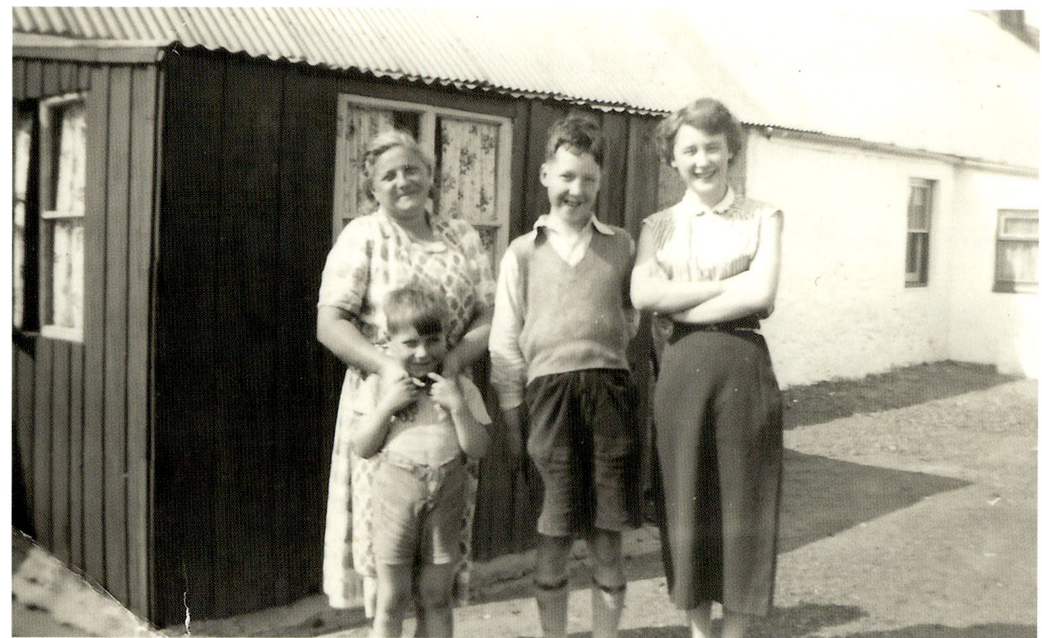

Isabella Riddler on the left outside her home. (Photograph courtesy of Dorothy Kirton)

She answered the advert and article I had in the Evening Express in 2012 and came round to meet me. Her son Ryan came along; he had been an apprentice joiner who helped rebuild the village with ABC Joiners and Scotia Homes and he told us it was a miserable, freezing place to work in the winter over 1991–92.

Moira was an eager source of information and was obviously proud of the village in her day and very entertaining to listen to. She was able to tell me stories about most of the families in the village. She scribbled a map and a list of the order of buildings with family names – who lived where – and this was invaluable when linking stories to houses.

This might not seem much but it was so important. By tying this to council valuation rolls, I've been able to define most, but not all, original house numbers. This was complicated by changes in numbers in the 1920s to 1940s.

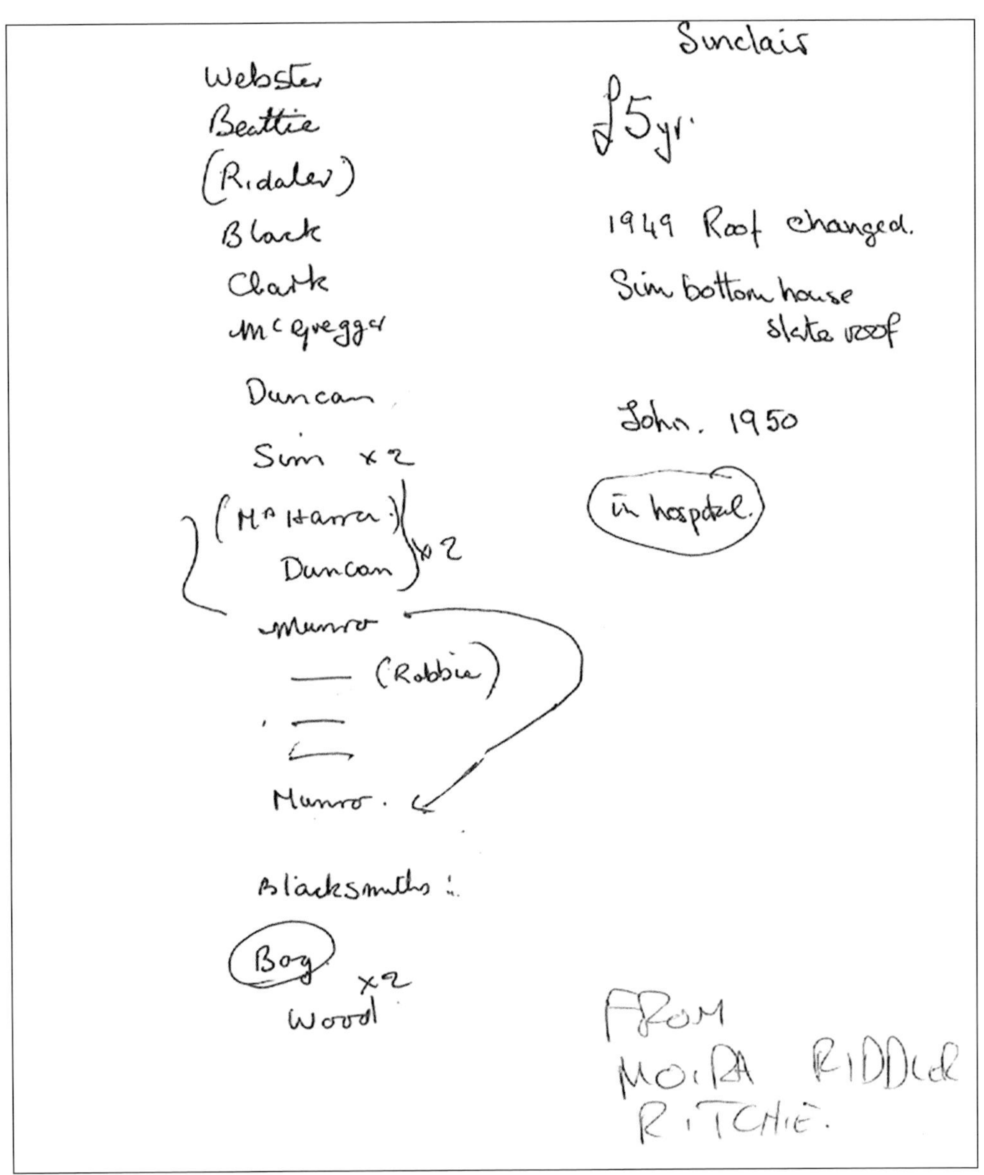

When my wife Rosa was having our children, I suggested that it would be great to have a home birth and have a child born in the village as I have met the family of the last one born here. Her reply was – 'No chance hombre, get me to a hospital!'

Seventy years later and we're still waiting.

Although Moira was born in Aberdeen hospital she was one of the last of the children to be brought up there and commented that it was a very lonely existence with no other playmates of a similar age.

The family left the village around 1963 and the house at No. 11 wasn't re-let to anyone else. The valuation rolls list it as uninhabitable just a year later and it disappeared from the register in 1967–68.

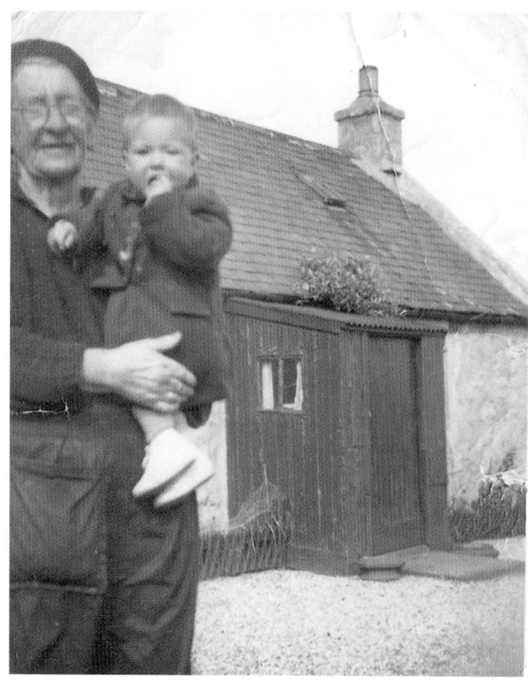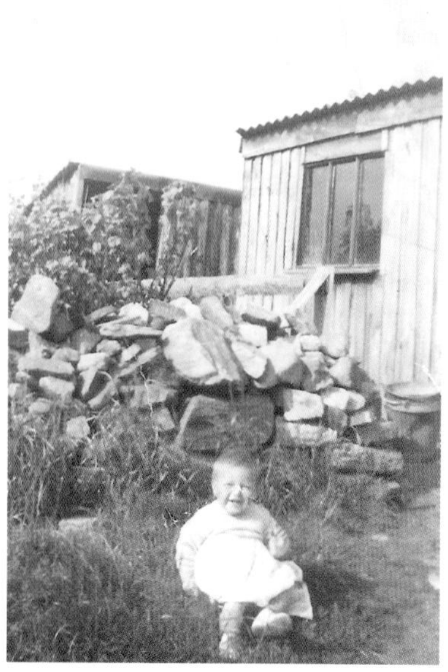

Above left: Here is Moira with Betty Sim.

Above right: This one is taken near the sheds and henhouses out the back of the village. Moira is around a year old.

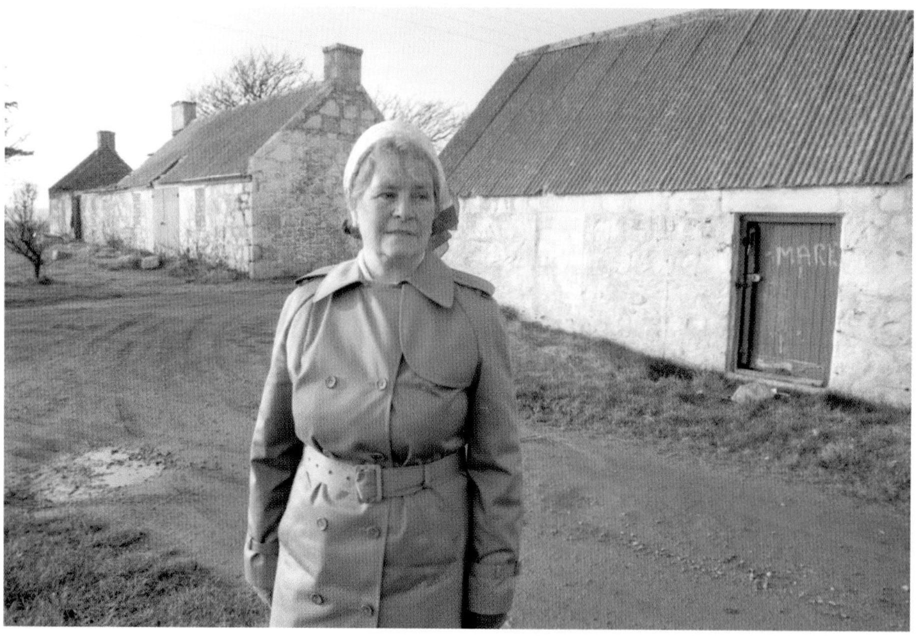

This photograph of ex-resident Mina King is outside Moira's old home in 1984. (Photograph courtesy of Aberdeen Journals Ltd. Used by kind permission of DC Thomson & Co. Ltd)

Nigg Kirkyard and War Memorial

Situated just off Wellington Road, Aberdeen, is the Nigg Kirkyard. This is the closest burial ground to Burnbanks and contains the graves of many villagers and also the war memorial that commemorates Burnbanks casualties from the First and Second World War. Three Burnbanks servicemen are listed and several others have links to Burnbanks. The three Burnbanks men listed are James Coutts, who died in 1917; John Taylor Robertson, 1918; and Frederick Beattie, 1941. Other casualties not from Burnbanks but connected are Alfred Colville and Alexander Eggo. Separate sections deal with each of these men.

The kirk has been closed for many years and all of the furniture including pews, pulpit and both sides of the upper balconies are now removed.

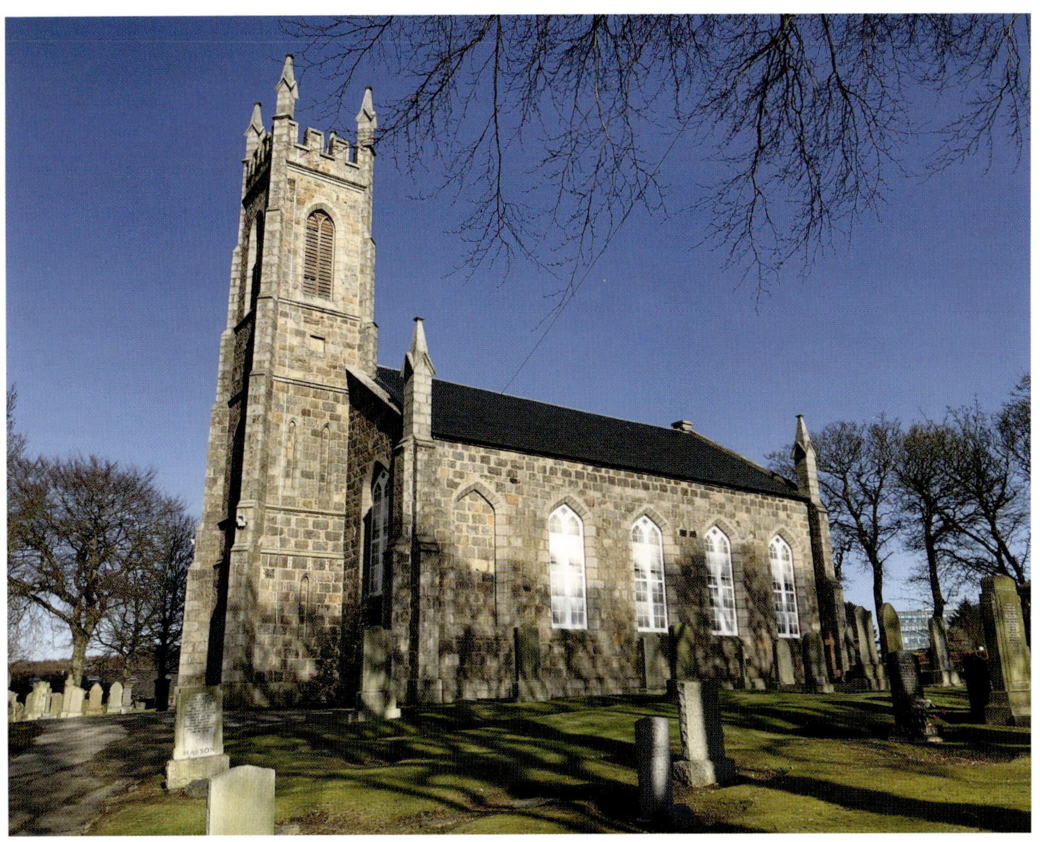

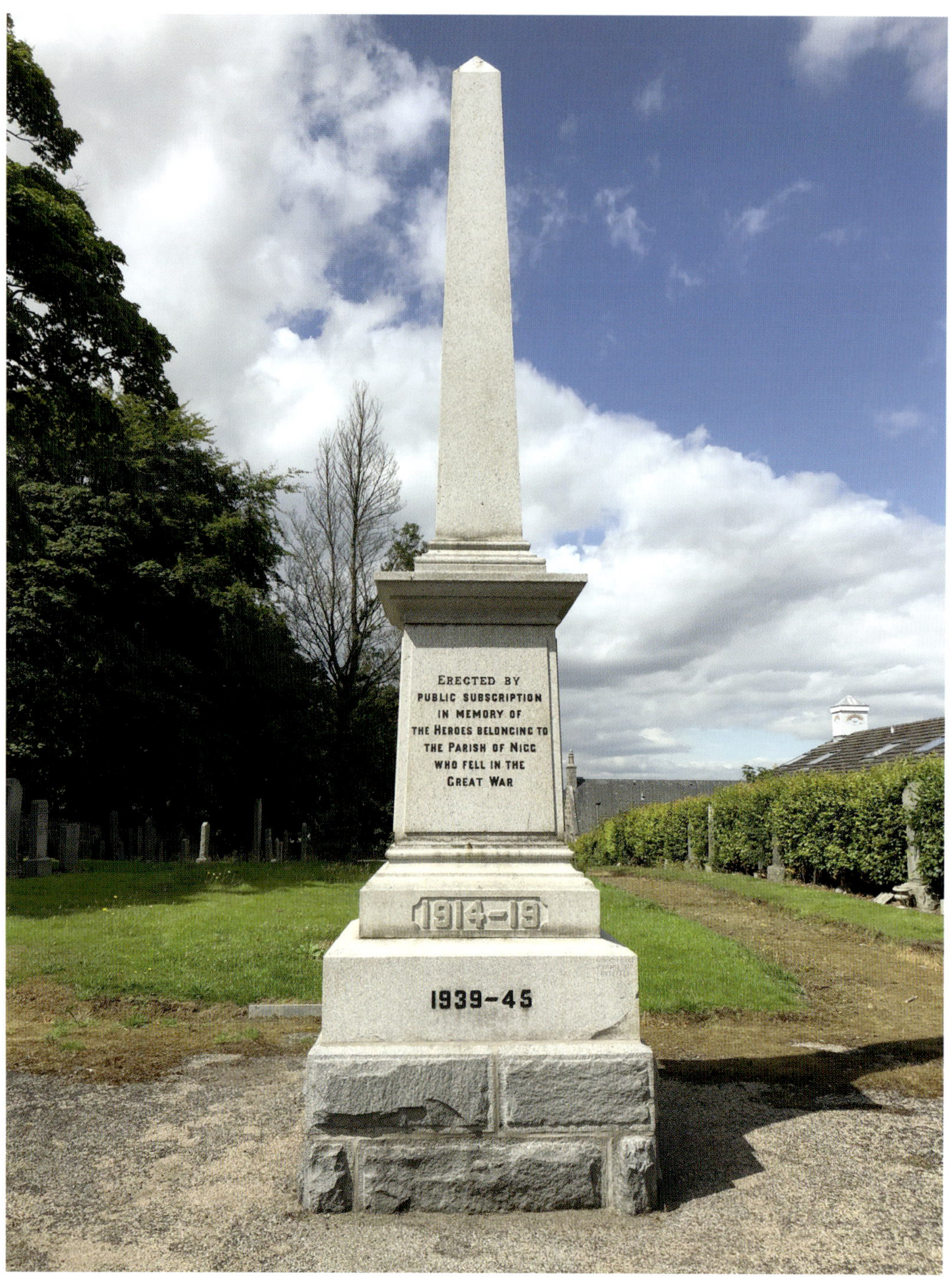

An unusual feature to deter vandals is that the windows are blocked with sheet steel but have window panels and frames painted on them to lessen the look of abandonment. The window shown below in the centre of the gable end is the only source of natural light.

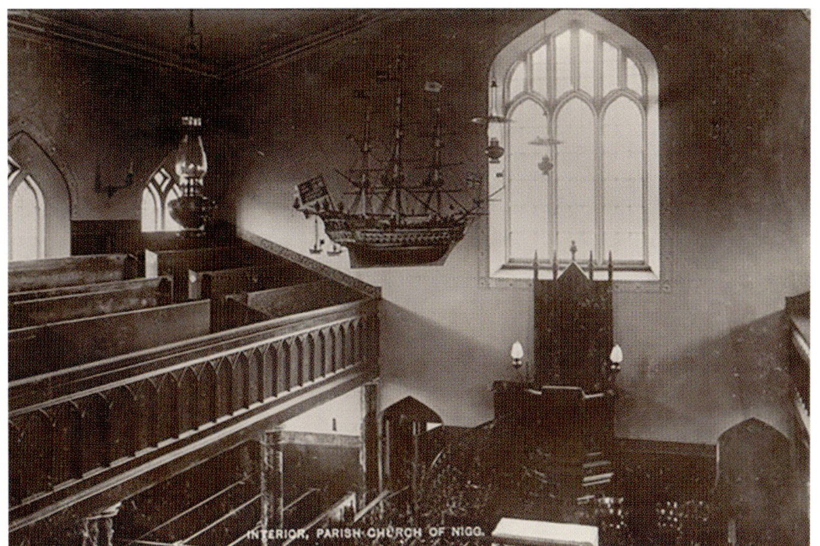

Interior of the Parish Church of Nigg. (From a postcard in the author's collection)

For many years, a model ship hung from the roof, donated by church member Captain Affleck who was thankful for being rescued from a shipwreck. After the kirk closed, this was transferred to Torry St Fitticks' parish church and now resides in Aberdeen Maritime Museum.

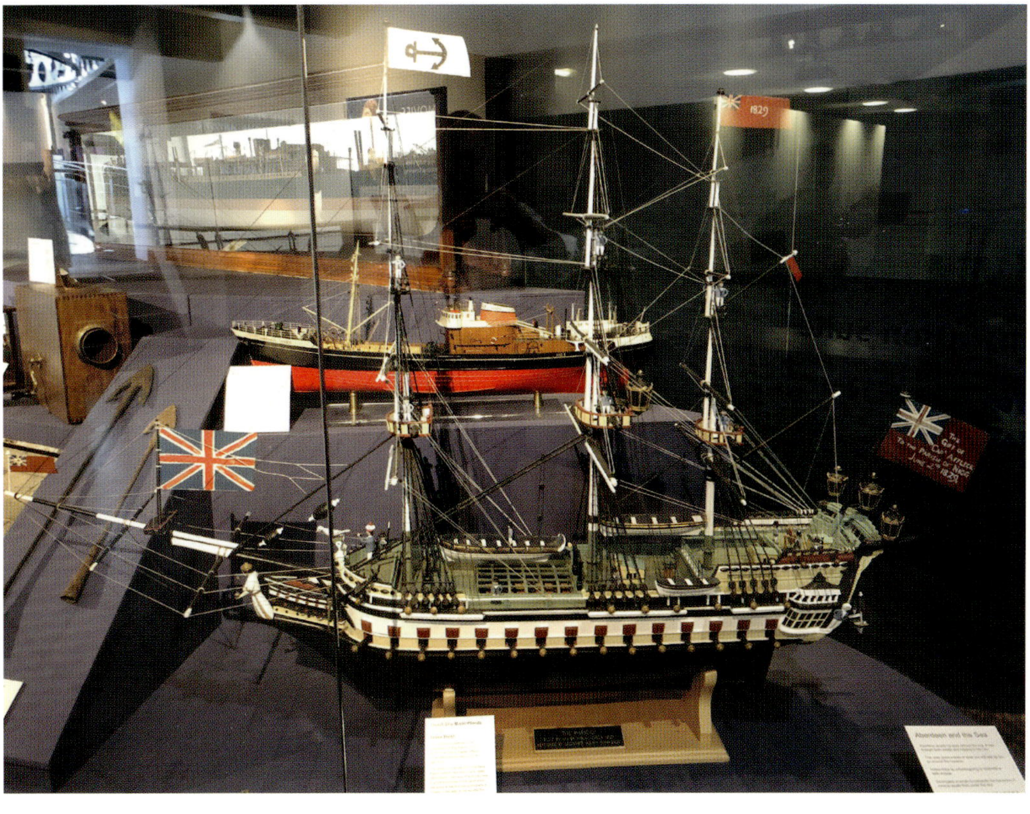

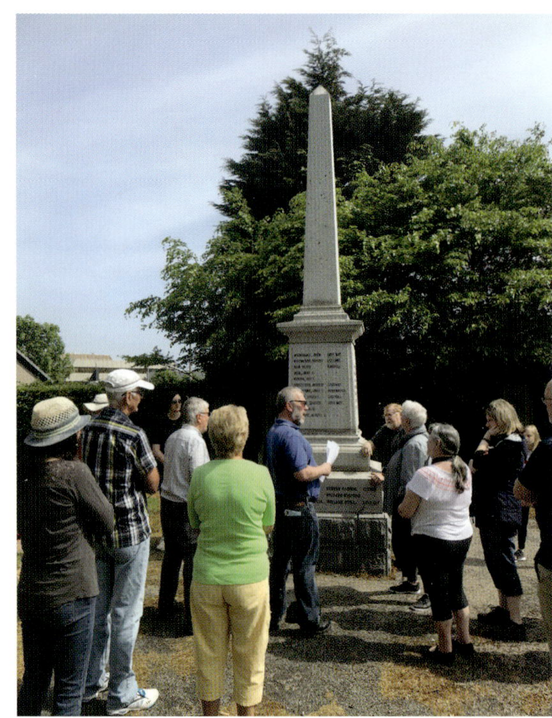

Left: I led a walking tour in 2018 covering several stories about Burnbanks people. I was really pleased when over twenty people turned up.

Below: At the Nigg Kirk War Memorial talking to Anne Park, who has done an amazing body of work compiling a database of all service casualties from the First World War from Aberdeen and the surrounding area. Look for the Aberdeen and North East Scotland Family History Society. (Photos by Pauline Gerrard)

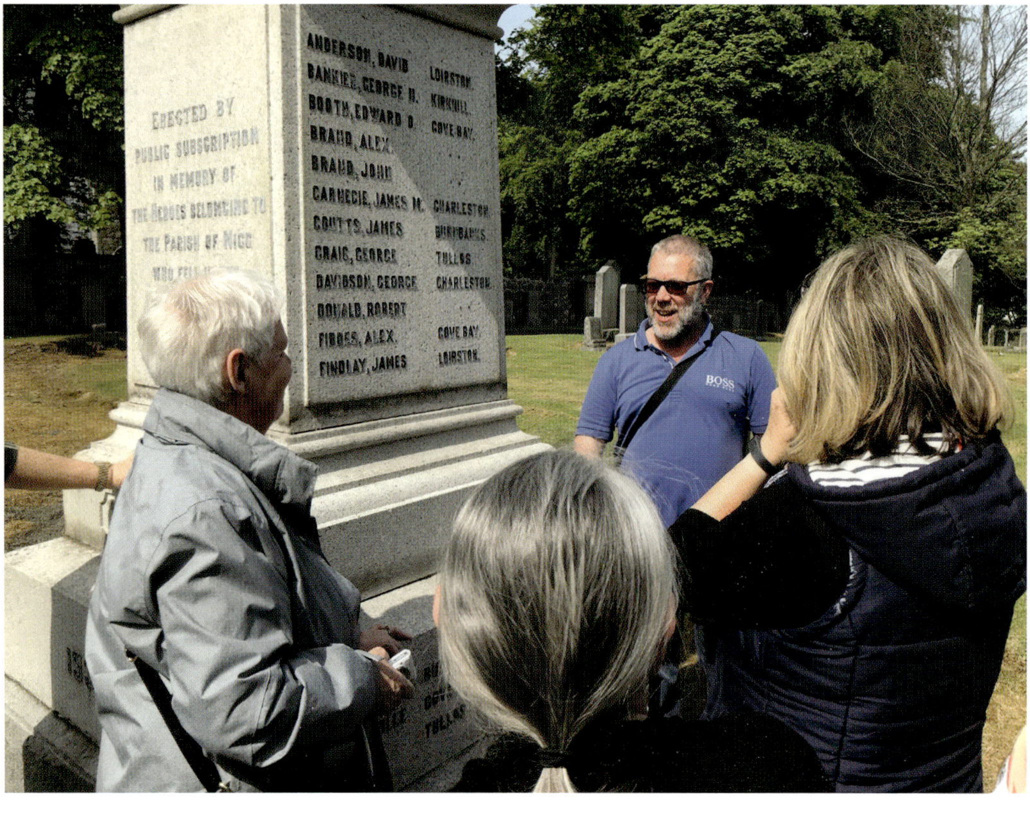

The Disgraceful Condition of a Country Churchyard

A report from the *Stonehaven Journal* of 19 October 1871 tells a shocking tale about Nigg Kirkyard.

The funeral was taking place of Alexander Morrice who was drowned during the works to redirect the River Dee, near Aberdeen harbour. Mourners were horrified to see the coffin of his father, who was buried nine years previously, lying on the grass next to the opened grave. The lid was broken and the remains were clearly visible.

The grave had become so overcrowded that it was deemed necessary to inter the fresher corpse at the bottom and rebury the older, decayed ones closer to the top. This meant the top coffin was less than 2 feet from the surface and it was noted that other graves in the cemetery had coffins mere inches from the surface.

Coffins had to be crushed to get everything back in and bones deposited in a steel box close to the headstone. Although the journalist considered the scene revolting, he was astonished that it caused little remark other than 'it is the custom'.

The kirkyard was extended in the 1880s, and again in 1919–20 just before the erection of the war memorial. Maps are available from the National Records of Scotland.

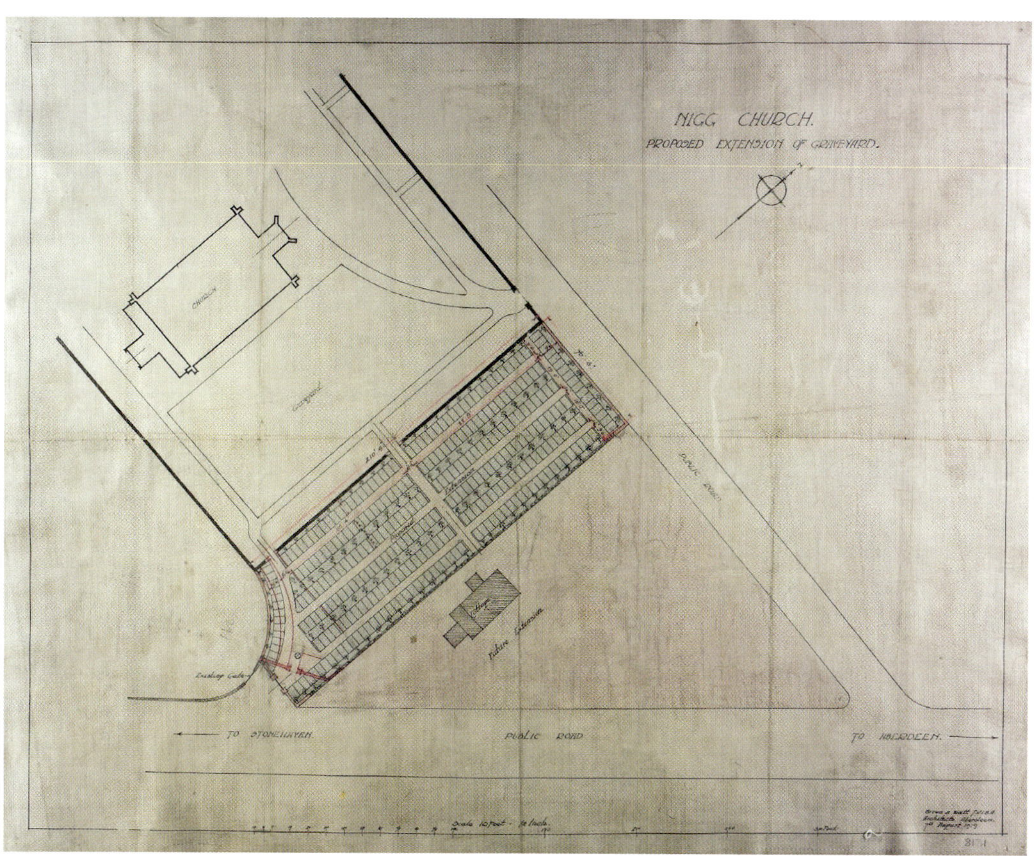

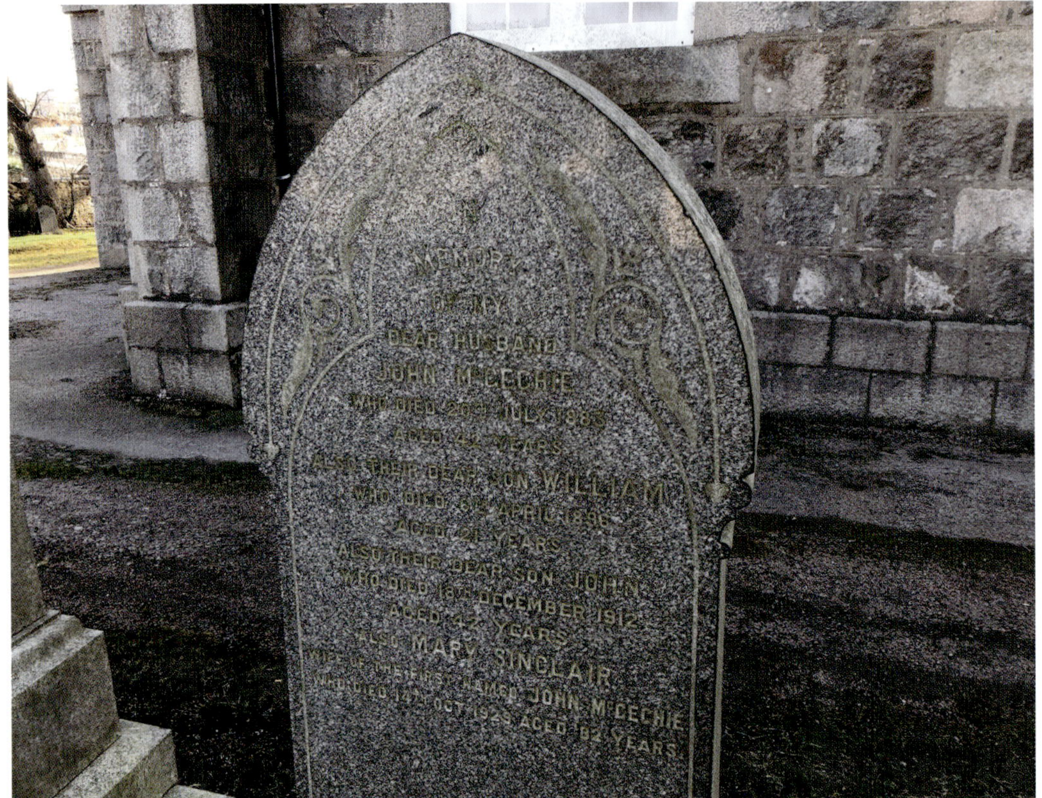

John McGechie Junior

This is the headstone of the McGechie family. Son John died in December 1912 aged forty-two when he committed suicide in the shed of his house in Burnbanks, which was behind the modern No. 5. His mother found him suspended by a rope but she couldn't release him and although she immediately went for assistance, Dr Skene of Cove attended and pronounced life extinct.

A few months previously, John had been injured in a cycling accident and had been in failing health.

Current Status

The cemetery is well tended by Aberdeen City Council and the war memorial was recently cleaned and re-lettered for the 100th anniversary of the end of the First World War.

The council is not accepting burials anymore except on previously purchased plots if space exists within a lair. There is a tree where ashes can be scattered.

James Shepherd Coutts and the SS *Norwood*

James was a ship's cook and he died during the First World War when his vessel SS *Norwood* was attacked in February 1917 close to Aberdeen harbour entrance by the German U-boat *UC-29* commanded by Ob Lt zur See Ernst Rosenow.

The *Norwood* was a coastal steamer owned by the Aberdeen, Newcastle & Hull Steamship Co. that operated regular passenger and cargo services from Hull and Newcastle to Aberdeen and the Northern Islands Orkney and Shetland.

The story of the *Norwood* could fill an entire book on its own but for the purposes of this chapter, we are concentrating on the life of James Coutts.

On a passage from Middlesbrough, the vessel had already entered the port of Aberdeen when it was ordered not to tie up and to make its way to Peterhead, some 30 miles north. Warnings had already been issued of U-boat activity in the area, so the exact reasons why the vessel was instructed to relocate even though it was already in a position of safety are not known, but it ultimately sealed the fate of all onboard. Eighteen men were lost.

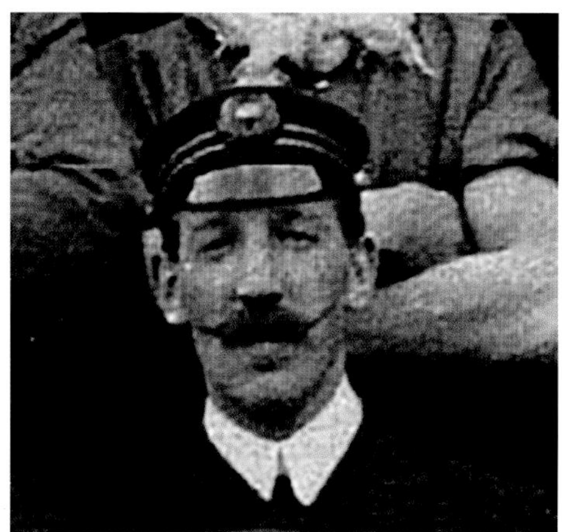

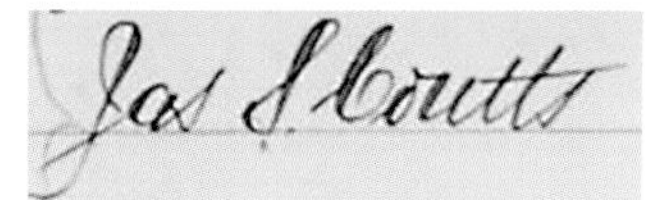

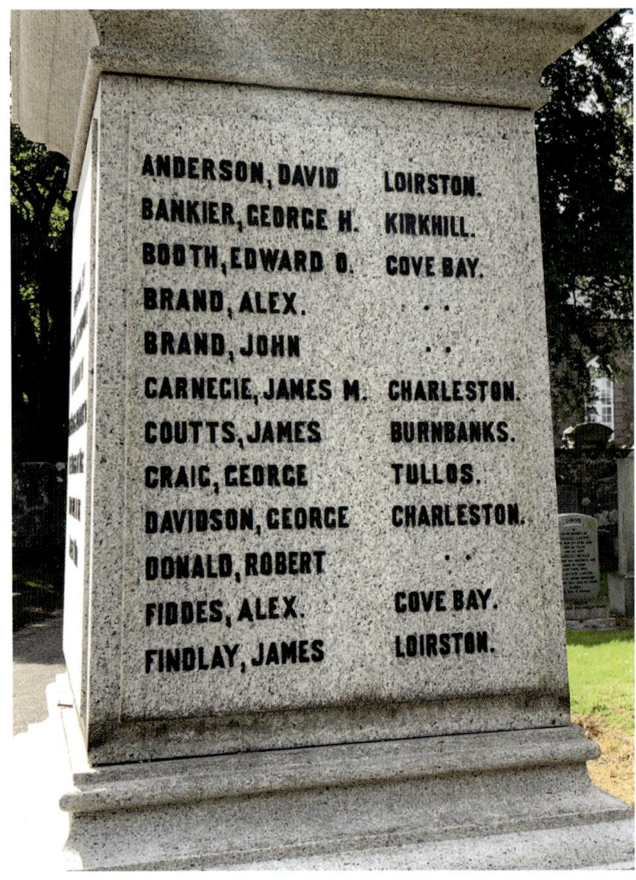

James Coutts is listed on the Nigg Kirkyard War Memorial.

The vessel departed for Peterhead but on arriving there, it was instructed to return again to Aberdeen. That was the last anyone saw of the vessel. Wreckage was later washed ashore that was identified as coming from *Norwood*, but no contact was made and no bodies were recovered. The location of the wreck is known, in 85 metres of water just a little to the east of Aberdeen harbour.

The *UC-29* was itself sunk a few weeks later off the coast of Ireland by an armed but disguised merchant vessel, a 'Q-Ship' called *Pargust* commanded by Captain Gordon Campbell who detailed that sinking in a personal memoir called *My Mystery Ships*. His description of the U-boat as it sank with a crewman clinging to the pointed bow brought great feelings of sadness for me. Once the submarine is incapacitated or sinking, the man is no longer an enemy; he then becomes a fellow mariner, a fellow mariner in distress.

A court of enquiry (but not a court martial) was convened to examine the circumstances of the loss of the vessel, and displeasure was expressed at both of the senior naval officers who were responsible for the safe-keeping and defence of the ports of Aberdeen and Peterhead. Blame was imported to the Peterhead SNO and he was removed from command.

The *Norwood* was built in Hall Russell & Co. Ltd shipyard in Aberdeen in 1895. This was the same shipyard where I completed an apprenticeship as a ship draughtsman from 1980 onwards.

During peacetime the vessel was a regular and popular ship which was highly regarded by passengers for a comfortable way to travel south. Think of the alternative form of transport at the time: long distances on a bone-jarring omnibus or a crowded, noisy, foul trip on a train. Forget about the rose-tinted spectacles memories of the majesty of steam trains; a gentle cruise on an accommodating ship with good food and drink with the attentive service of the captain and crew was the way to travel.

During the First World War, travel by sea was very dangerous due to the German U-boats patrolling the North Sea and attacking any ships, warships or merchantmen. Because of this passenger services were restricted and the *Norwood* was requisitioned for war duties transporting personnel and cargo at the directions of the War Office.

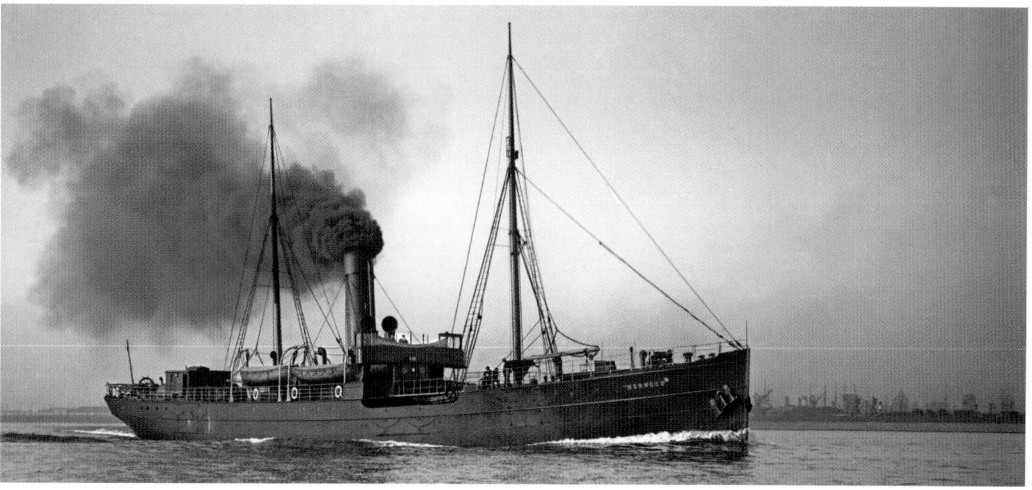

Above: (Photograph © Hull Maritime Museum)

Right: Ernst Rosenow from German Navy Crew Chronicle 1891–1918 published on Ancestry and memorial project www.denkmalprojekt.org.

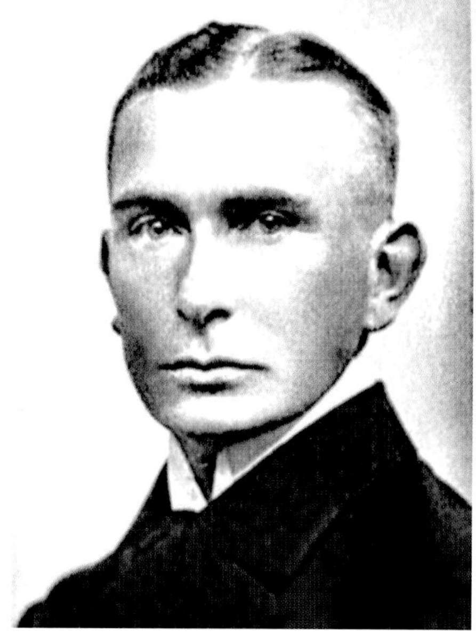

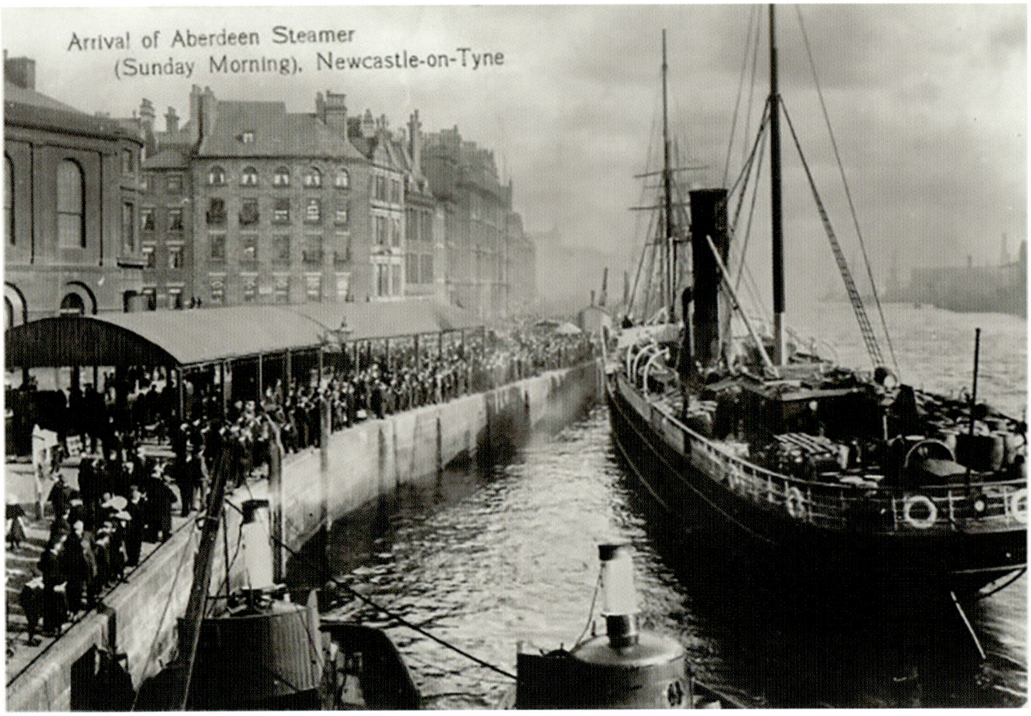

The *Norwood* arriving at Newcastle *c.* 1910. The amount of people lining the quayside shows the popularity of the vessel. (Postcard from the author's collection)

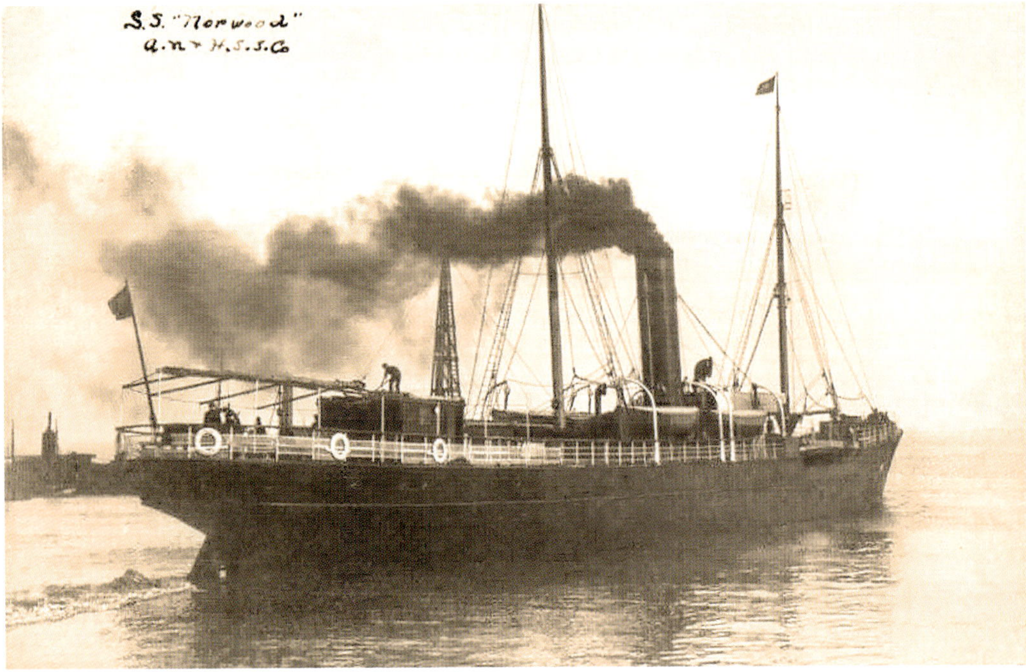

The *Norwood* leaving Hull in 1904. (Postcard from the author's collection)

The many threads of the research have yielded a fascinating story. We traced all the crew, their home addresses, their families, the operation of the company before and during the war and we also dipped into the lives of the U-boat and crew.

Researching James and the *Norwood* has taken up a large amount of time but it's been an amazing journey. For a long time, I couldn't find a direct link from James to Burnbanks and it was a great concern that so much time had been spent, but other than the war memorial inscription, I couldn't link him to the village.

All other references seem to show him as living in Walker Road, Torry, at the time of his death, which is around 3 miles from Burnbanks. Census returns and his marriage certificate show him living in Leith in 1901–06.

Valuation rolls show a lot of movement, but he seems to have spent a fair amount of time in the Rosemount area of Aberdeen.

To my great relief, the link to Burnbanks was proven. I found that his first wife, Elizabeth Fingzies Coutts, had died in 1912 in Rosemount, Aberdeen, aged only thirty-one years old from acute pneumonia. His second wife was called Helen Campbell and their marriage certificate, dated 1914, confirmed that she came from Burnbanks, living with her parents Alexander and Jeanie Campbell in Nos 10 and 11.

James had three children with his first wife: twin daughters Elizabeth and Helen, born 1906; and another daughter, Pearl, born in 1911. Sadly they also had a second set of twins, Grace and James, who died in 1908 and 1909 respectively. James and Helen had one child, Jeanie Coutts, in 1914. Jeanie was one of the residents who came to the village on the open day after the rebuild and was known as Jean Ingram.

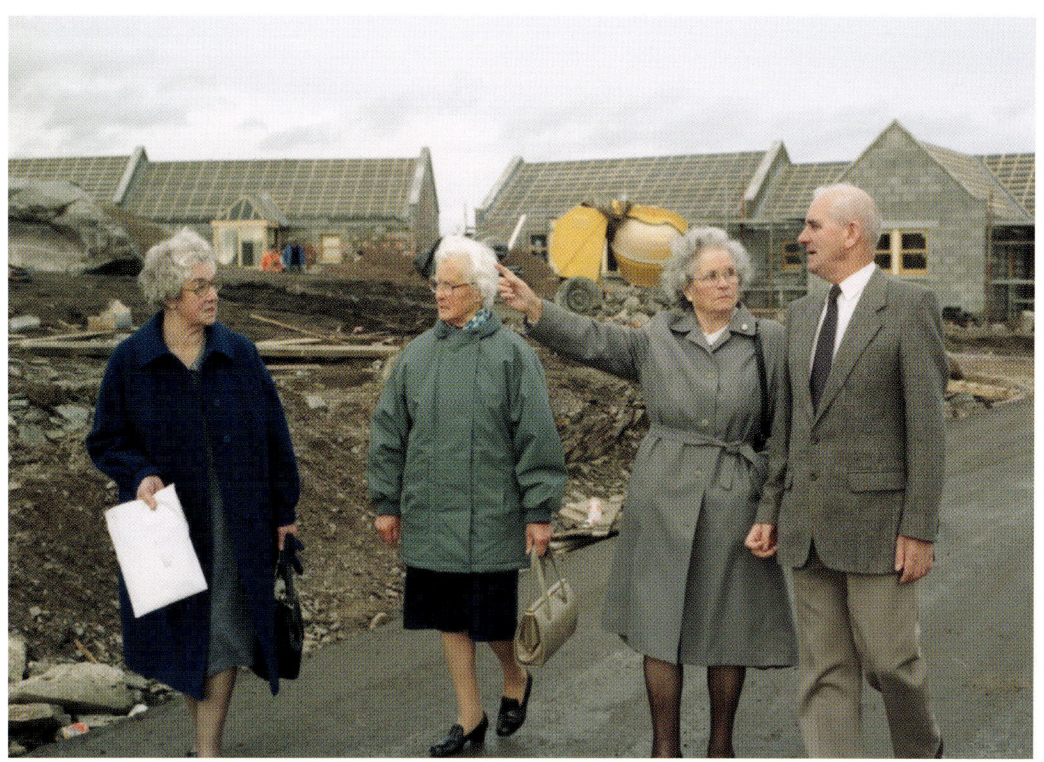

Jean is on the left with her old house No. 10 and 11 directly behind her.

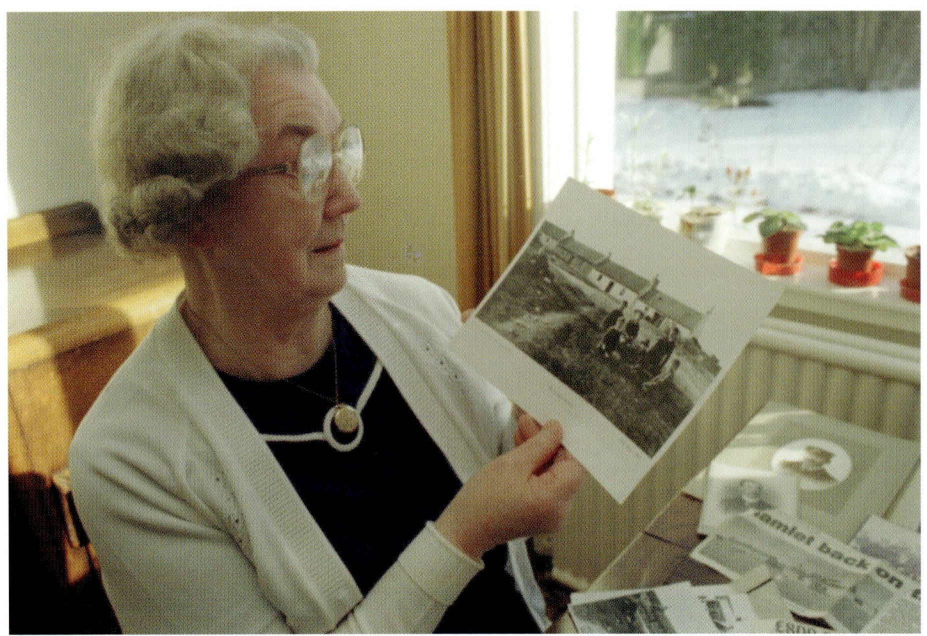

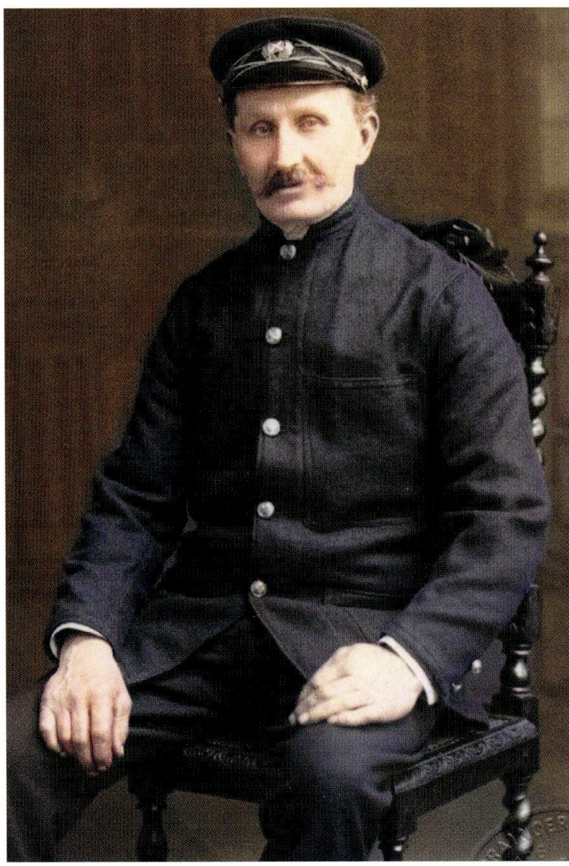

Above: A picture of Jean from an article in 1991. She is holding the 1921 postcard and photographs of her father are on the table. (Both photographs from Aberdeen, Journals Ltd. Used by kind permission of DC Thomson & Co. Ltd)

Left: David Geddes' photo of his great-grandfather Lewis Morrison in the Aberdeen, Newcastle & Hull Steam Co. uniform.

In the course of researching, I made contact with David Geddes, an avid amateur historian. His great-grandfather, Lewis Morrison, was the *Norwood's* carpenter.

As the research expanded, we made contact with more descendants and although it is over 100 years since the vessel was lost, we all feel that these men are calling out to have their story told and to be remembered. At the time of writing, we have contacted descendants of twelve of the eighteen men.

Between us all, we have gathered quite a few interesting photographs and artefacts and many documents from the National Archives, National Maritime Museum and Aberdeen City Archives.

All families of casualties in the First World War were given a commemorative scroll from the government, a letter from the king thanking the family for the sacrifice of their loved one and a bronze plaque that came to be known as the 'Dead Man's Penny'. The Dead Man's Penny given to AB Charles Massie and the victory medals for John Booth are in Aberdeen Maritime museum.

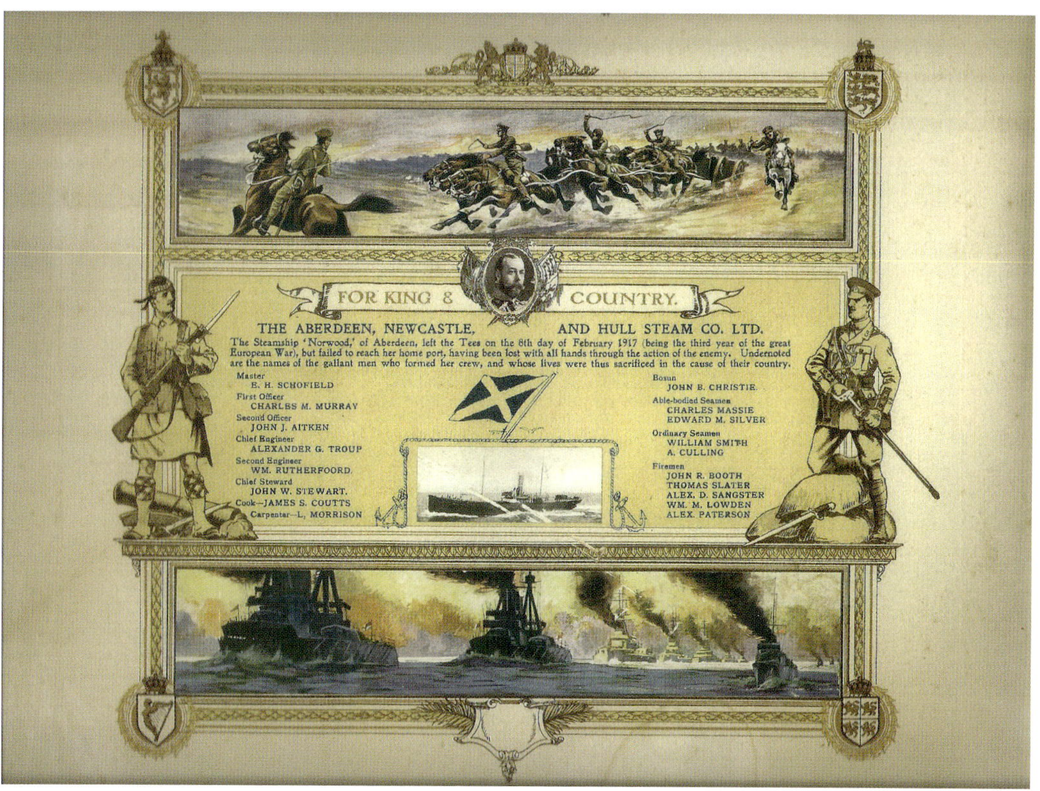

Johanna Martensen's ancestor First Mate Charles Murray also received a commemorative scroll from the Aberdeen, Newcastle & Hull Co.

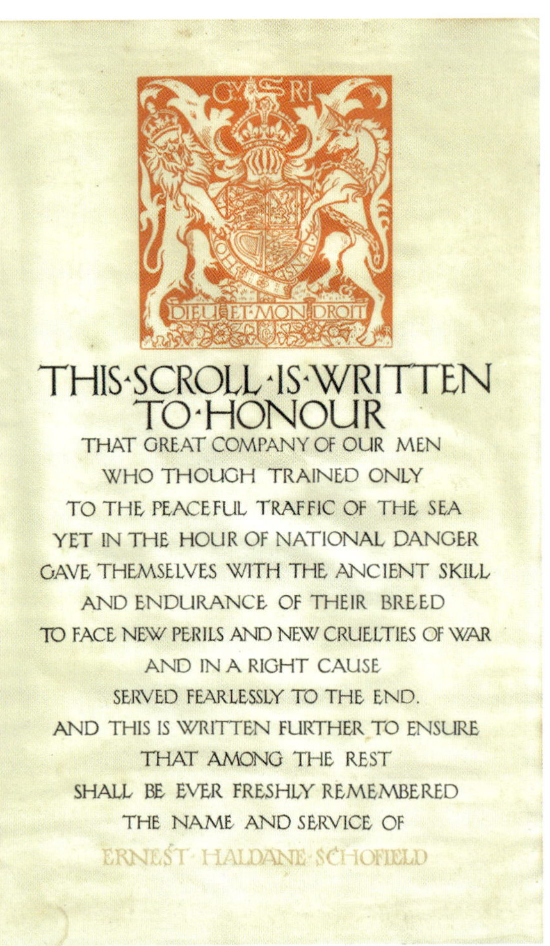

Captain Schofield's honour scroll.

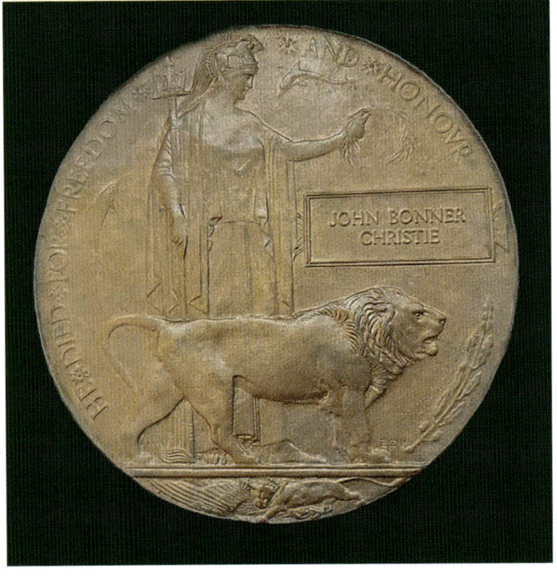

Bosun John Bonner Christie's bronze plaque.

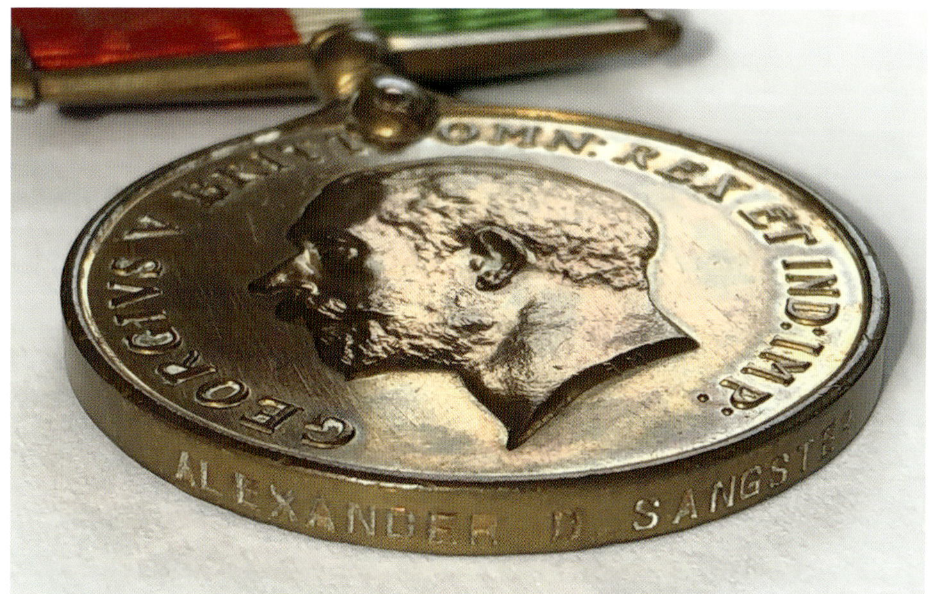

Alexander Sangster's victory medal.

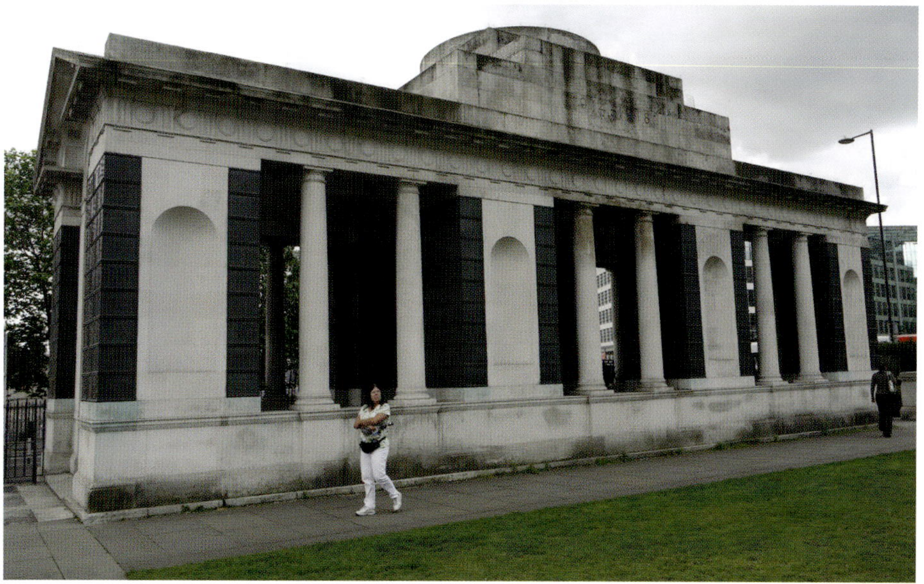

The Mercantile Marine War Memorial at Tower Hill, London.

I visited this monument in 2012. It is situated close to Tower Bridge and the Tower of London. There are 24,000 names inscribed on the panels around a sunken garden for the Second World War and 12,000 for the First World War. Graveyards and monuments can be cold, barren places but it was summer and it was good to see this one was full of people in deckchairs having lunch or enjoying the summer sun during the 2012 Olympics. If the opportunity arises, visit this place, choose a vessel at random and read aloud the names of the casualties.

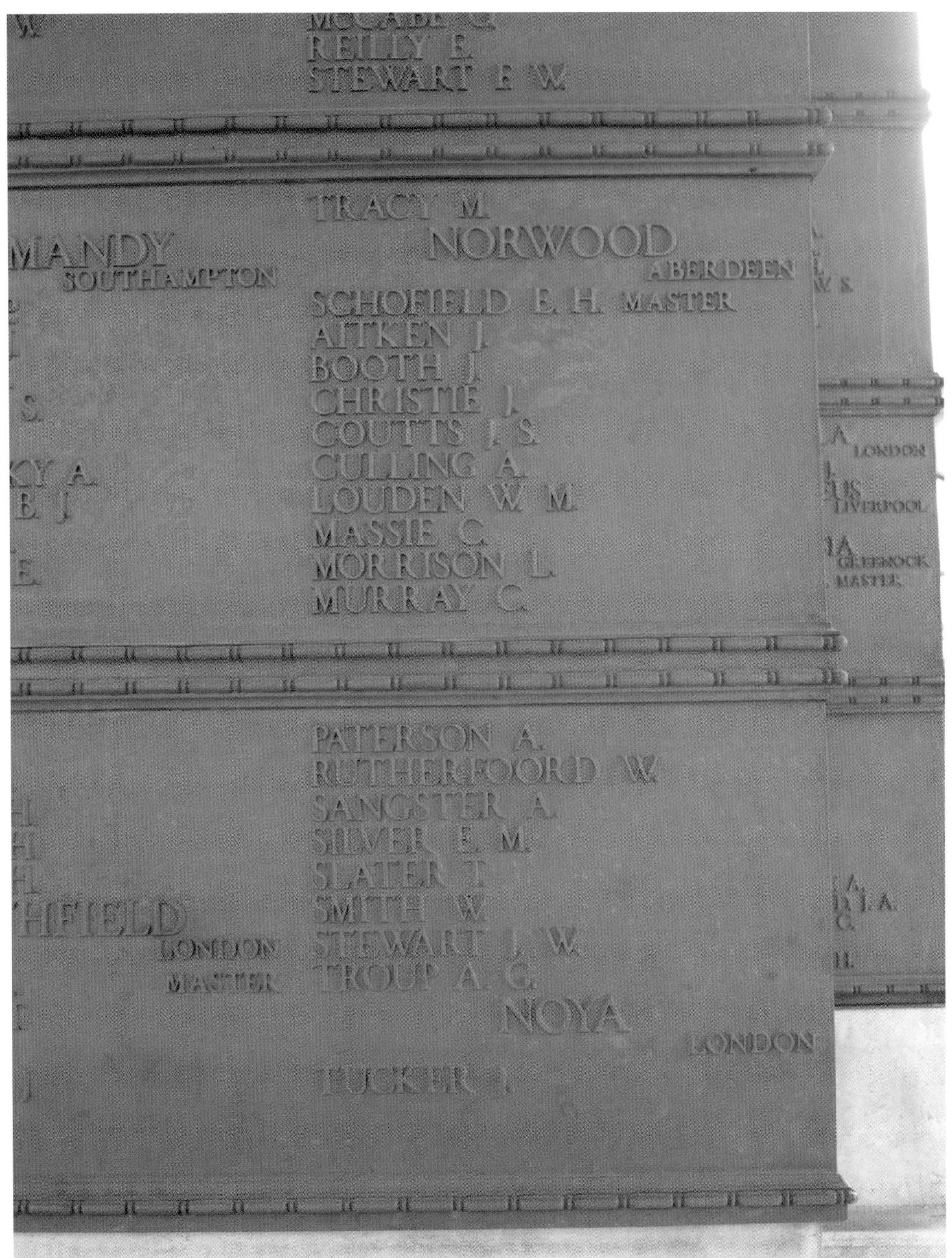

The panel to commemorate the crew of the *Norwood*.

After the First World War ended, Coutts' widow, Helen, returned to live with her family in Burnbanks Village. It is unclear what happened to James' children from his first marriage. Helen remarried in 1925 and the marriage certificate gives her address as 11 Burnbanks.

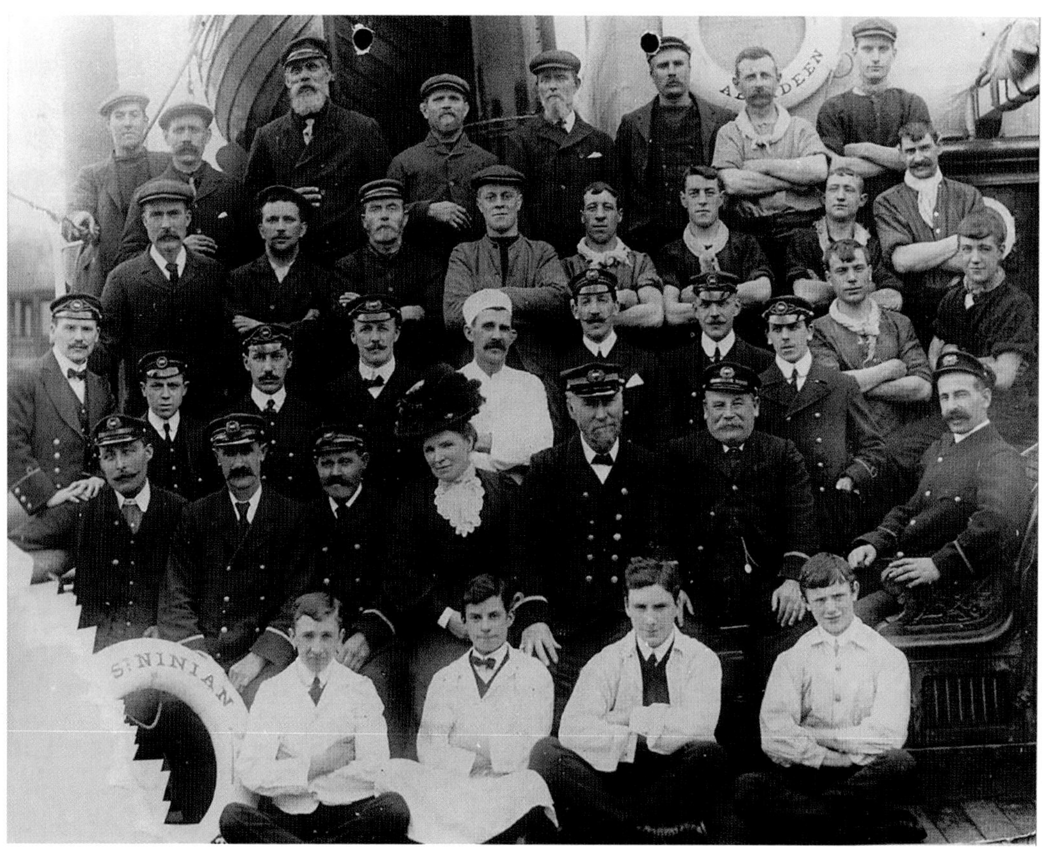

One final photo of James Coutts from happier times before the First World War. James is to the right of the man in chef's whites in the centre of the photograph. This one is dated 1910, when James was Chief Steward on SS *St Ninian*. I love this photograph as I have spent a large part of my working life at sea on various vessels and the crew line-up could be one of the modern vessels I work on. The middle rows are filled with the officers and supervisors, the back two rows are the deck crew and engine room staff, no different to the hard-working tough men we see today, and the young fresh-faced boys on the front rows are just starting out on a career at sea. (Courtesy of the Lerwick Museum Collection)

The SS *Norwood* Crew

Captain Ernest Haldane Schofield
Charles Murray – First Officer
John James Aitken – Second Mate
John Bonner Christie – Bosun
Lewis Wilson Morrison – Carpenter
Alexander Paterson – AB
Edward Maxwell Silver – AB
Arthur Ernest Albert Culling – Ordinary Seaman
William Smith – Ordinary Seaman
John Wattie Stewart – Steward
James Shepherd Coutts – Ship's Cook

Alexander Gibb Troup – Engineer
William Rutherfoord – Second Engineer
Charles Massie – Fireman
Thomas Slater – Fireman
Alexander Sangster – Fireman
John Rae Booth – Fireman
William Murray Louden – Fireman

Some of James' Shipmates

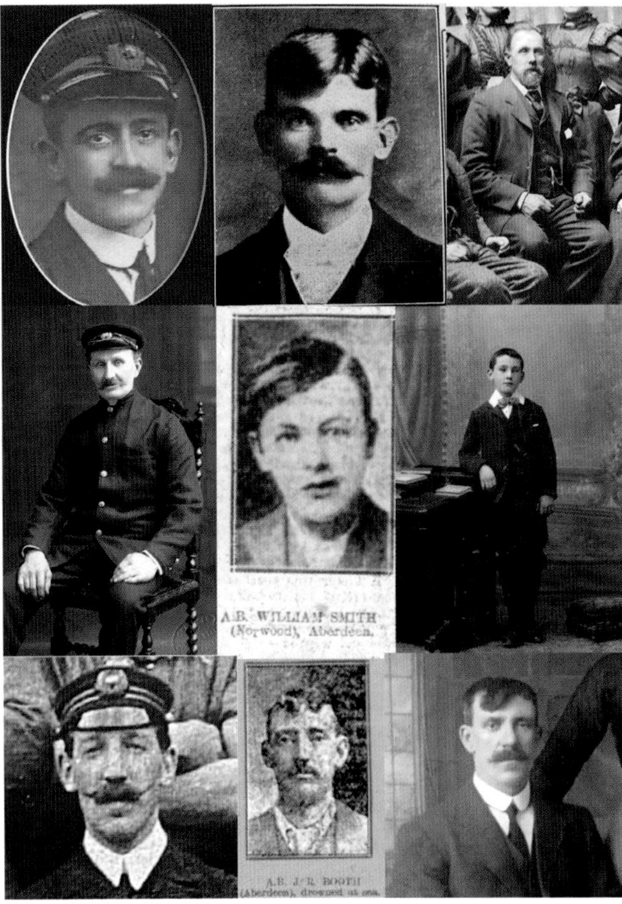
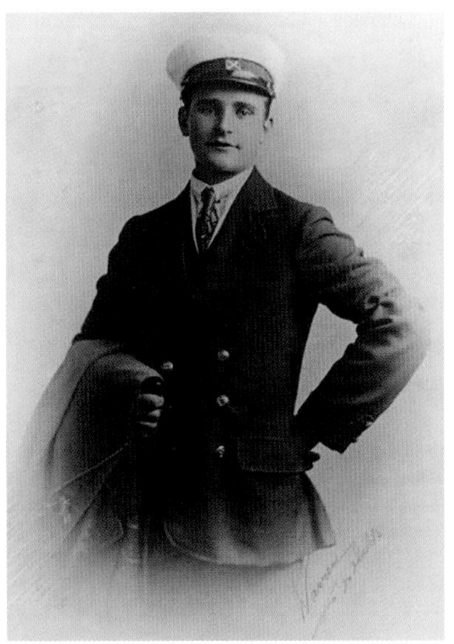

Above left: Charles Murray (from Johanna Martensen), John Aitken (from Orkney Museum), John Christie (from Liz Brown), Lewis Morrison (from David Geddes), William Smith (from Aberdeen Journals Ltd), John Wattie Stewart (from Shiona Airlie), James Coutts (from the Lerwick Museum), John Rae Booth (from Aberdeen Journals Ltd), and Thomas Slater (from Bob Nichol).

Above right: Arthur Ernest Albert Culling. (Photograph courtesy of Alan Cowburn)

11

Private John Taylor Robertson

S/41291 – 2nd Battalion Seaforth Highlanders
Formerly with the Gordon Highlanders S/18152
  John Taylor Robertson died on 20 October 1918 just a few weeks before the end of the First World War, aged only twenty years old. His battalion was involved in fighting near Cambrai in Northern France. His parents were Mitchell and Mary Robertson of No. 19 Burnbanks (the modern house No. 7). Mitchell was an agricultural labourer and horseman.

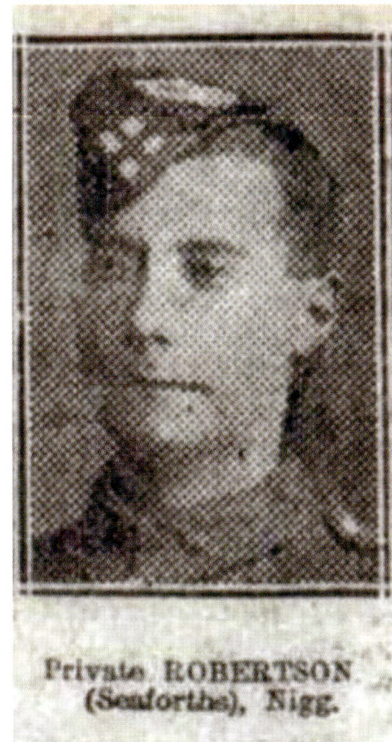

Above: From Aberdeen Weekly Journal, 29 November 1918. (Used by kind permission of DC Thomson & Co. Ltd)

Right: (From Nigg Kirk War Memorial)

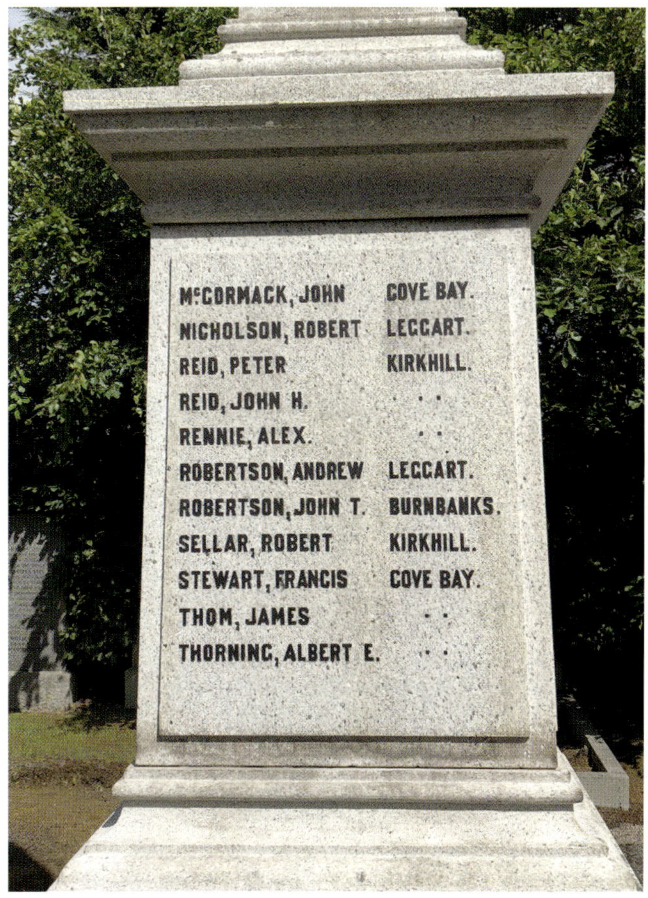

aged 27. Walter A. Reid, C.A., Woodbank, Aberdeen,
ROBERTSON.—Killed in action on 20th October, 1918.
Private John Taylor Robertson, Seaforth High-
landers, eldest and dearly beloved son of
Mitchell and Mary Robertson, Burnbanks, Nigg,
aged 20 years. Sadly missed and deeply mourned.
American and Canadian papers please copy.

(From the British Newspaper Archive, *Aberdeen Journal* 19 November 1918. Used by kind permission of DC Thomson & Co. Ltd)

John Robertson is a very common name in Scotland and there are more than 450 John Robertsons listed as casualties in the Commonwealth War Graves Commission website from the First World War. The key to finding John's correct records was his father's forename Mitchell, which is a less common name and it made the whole family easier to find.

The Service Return Death Certificate lists his cause of death simply as 'Killed in Action'. His Commanding officer on the day was Major R. Laing DSO MC (Acting Lt Colonel) Commanding Officer 14 October until 31 October

An excerpt from the 2nd Battalion Seaforth Highlanders War Diary WO-95-1483-7_1 from the National Archives for the date of John's death is transcribed here, but no specific enlisted men's casualty details or names are usually mentioned in these diaries.

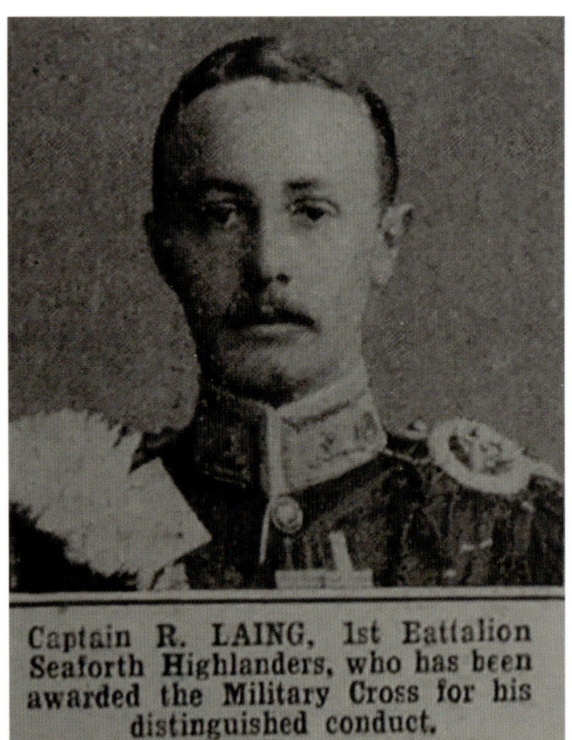

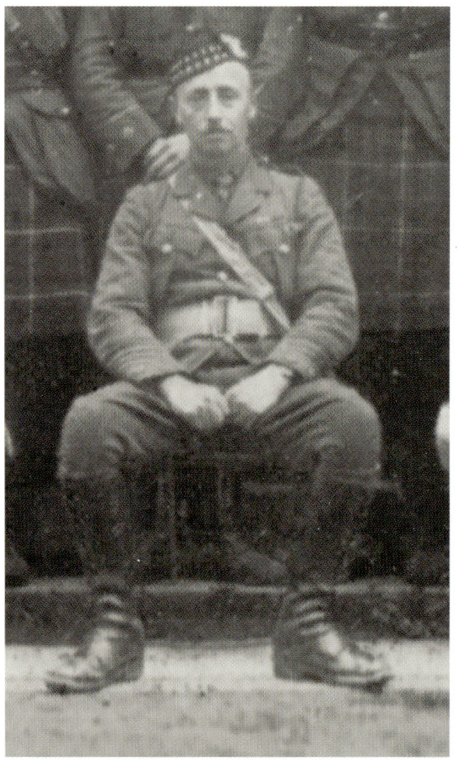

Above left: The War Illustrated, 8 May 1915. (*UK Photo Archive WW1 photos*)

Above right: Major Laing photographed in 1917. He seems to have aged a lot in two years. (*UK Photo Archive WW1 photos*)

If an officer was killed or injured, their details would generally be recorded in the War Diaries in a monthly summary.

20th October 1918
Companies moved up at midnight to east bank of SELLE river at SAULZOIR to assembly positions for attack, D-company on the right, A-Coy, C-company, B-company on left.

Zero hour was 2AM & the attack went forward under a heavy barrage and in pelting rain. Objectives were gained and forty-nine-prisoners & nine machine guns were captured-casualties about twenty five. Men lay out in soaking rain all day and late in the afternoon we had pushed forward and established an outpost line on western outskirts of VERCHAIN The 10th Battalion attacked on a one battalion front, with (indecipherable) in reserve

Battalion HQ moved up to SAULZOIR in the afternoon. Shelling resistance was not serious and artillery reply feeble. The men had no coats and got soaked to the skin. The attack on the right went well and in the whole operation over 3000 prisoners were captured, the front of attack being from DENAIN & LE CATEAU.

Signed by Major R Laing DSO MC(Acting Lt Colonel)

John was initially buried in Saulzoir Communal Cemetery Extension. After the war ended, there was a huge programme, which was ongoing for many years, to clear the battlefields of explosives and casualties. They would exhume remains, identify them where possible, gather together and re-inter casualties in purpose-built cemeteries so that the graves could be looked after in perpetuity. There was also a pressing need to gather up human remains to be able to return the land to agriculture and to prevent harrowing incidents where the remains came to the surface in the future. Further reading regarding the horrendous tasks and teams of men assembled to carry them out can be found in online articles: refer to www.1914-1918.net, or articles regarding Battlefield Clearance by Terry Carter or the highly detailed writings of Peter Hodgkinson.

On exhumation from Saulzoir five years after he died, John was identified by the temporary cross erected when he was first buried, his clothing, kilt and numerals. Numerals could mean his service number written on personal effects or battalion number badges on his uniform. He was reburied in St Souplet Cemetery in France, in Plot-I Row-B Grave-2.

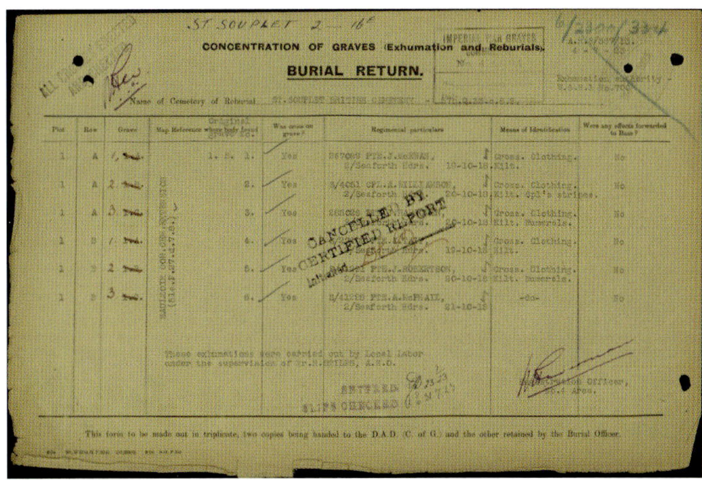

The exhumation and reburial records for John. (Commonwealth War Graves Commission)

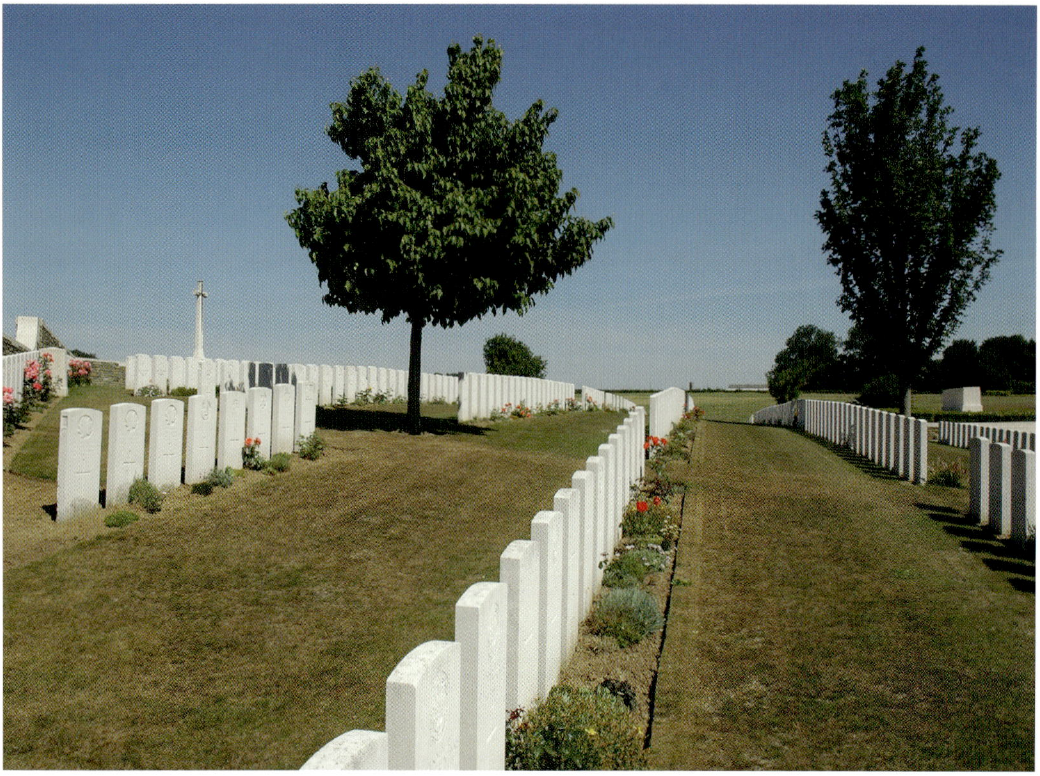

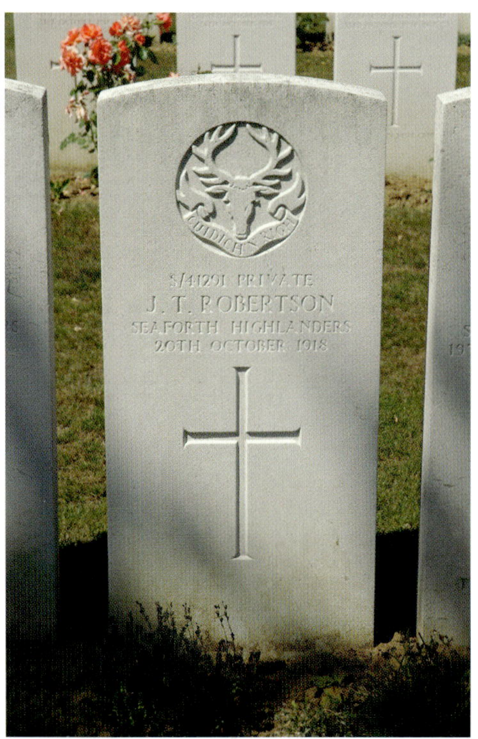

Above: The photograph above shows the graveyard. John's grave is directly in line with the trunk of the tree on the right. (Both photographs are courtesy of the Commonwealth War Graves Commission and the War Graves Photographic Project)

Left: Pte John Taylor Robertson's grave in St Souplet.

12

Private Frederick Beattie

2nd Battalion Queens Own Cameron Highlanders s/n 2937863
Frederick Beattie was born in Burnbanks in 1912, the fourth son to William Beattie and Elspeth Barron. His family lived in No. 17, which is the location of the modern No. 22. There were twelve children but one died at only a week old.

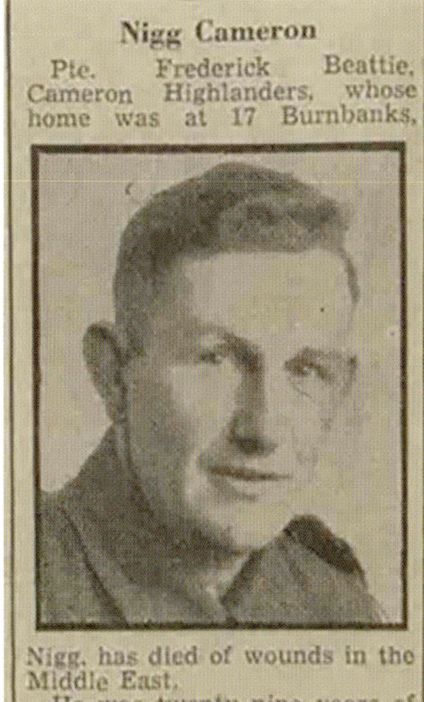

Nigg Cameron

Pte. Frederick Beattie, Cameron Highlanders, whose home was at 17 Burnbanks, Nigg, has died of wounds in the Middle East.

He was twenty-nine years of age and leaves a widow and one son.

Before the war Pte. Beattie was employed with an Aberdeen firm of contractors, and prior to that he was a farm servant.

He was the fourth son of Mr and Mrs W. Beattie, Loirston Road, Cove Bay.

(From the British Newspaper Archive, Aberdeen Weekly Journal 8 Jan 1942. Used by kind permission of DC Thomson & Co. Ltd)

When I placed the advert in the local newspaper in 2011 appealing for information about Burnbanks, descendants of two of the Beattie children contacted me: Margaret McGill, daughter of John Beattie; and Moira McIntosh, daughter of David Beattie.

Moira gave me some very interesting photographs of the family group and this led to me identifying the children from the 1921 postcard.

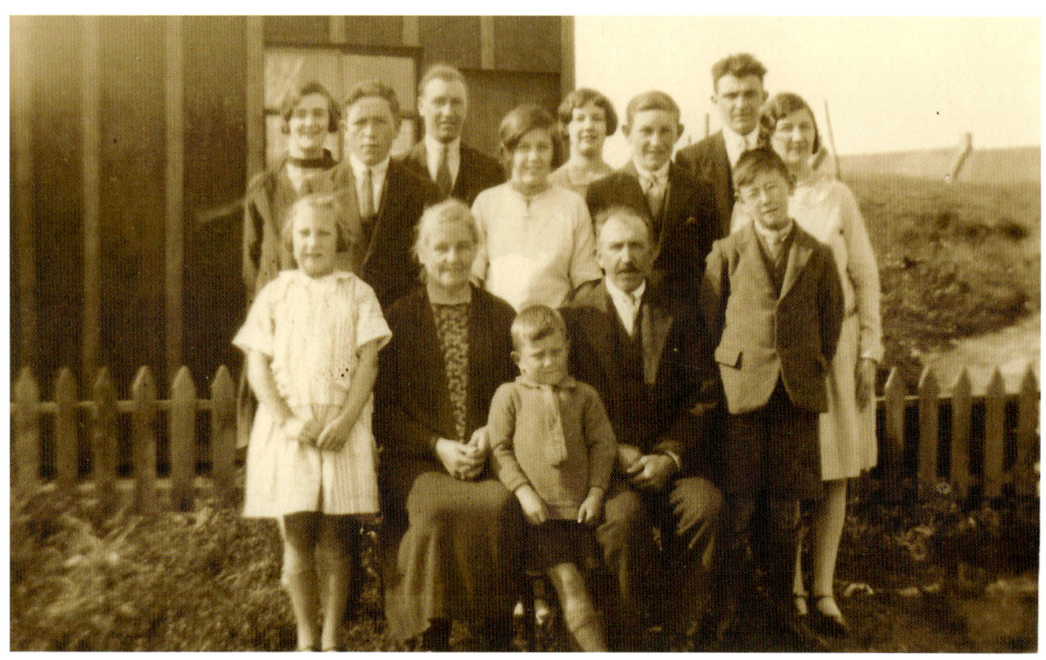

Freddie is third from the right in the back row. Moira McIntosh's father, David, is the boy with glasses on the right of the front row. Margaret McGill's father, John, is in the back row, second from the left. Back row: Elsie, John, Andrew, Annie, Lily, Freddie, William the eldest son, Jean the eldest daughter. Front row: Barbara (Bunty), Elspeth Barron, George, William Snr, David.

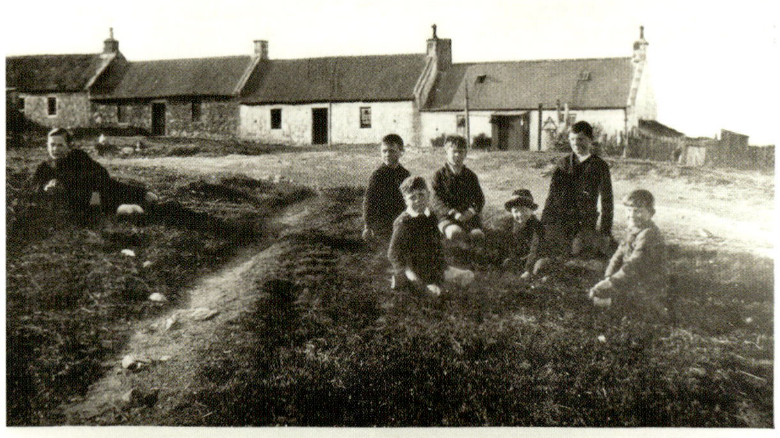

The 1921 postcard. Freddie Beattie is the child seated on the extreme right. The children are, left to right: back row: Andrew, John, unindentified, Jeanie Coutts, William the eldest son. Front row: David, Freddie

We have the 1921 postcard framed on a wall in our house and every time I passed it, the child on the right always seemed to catch my eye. I felt I knew him. The group of children have some quite distinct features: some have high foreheads, some have sharp noses and down-turned mouths; others have prominent cheeks and 'big lugs'. Whilst studying Moira's photographs, these same traits seemed to be present in the Beattie family. It was then that I knew I had identified the children. The child on the right is Frederick Beattie, eight years old at the time of the photgraph.

Freddie died on 5 December 1941 in Egypt during the Second World War and the cause of death is listed as 'Died of Wounds'. I believe he was injured on the 4th and died the following day.

As well as being commemorated on the Nigg Kirk War Memorial, he is also listed on the El Alamein War Memorial in Egypt but unfortunately he has no known grave.

There are over 7,200 burials in the cemetery with 800 being unidentified. Freddie may be there, but another possible location could be Halfaya Sollum Cemetery, which has several casualties from his battalion who died on the same day.

Second Lt Andrew Ian Ross, born in 1919 in Tayport, was in the same battalion and was killed on the same day as Freddie. He was injured during an attack on Bir el Gubi

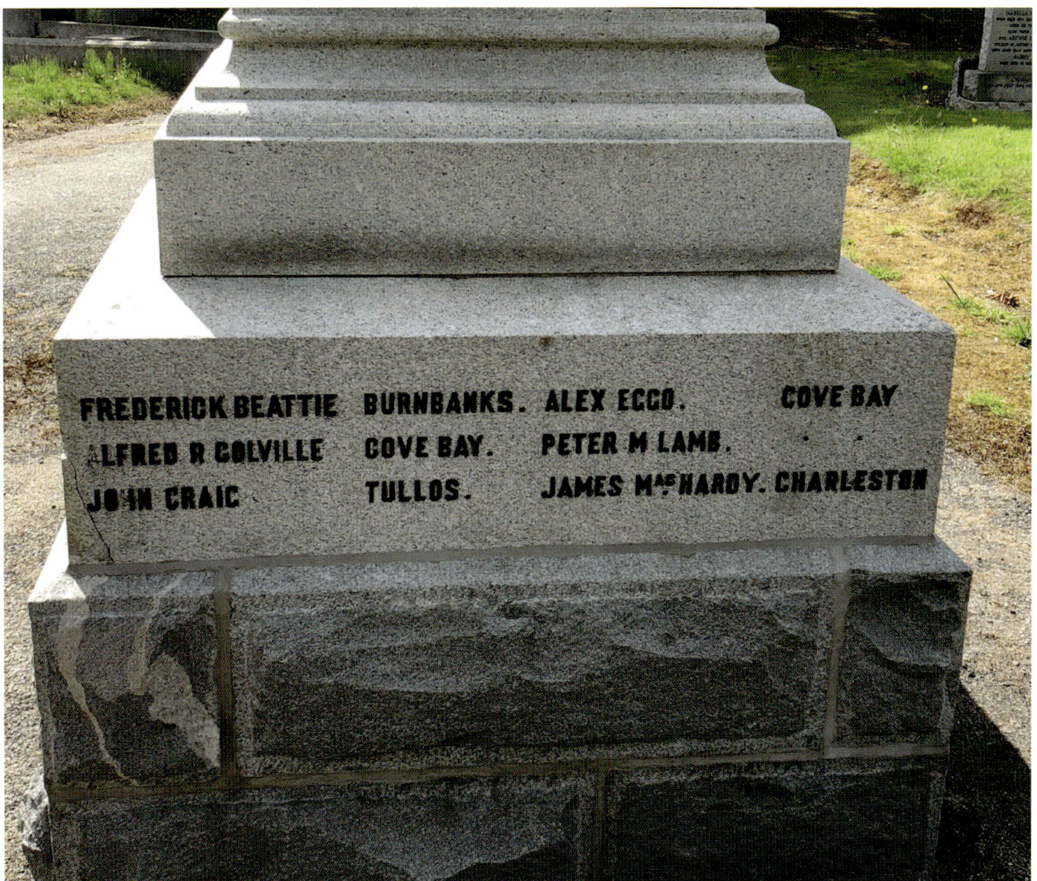

Nigg Kirk War Memorial.

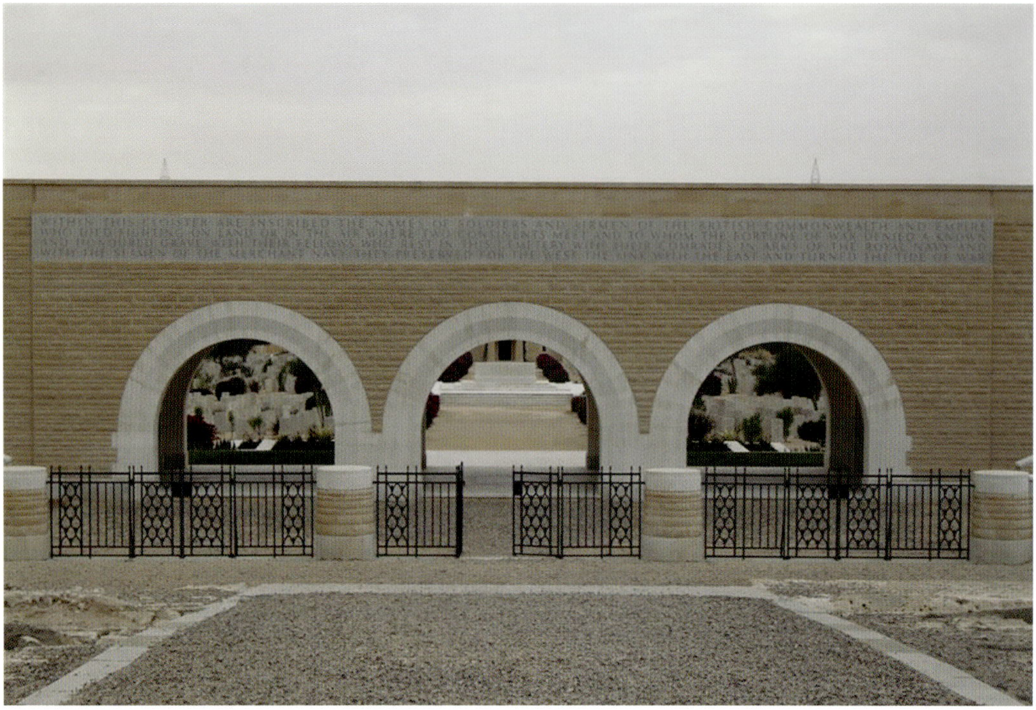

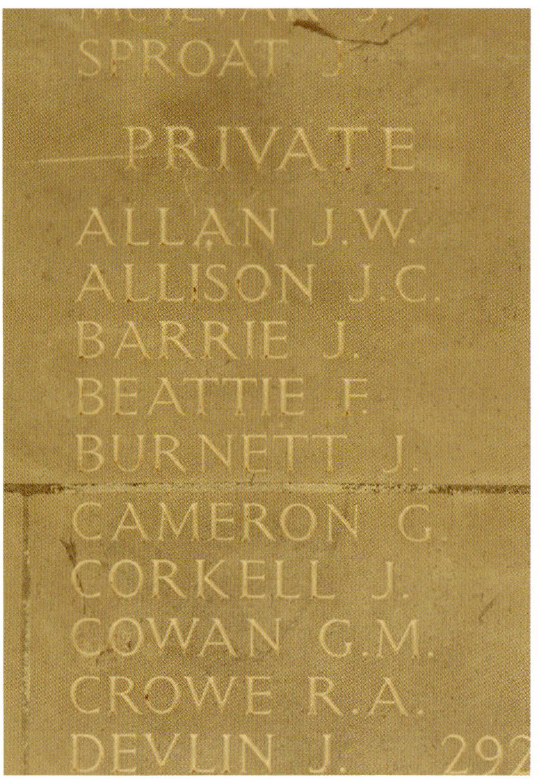

Above: The Alamein Memorial Cloisters that list casualties with no known grave. (Courtesy of the Commonwealth War Graves Commission and the War Graves Photographic Project)

Left: Column 71 from the Cloisters. (Courtesy of the Commonwealth War Graves Commission and the War Graves Photographic Project)

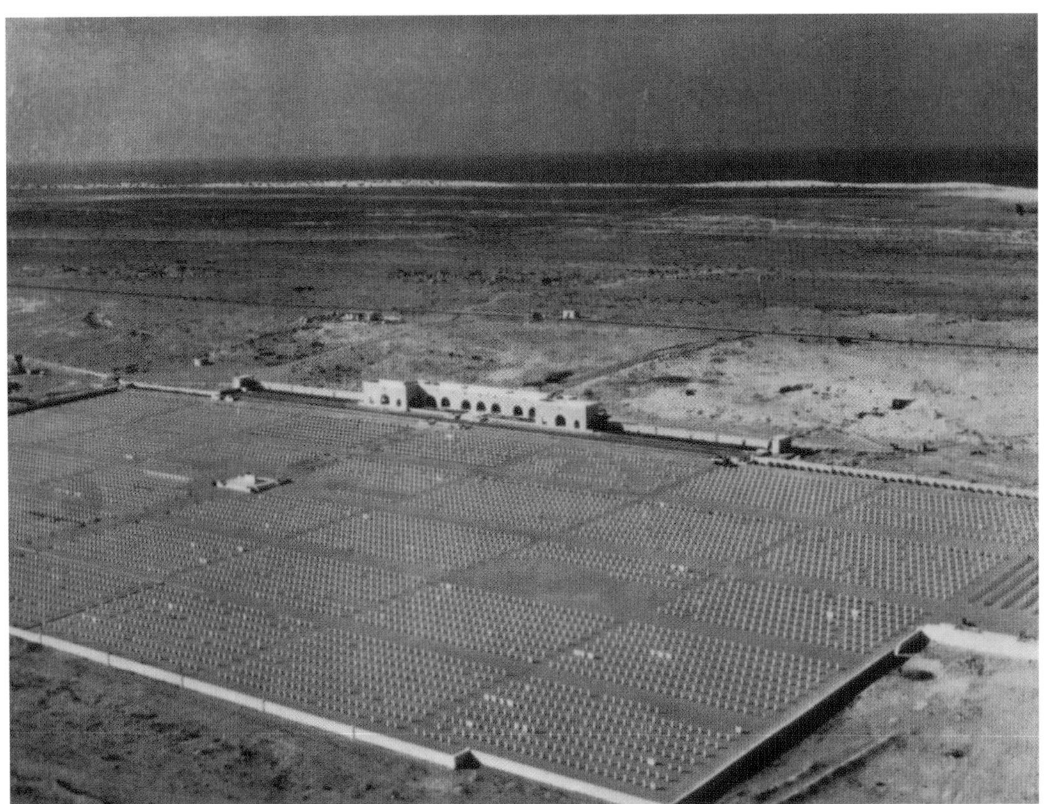

Alamein Cemetery from the air.

and transferred to an Advanced Dressing Station. The dressing station came under a bombing attack and Lt Ross was killed. He was buried in Halfaya Sollum Cemetery. I can only speculate but if Freddie was injured the previous day, he may have ended up at the same dressing station. There are several unidentified casualties from that attack buried at the same location.

A sad point to note is that he could have ended up anywhere – we will never know. It would have been heartbreaking for the family but that is the common reality of war.

In 1939, just before the beginning of the Second World War, he married Barbara Colville from Cove. After Freddie died, Barbara stayed in the Cove area and was the postmistress for many years.

Her brother Alfred Ross Colville was also killed in the Second World War in 1940 and amazingly is listed below Freddie on the Nigg Kirk War Memorial.

Private Alfred Ross Colville

2nd Battalion Seaforth Highlanders s/n 2821665
Died 2 June 1940

Alfred was initially buried in St Maxent-en-Vimeu and reburied 90 kilometres away in Longueval Cemetery in Northern France in 1948.

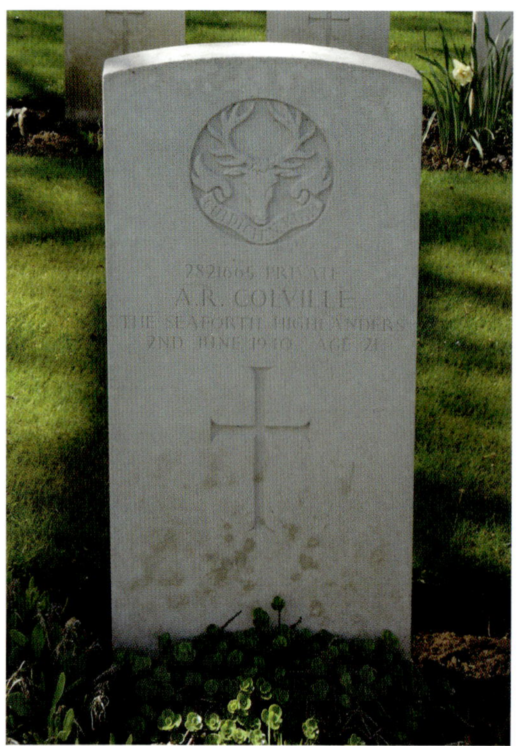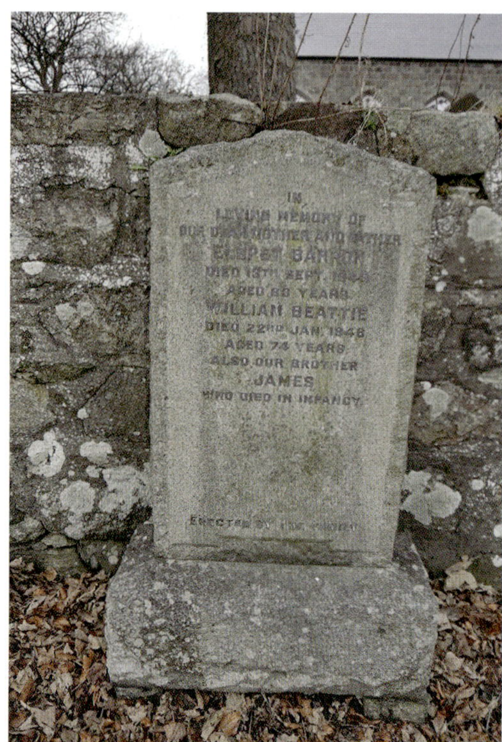

Above left: (Courtesy of the Commonwealth War Graves Commission and the War Graves Photographic Project)

Above right: The Gravestone of Freddie's parents, William Beattie and Elspeth Barron, in Nigg Kirkyard, along with his brother James who died in infancy.

13

Alexander and Amelia Eggo

Alexander Nichol Eggo was not a Burnbanks man but had connections to the village and it is a tragic story worthy of inclusion.

He was lost during the Second World War on the Motor Tanker *MV Cordelia* on 3 February 1943 in the North Atlantic. He was only sixteen years old, not old enough for combat but he was onboard as a mess boy.

The years that separate us from this incident may dull the impact, especially given the huge amount of casualties during the major conflict periods, but this does not change the fact that this was a child of sixteen. Alexander was the youngest casualty but there were nine teenage casualties in total from a crew of forty-seven. The vessel was carrying a cargo of 12,000 tons of Admiralty fuel oil and was en route from New York to the Clyde.

Alexander is commemorated on the Nigg War Memorial and is stated as being from Cove Bay. The screenshot from the British Newspaper Archive says he was living with his grandparent from Gourdon, a fishing village a few miles to the south.

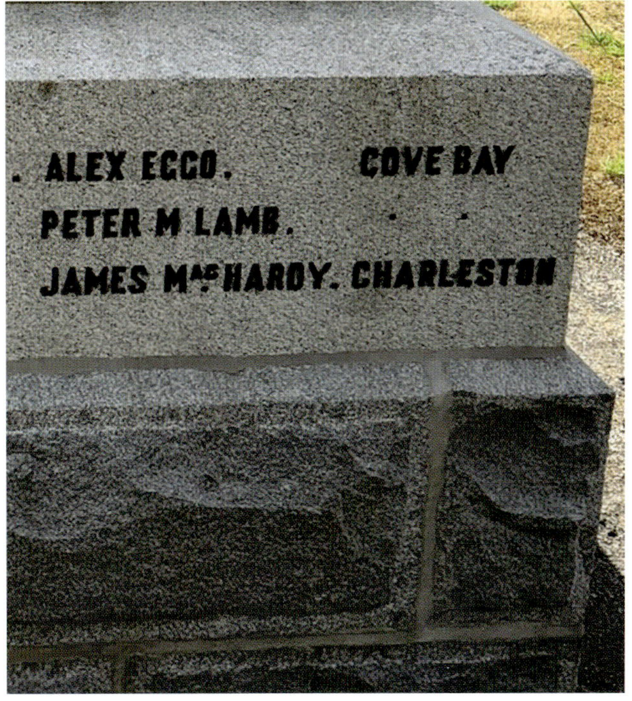

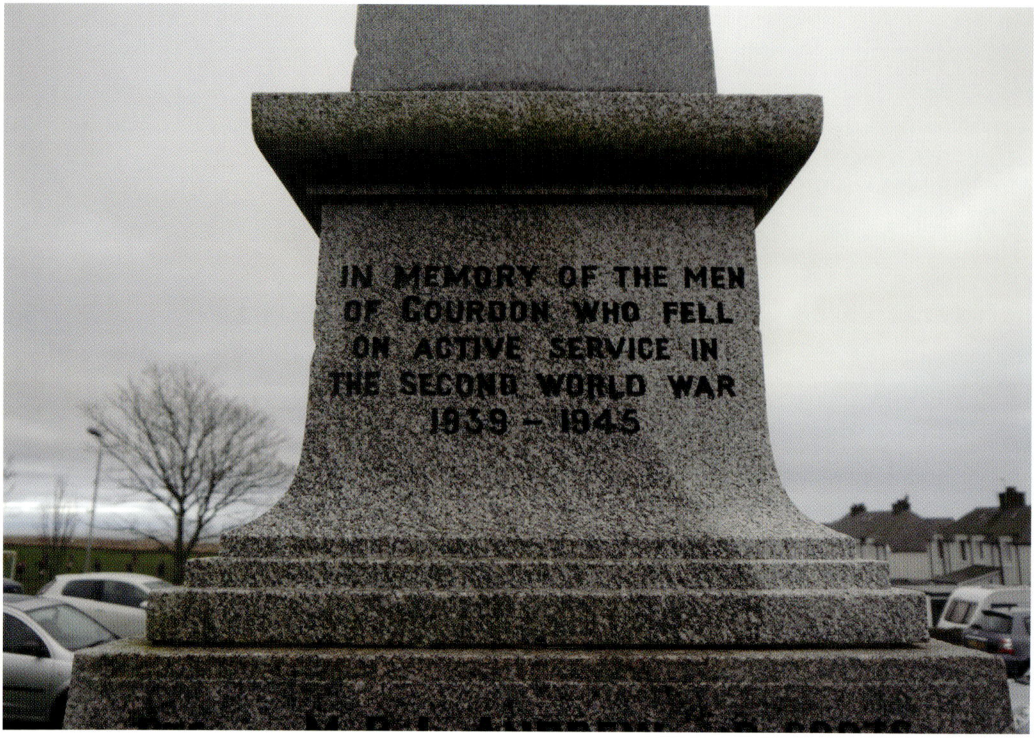

He is also commemorated on the Gourdon War Memorial.

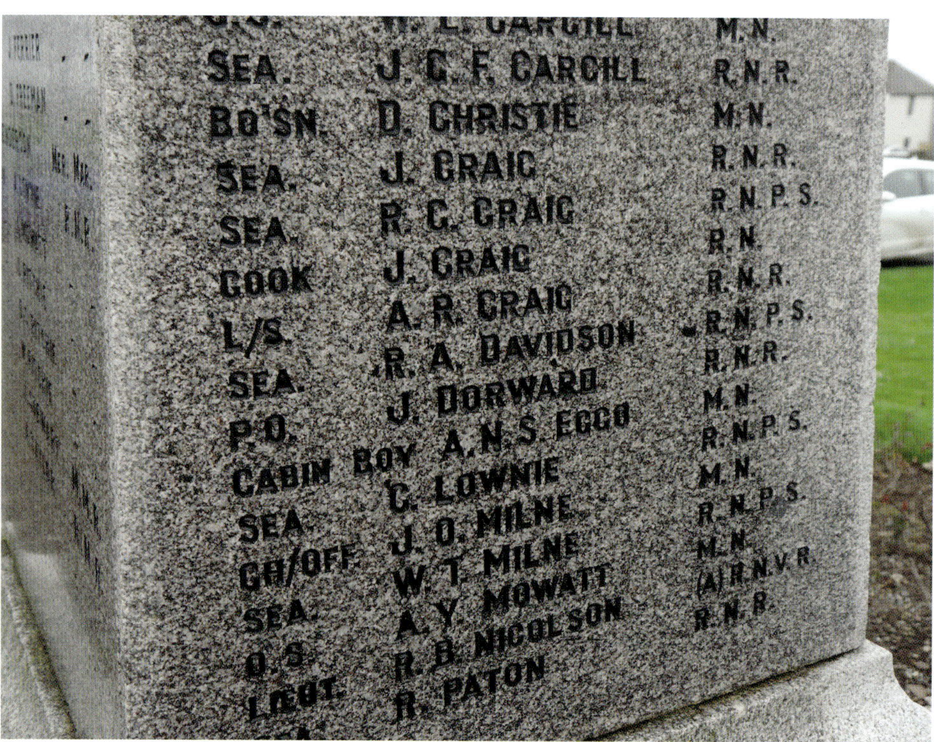

Alexander's sister Amelia (Amy) Eggo lived in Burnbanks. Their mother Amy died in 1930 from septicaemia following a miscarriage aged twenty-two. Alexander would have been three when she died and Amy junior would have been two years old. The children were split up and Amy junior went to live with her Aunt Elizabeth, who was married to John Munro of No. 17 Burnbanks. Alexander went to live with his grandparents, Mr and Mrs Alexander Nicol Smith.

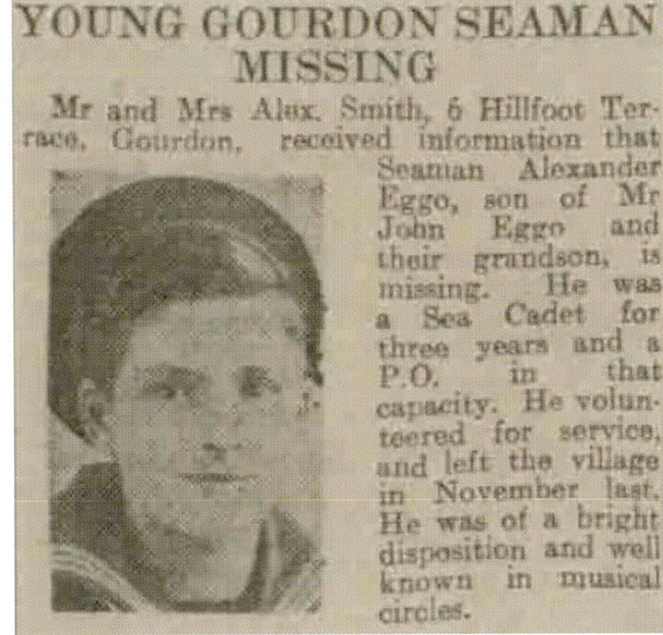

YOUNG GOURDON SEAMAN MISSING

Mr and Mrs Alex. Smith, 6 Hillfoot Terrace, Gourdon, received information that Seaman Alexander Eggo, son of Mr John Eggo and their grandson, is missing. He was a Sea Cadet for three years and a P.O. in that capacity. He volunteered for service, and left the village in November last. He was of a bright disposition and well known in musical circles.

Right: The *Dundee Courier*, 1 April 1943. (From the British Newspaper Archive. Used by kind permission of DC Thomson & Co. Ltd)

Below: (Vessel picture courtesy of Tony Allen of www.wrecksite.eu)

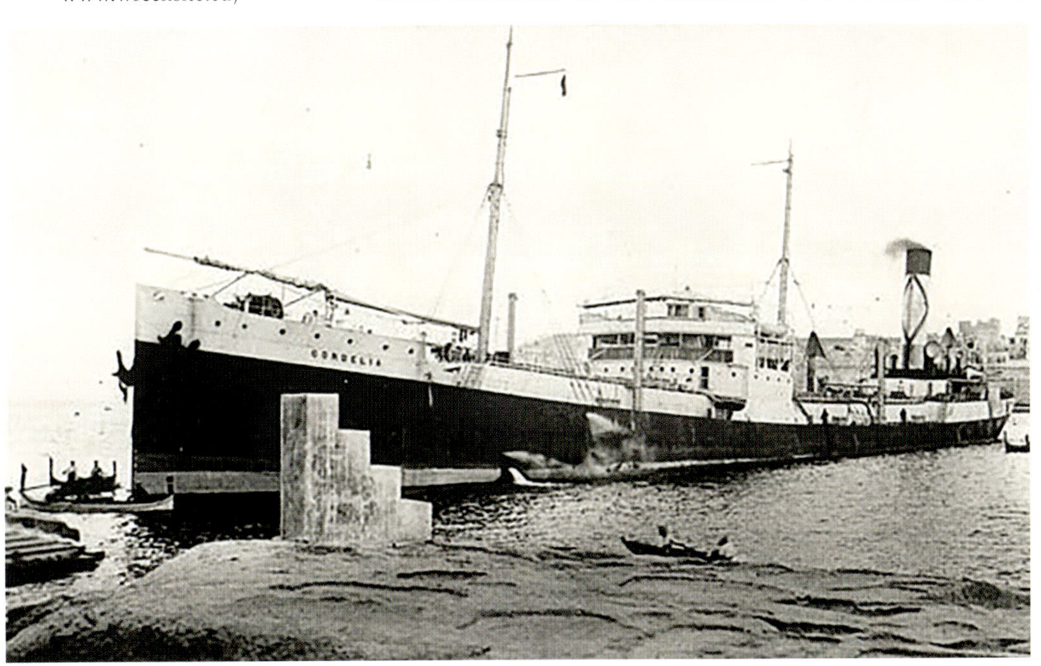

Information about the Sinking from www.uboat.net

At 21.54 hours on 3 Feb 1943 the unescorted Cordelia (Master Edward Marshall), a straggler from convoy HX-224, was torpedoed and sunk south of Iceland by U-632 commanded by Korvettenkapitän Hans Karpf. The master, 37 crew members and eight gunners were lost. The sole survivor, chief engineer I.C. Bingham, was taken prisoner by the U-Boat and carelessly mentioned the convoy SC-118 which was reported to the U-Boat High Command. The convoy was subsequently attacked with the loss of nine ships. The survivor landed at Brest on 14 February and was taken to the German POW camp Milag Nord.

It seems very harsh to name the survivor and to blame him for further losses and one wonders how true the accusation is. The National Archives hold a 'Narrative of Survivor of *MV Cordelia*' taken from Chief Engineer Bingham after he was repatriated to the UK and gives a harrowing account of the sinking.

Alexander Eggo is not mentioned by name but Bingham's testimony notes that the Chief Steward and a cabin boy were stocking stores in a compartment below him when the first torpedo struck and although he went to look for them, he could see no signs of life.

Along with six crewmates, Bingham managed to launch a life raft from the Foc'sle area.

After dispatching more torpedoes and shellfire to sink the vessel, the U-boat came alongside the drifting life raft and the crew refused to pick up any survivors; they only wanted the captain, who was already presumed dead at that time and Chief Engineer Bingham.

The ship's carpenter, William Goss, twenty-five years old, attempted to jump onto the submarine but was given a life jacket and cast back into the sea. February in the North Atlantic close to Iceland and in rough seas meant that they would not survive for long.

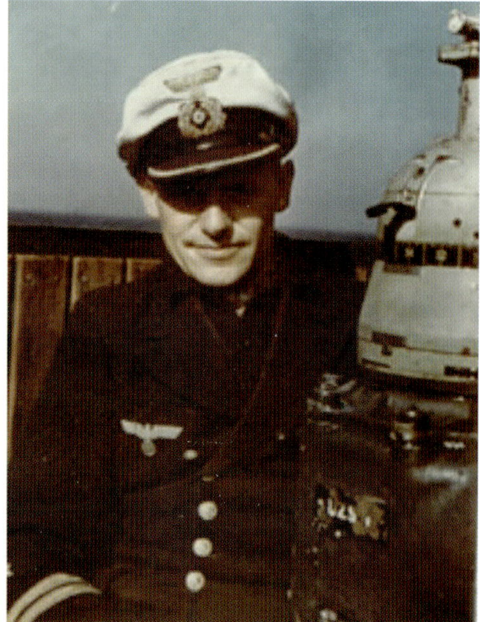

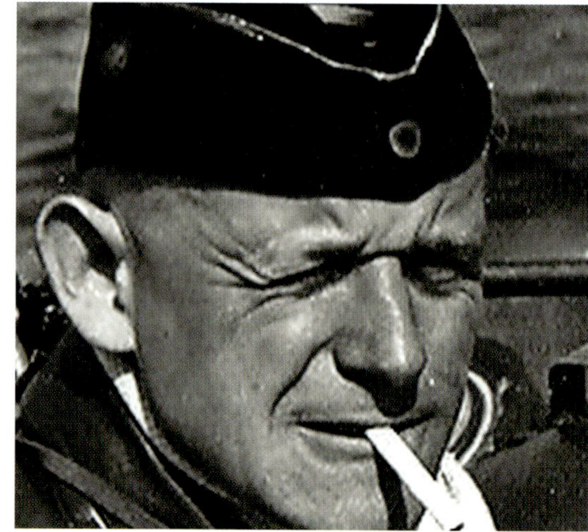

Above: (From Tetang Saya)

Left: Captain Hans Karpf onboard U-632. (Photograph courtesy of www.uboat.net)

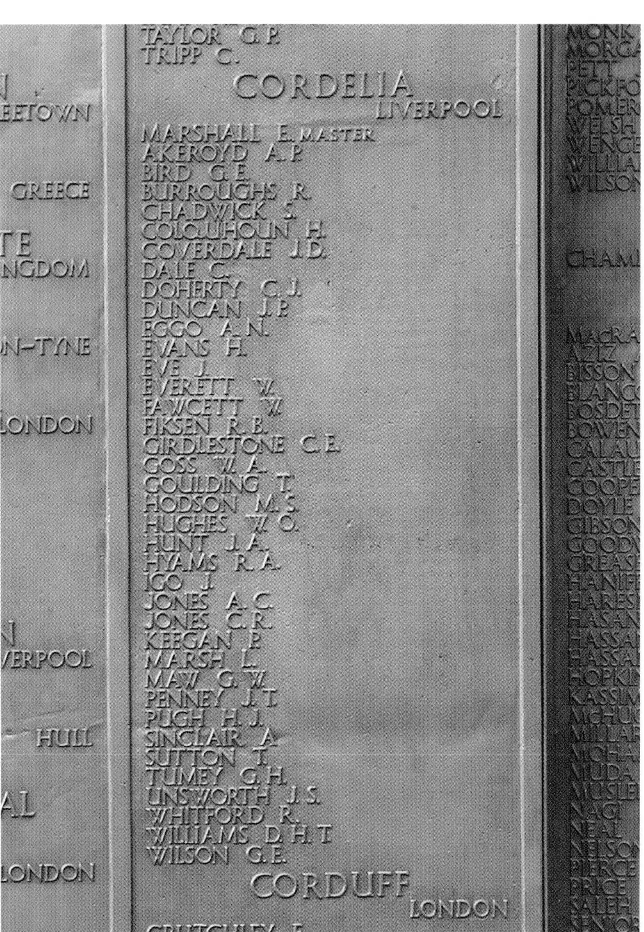

A view of the panel at the Tower Hill Memorial for Second World War losses. Alexander is on the eleventh line. (Courtesy of the Commonwealth War Graves Commission and the War Graves Photographic Project)

U-632 was also sunk a few weeks later with the loss of all hands.

Alexander Eggo is also commemorated along with his shipmates in London on the Tower Hill Memorial for Merchant Seamen.

14

Charles (Chick) Duncan

Charles was born in 1900 in No. 5 Burnbanks – which was the old number for my house – one of the sons of Henry Duncan and Elizabeth Campbell, and he had a very interesting early life.

He joined the army on 19 September 1914 to serve in the First World War, but was dishonourably discharged only twenty days later for being underage.

There have been several books written about boy soldiers who managed to join the forces even though they were underage, and it seems that our Charles was one of these.

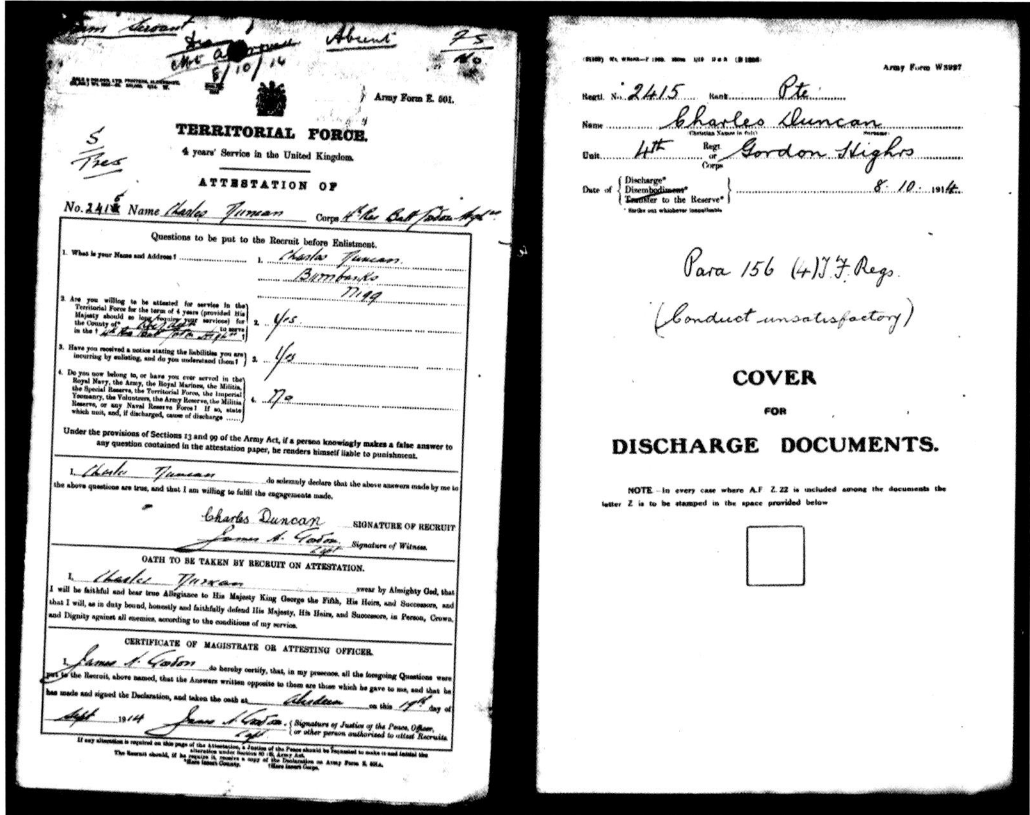

This is Charles' Attestation Form (enrolment and statement of truth). His Medical Inspection Report lists his 'apparent age' as seventeen. His discharge documents for 'conduct unsatisfactory' were created only twenty days later.

In 1921 Charles emigrated to Canada. There was a huge drive to have people of all ages and with a wide range of skills to populate Canada and ships often travelled full of young emigrants.

The ticket above is a third-class from Glasgow to Halifax Nova Scotia onboard the *Saturnia* sailing on 31 March 1921. Charles' passage included onward rail travel to Toronto and he was due to meet up with his brother-in-law W. Logan.

Right: From the British Newspaper Archive *Motherwell Times*, 9 May 1924. (Used by kind permission of DC Thomson & Co. Ltd)

Below: One such ship was the TSS *Saturnia* operated by the Anchor-Donaldson Line in Glasgow.

EMIGRANTS FOR CANADA.

A large party of Scottish emigrants left the Clyde for Quebec and Montreal on Thursday by the Anchor-Donaldson liner T.S.S. "Saturnia." There were 100 cabin and 500 third-class passengers. These emigrants have been drawn from practically every part of Scotland, especially from the agricultural districts. Many of them are proceeding there under assisted passage schemes, and in this connection the Ontario Government are largely represented. A great many opportunities seem to be afforded to domestic servants in Canada, and 50 girls of that class left by the "Saturnia." The land is also attracting the young men, and the greater part of the vessel's complement are composed of farm and labouring classes. There are eight miners and ten engineers and mechanics, as well as men representing practically all other trades, also several families of eight, seven, six and five members, who are going out to find employment.

ALARMING OCCURRENCE

CHAR-A-BANC B[...]

Wishaw Driver [...]

A Wishaw motor driver [...] Hunter appeared before Baili[...] Monday morning on a charge [...] an omnibus at Motherwell [...] was an unauthorised stance, [...] was necessary to pick up o[...] sengers.

In pleading guilty, accuse[...] knew he was doing wrong. The Fiscal stated that on [...] 19, about half-past six at ni[...]

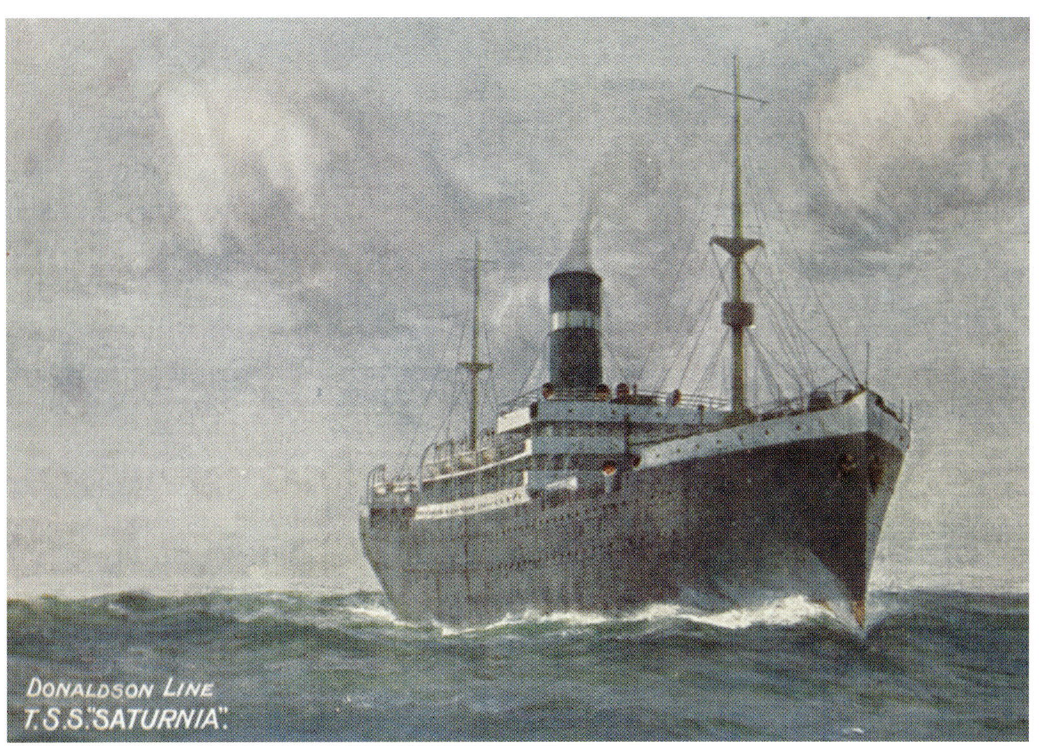

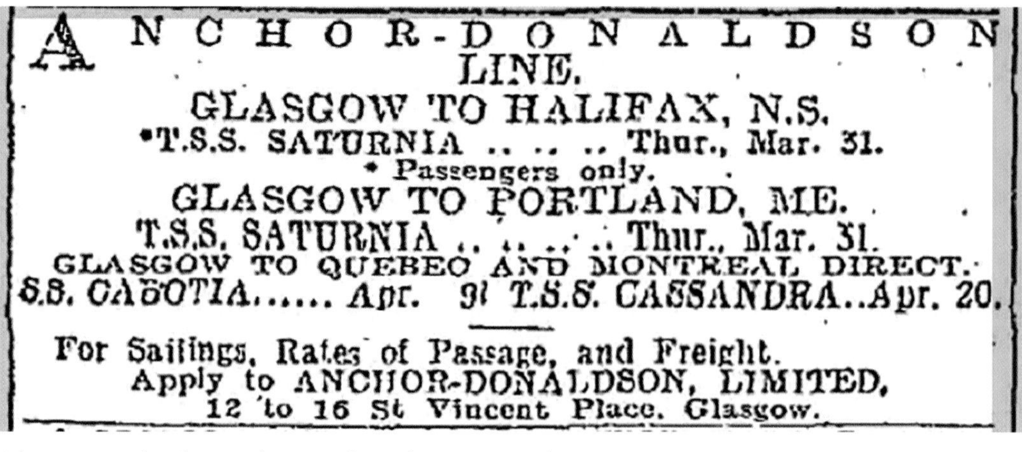

Advertisement for the March 31st sailing of *Saturnia* in *The Scotsman* newspaper.

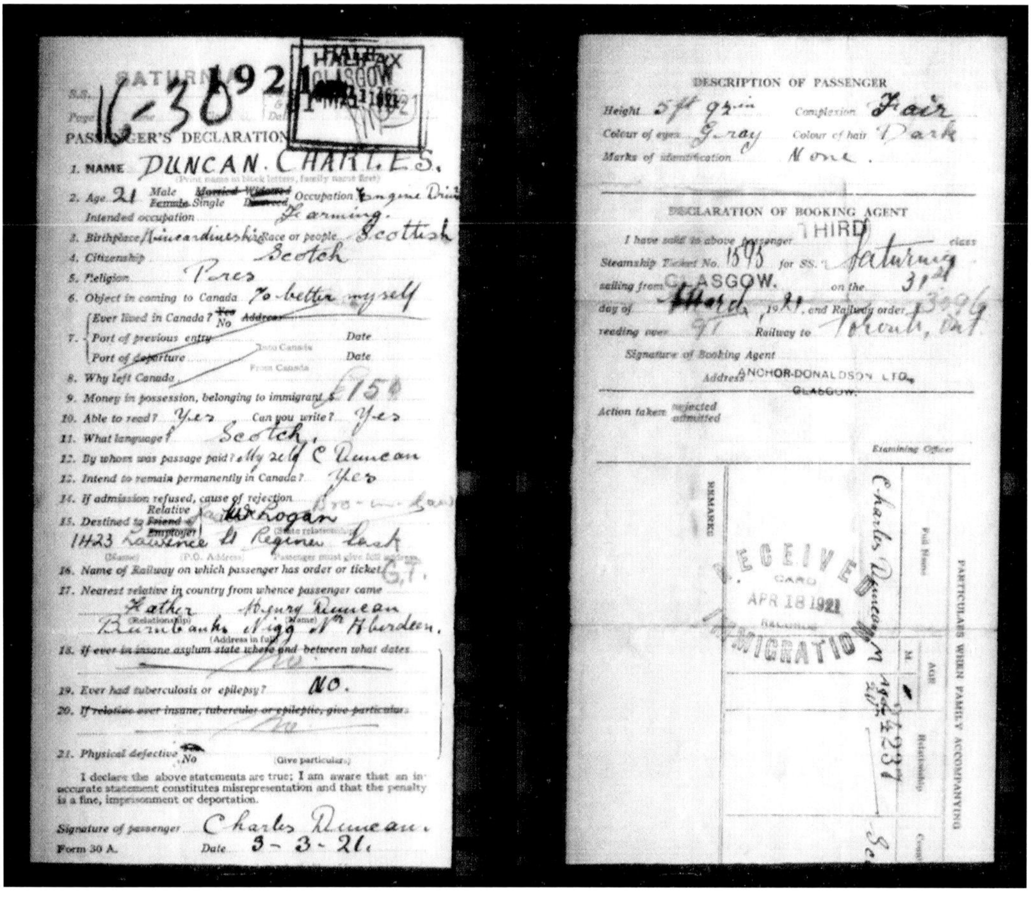

This is Charles Duncan's Passenger Declaration on arrival in Canada. The document has a personal description of him, his next of kin, his intentions in Canada and how much money he had. (Courtesy of Ancestry.co.uk)

Name of Ship *"Saturnia"*
Steamship Line—ANCHOR-DONALDSON.
Date of Departure 31st March 1921
Where bound *Halifax & Portland*

NAMES AND DESCRIPTIONS OF BRITISH PASSENGERS EMBARKED AT THE PORT OF GLASGOW.

388 Souls Forward — Halifax

	(1) Contract Ticket Number	(2) Names of Passengers	(3) Class	(4) Port at which Passengers have contracted to land	(5) Profession, Occupation, or Calling of Passengers	Acc. by husb./wife M	Acc. by husb./wife F	Not Acc. M	Not Acc. F	Children 1–12 M	Children 1–12 F	Infants M	Infants F	England	Wales	Scotland	Ireland	Brit. Possn.	Foreign	(8) Country of Intended Future Permanent Residence
						43	43	155	71	37	32	4	3			388				
✓	1586	Bain, Mrs Mary	3rd	Do.	Ho'wife				25							1				Canada
✓	〃	〃 Miss Lena	〃	Do.	nil						2½					1				✓
✓	〃	〃 Annie	〃	Do.	Mill-worker				26							1				✓
✓	1594	Taggart, Mr James	〃	Do.	Machinist			33								1				✓
✓	1595	Duncan, Mr Charles	〃	Do.	Eng. Driver			21								1				✓
✓	1602	Davidson, Mrs Margt	〃	Do.	nil				75							1				✓
✓	〃	〃 Jean	〃	Do.	Ho'wife				45							1				✓
✓	〃	〃 Miss Margt	〃	Do.	Factory work				19							1				✓
✓	〃	〃 Helen	〃	Do.	do.				18							1				✓
✓	〃	〃 Wilhelmina	〃	Do.	nil						11					1				✓
✓	1637	Duffy, Mrs Annie	〃	Do.	Ho'wife				49							1				✓
✓	1640	Henderson, Mr Alex	〃	Do.	French cleaner	35										1				✓
✓	〃	〃 Mrs Jeanie	〃	Do.	Ho'wife		31									1				✓
✓	〃	〃 Miss Cath	〃	Do.	nil						11					1				✓
✓	〃	〃 Mary	〃	Do.	nil						10					1				✓
✓	〃	〃 Helen	〃	Do.	nil						9					1				✓
✓	〃	〃 Mstr William	〃	Do.	nil					7						1				✓
✓	〃	〃 James	〃	Do.	nil					2						1				✓
✓	〃	〃 Miss Eliz	〃	Do.	nil						1					1				✓
✓	1641	Munro, Mr Alex	〃	Do.	Machineman	22										1				✓
✓	〃	〃 Mrs Cath	〃	Do.	Ho'wife		23									1				✓
✓	1643	Burke, Mr Joseph	〃	Do.	Miner	36										1				✓
✓	〃	〃 Mrs Mary	〃	Do.	Ho'wife		28									1				✓
✓	1644	King, Miss Hilda	〃	Do.	Domestic				40							1				✓
✓	1647	Barr, Mrs Mary	〃	Do.	Ho'wife				20							1				✓

Above: This is an excerpt from the passenger list for the 31 March 1921 sailing commanded by Captain David Taylor. Charles has ticket no. 1595.

Right: Captain Taylor pictured later in life during his last sailing prior to retirement.

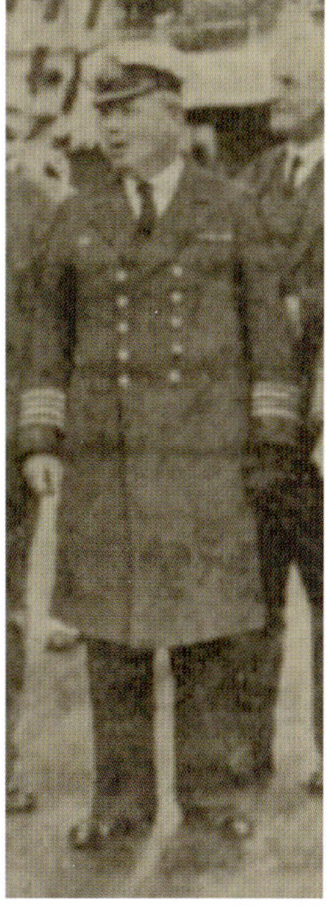

I've managed to buy several items of memorabilia for the TSS *Saturnia* – postcards, photographs, deck plans and the badge below.

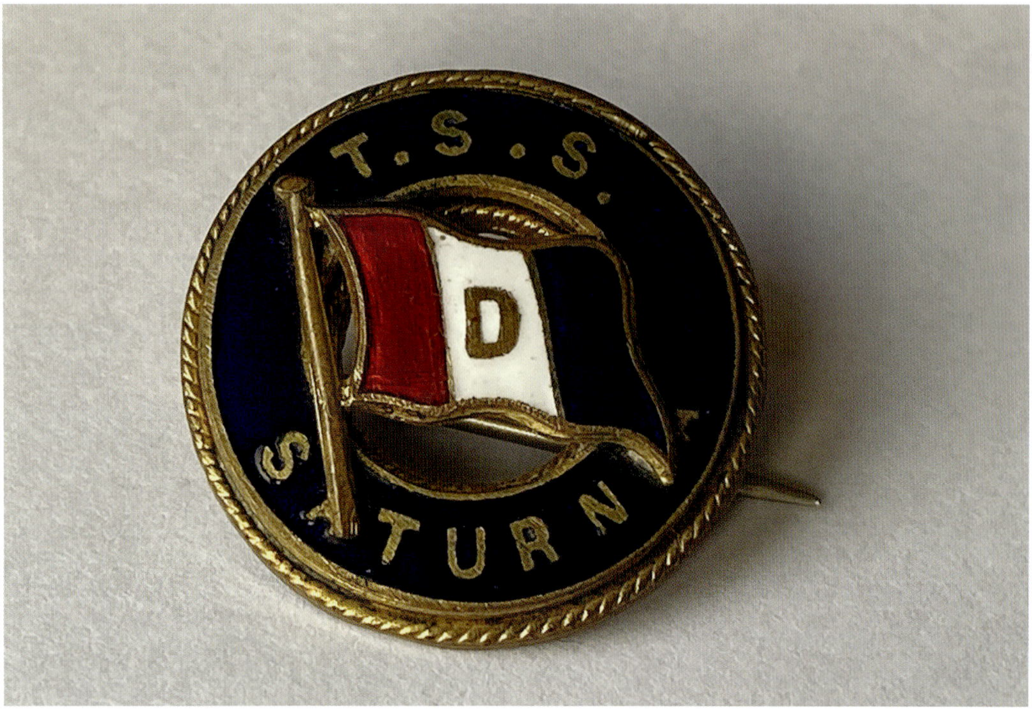

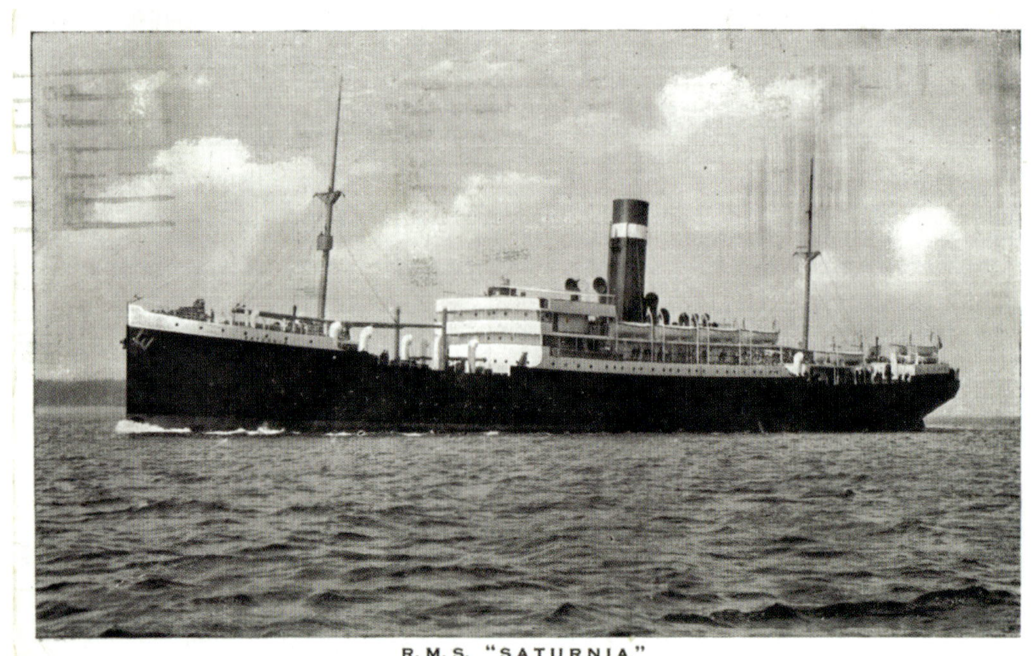

The postcard opposite was sent from another passenger, unconnected but on the same voyage that Charles was on and was sent to Mrs J. Sneddon of Glasgow. The reverse reads, 'This is a better picture than the one you got at the docks. We are starting to make preparations for landing, Andrew'.

He spent the rest of his life in Canada and had a visit from his sister Jessie Duncan Maharey in 1964 which was covered in the local press. Jessie was the wife of Jim Maharey and she later became one of the last remaining inhabitants of Burnbanks before the village was finally abandoned in the 1980s.

He hadn't seen his sister for forty-four years at that point. He died just a few years later on 22 August 1968 in Regina, Saskatchewan, Canada, at the age of sixty-eight and was buried there.

The Anchor Donaldson Line ceased trading many years ago but the office in St Vincent Street in Glasgow has been sympathetically restored and is now a beautiful bar and restaurant. The walls are full of photographs, posters and memorabilia spanning the entire history of the company and is certainly worth a visit.

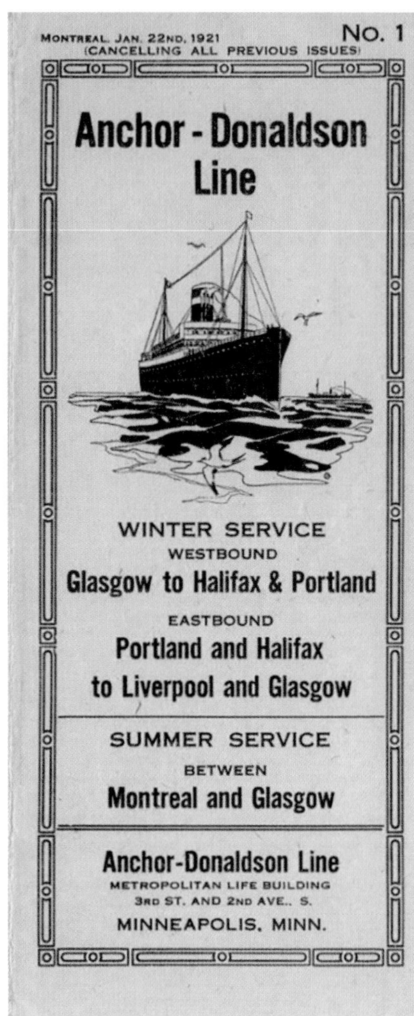

An onboard brochure from the author's collection detailing deck plans, transportation costs and terms and conditions.

Captain Robert Parrott and the Paddle Steamer *Prince Consort*

Several shipwrecks have happened close to Burnbanks Village over the years but one of the most interesting ones happened to the Paddle Steamer *Prince Consort* in 1867.

The ship was operated by the Aberdeen, Leith & Clyde Shipping Co. and had a regular well-supported route from Aberdeen to Leith and the Orkney and Shetland islands.

The ship was commanded by Captain Robert Parrott. It was 222 feet long and iron-hulled, only nine years old but it had already been involved in two previous serious incidents.

On 11 May 1867, the fishermen of Burnbanks were at the Haven preparing their boats and nets. There was a dense fog, no wind, but a heavy ground swell and all was very still but being close to midsummer, there would have been light to work, so everyone was about at five o'clock.

A cry went up: 'there's a ship coming on to the rocks'. A bell was ringing fast and loud to warn the crew and passengers but nothing could be done to prevent the slow crunching, groaning and screeching as the *Prince Consort* struck the rocks.

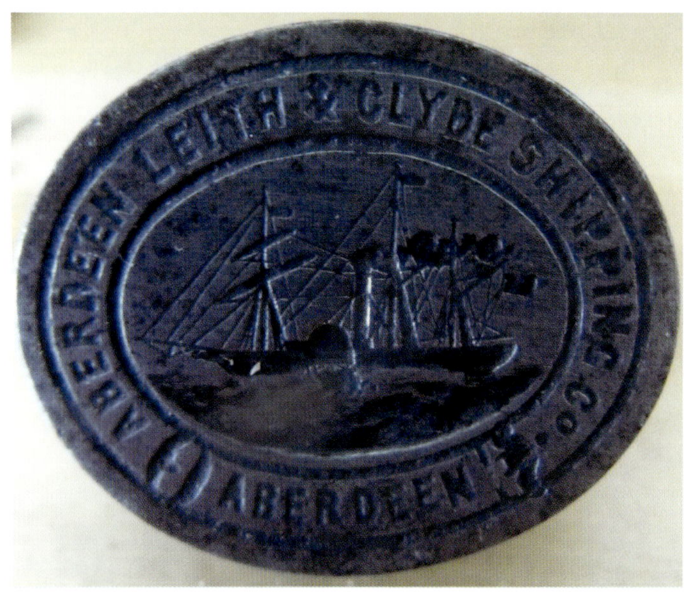

A stationery embossing stamp from the Aberdeen, Leith & Clyde Shipping Co.

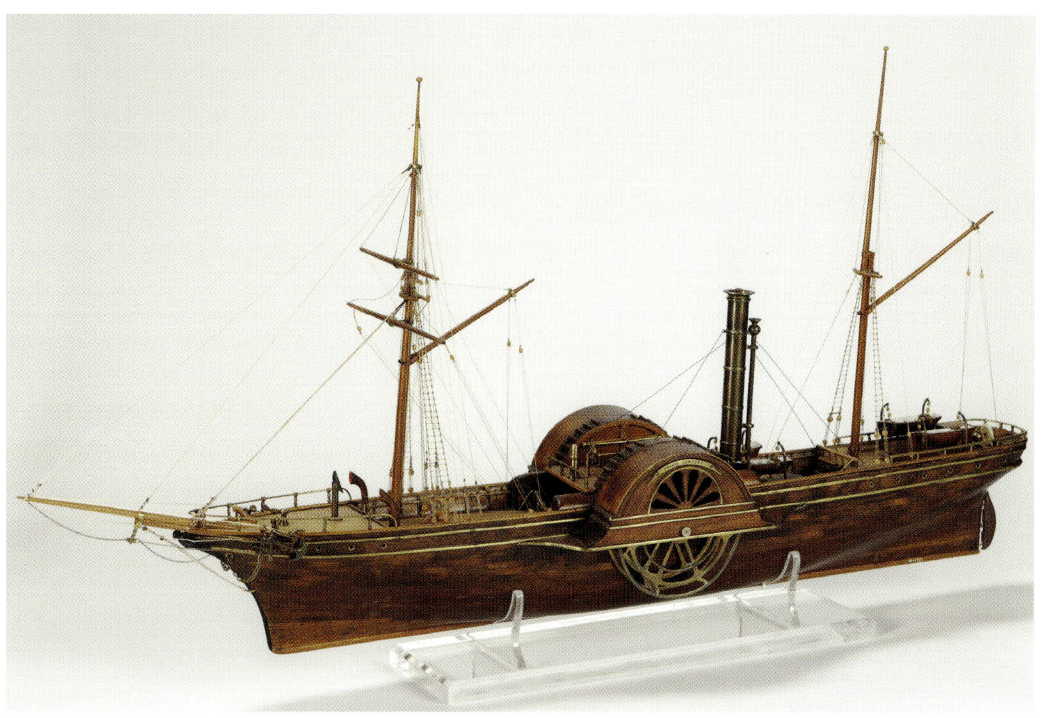

A beautiful wooden model of the *Prince Consort*. (Photography courtesy of the Aberdeen Maritime Museum)

Everyone knew the boats would be required to render assistance, so all available men set about putting to sea.

The *Prince Consort* had left Leith the previous day and had made very slow progress due to fog. Accurate passenger records were not kept but it was estimated between seventy to ninety and possibly as high as one hundred passengers were onboard. It stopped on many occasions to take depth readings using a lead weight and marked rope. The speed was reduced but errors were made with position and expected depths under the hull. At the Board of Trade Enquiry into the reasons for the wreck several weeks later, it was found that the lengths of rope on the sounding line were incorrectly marked due to rope being cut by a paddle and not repaired. Something as simple as that had huge consequences and caused the vessel to be lost. The inaccurate recordings led the captain to believe the vessel was much further out in deeper water and in no danger of being too close to land.

A depth sounding was being taken at the exact time when breakers on the shore were heard and seen through the fog. Even though evasive action was taken immediately, it was too late and the vessel struck the Hasman Rocks. It swung around 180 degrees to point south but then struck another rock close to Burnbanks harbour and was stuck fast.

The captain ordered the ship's boats to be prepared and lowered. Rescue boats from Burnbanks and Altens were on the scene very quickly and proceeded to take off all the passengers and crew. They were taken to Altens Haven and Burnbanks.

Captain Parrott was still onboard as the vessel broke in two and sections were already under water. His Chief Mate Robert Wilson pleaded with him to leave the vessel but although he knew all passengers and crew were off, he didn't want to leave. Differing reports detail Parrot stepping off as the last section slipped under water and others have him forcibly removed and deposited into a rescue boat by the Chief Mate.

The vessel was now completely wrecked in a very short time. Wreckage was strewn along the coastline for some distance and coastguards from Cove Bay were on the scene to take control of the incident and to prevent any looting – according to the coastguard, Mr Thomas Wakeham, the people onshore behaved admirably. He instructed the rescue boats to return to sea and recover as much of the cargo and personal effects as they could.

Captain Parrott and the Chief Mate were segregated from other crew and passengers, presumably to prevent collusion of stories, and taken to No. 11 Burnbanks. This is the modern No. 12.

Passengers and crew were taken to other houses in Burnbanks and Altens and given food and drink and changes of clothes, then transferred to Aberdeen.

Later in the day Captain Parrott was seen back at the clifftop viewing the wreck site. Only the tops of the paddle boxes and the funnel were still visible. The shore was littered with wreckage of broken timbers, furniture, cargo and luggage. The poor man was devastated, in shock and showing great distress at the loss of his vessel, but must have been thankful there were no casualties.

Knowing the position of the wreck, it is incredible that there were no fatalities or serious injuries; it is a harsh environment and even on calm days, you would not want to be in a position of being in the water so close to the rocks and crags.

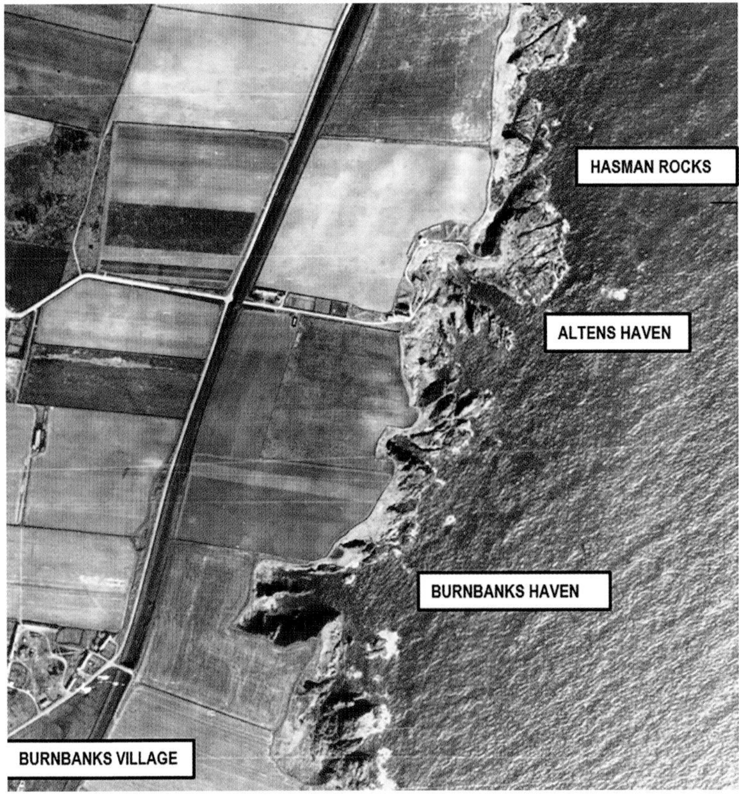

(Photograph from the National Collection of Aerial Photography with annotations by the author)

A three-day Board of Trade Enquiry into the circumstances of the loss of the vessel was conducted at Aberdeen court with many witnesses being called, giving eyewitness testimony and expert opinions. Parrott's character was called into question as is usual in these cases. Was he competent, was he sober, how did he conduct himself under the circumstances?

All accounts defended the captain and although he was reprimanded for allowing the vessel to go to sea with a defective depth sounding line, he was praised by the court for swift decisive actions that helped save the passengers and crew. His Master's Certificate was returned to him amidst great applause from the court.

After the sinking inquiry, the Board of Trade recommended that the fishermen involved in the rescue of passengers should receive cash rewards: several of the men received £2 each; boat owners were awarded more to compensate for any damages to their vessels.

The men of Nigg Bay were given £25 between them and being first on the scene and responsible for rescuing most of the passengers and crew, Altens salmon fishers were given three guineas each.

A total of over £75 was distributed amongst those involved in the rescue and recovery operation. A row broke out between Altens and Burnbanks because they felt the distribution of the awards was unfair. They stated that only two Burnbanks boats had rendered assistance after all passengers and crew were already safely ashore, yet seventeen men lined up to claim a reward. Tough luck to the Altens men, 'Shy bairns dinna get any sweeties!'.

Captain Parrott's Master's Certificate, 1851. (Courtesy of Ancestry.co.uk)

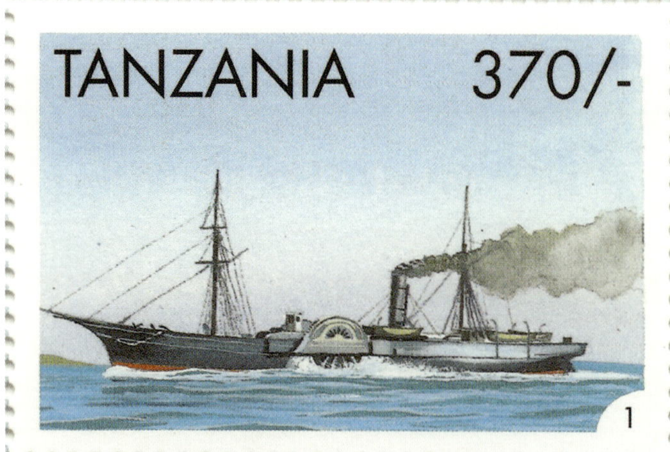

The *Prince Consort* on a stamp from a 1999 collection of ships of the nineteenth century from Tanzania.

Even though this was his third shipwreck with the same vessel within seven years, Captain Parrott was still a very highly regarded man by employers, shipmates and passengers and received awards for saving all the passengers.

Aberdeen University Special Collections hold records and minutes for Aberdeen, Leith & Clyde Shipping Co. and Captain Parrot receives regular mentions, and this is a measure of how highly he was regarded. He was lined up for a new replacement ship which was to be called St Clair, a vessel name closely associated with Aberdeen and the Northern Islands run since then.

By July of the same year of the loss, Parrott is reported as being unable to take up command of the replacement due to illness. He was relieved of command but on full pay until he died. He died very soon afterwards on 6 April 1868 at the age of only fifty-one. He had a brain tumour and for the last three months of his life was totally blind. Many tributes were paid in the press and in the company minutes.

Parrott's Early Life Before the First Incident

His first wife Annette Lewis died in 1849 at the age of only twenty-six, at No. 19 Marischal Street, Aberdeen. They already had two children, Charles and James, but Annette died in childbirth along with their third child. The child is unnamed and only listed as SBC (Still-Born Child) in the register of lairs.

Her younger sister Matilda Lewis came to Aberdeen to look after the children to allow Robert to return to sea. Fifty years later, the local papers refer to a story from 1849 called the Marischal Street Tragedy.

Sister-in-law Matilda fell in love with Robert but it seemed to be a case of unrequited love. The newspaper reports listed 'temporary insanity' causing Matilda to commit suicide in the same year her sister died by hanging herself in the same room as the children. Neighbours reported loud wailing and crying from the children. A locksmith was sent for and the door of the house breached. Inside were the children around their deceased aunt, still hanging from a four-post bed, the children pleading with her to talk to them. The children were seven and two years old at the time.

Those present said it was the most heart-rending scene and it was a long time before Aberdeen forgot about that.

Captain Parrott remarried in 1851 to Margaret Milne.

Captain Robert Parrott and the First *Prince Consort* Incident

In 1860, after only two years of service, the *Prince Consort* was involved in the first incident where it run aground and collided with the Noss Head Crags, near Wick in northern Scotland. Again, thick fog was the cause of the incident. Landmarks were invisible and navigational estimates were incorrect; the vessel had sailed backwards and forwards several times and missed the entrance to Wick.

Slow passage and attentive lookouts were employed but the Noss Head Crags were sighted directly overhead and only one half of the ship's length away. Evasive action was too late to be effective and the vessel struck hard. All damage was above the waterline, so the vessel was never in danger of sinking. It lost its bowsprit and figurehead and the bow was extensively damaged – effectively a bloody nose. A rumour spread on land that the vessel was lost but the local press and the company offices quashed the rumour very quickly. The passengers were safely disembarked in Wick with no serious injuries reported.

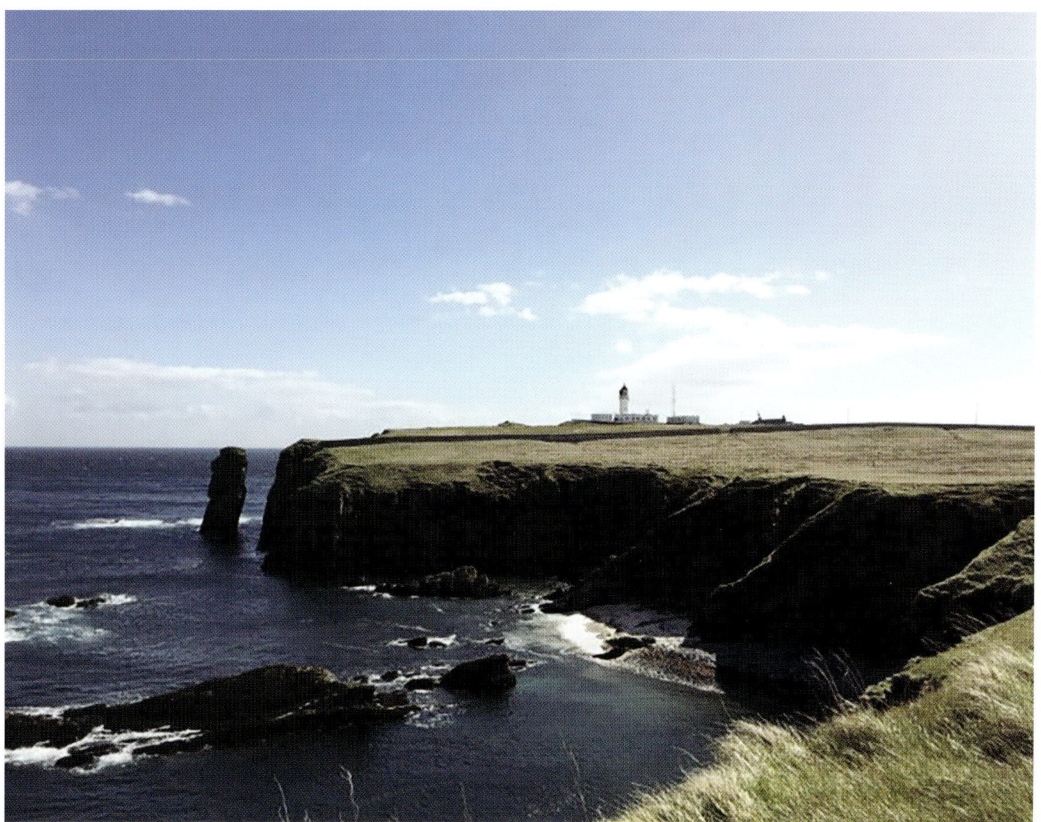

Noss Head, near Wick.

Captain Robert Parrott and the Second *Prince Consort* Incident

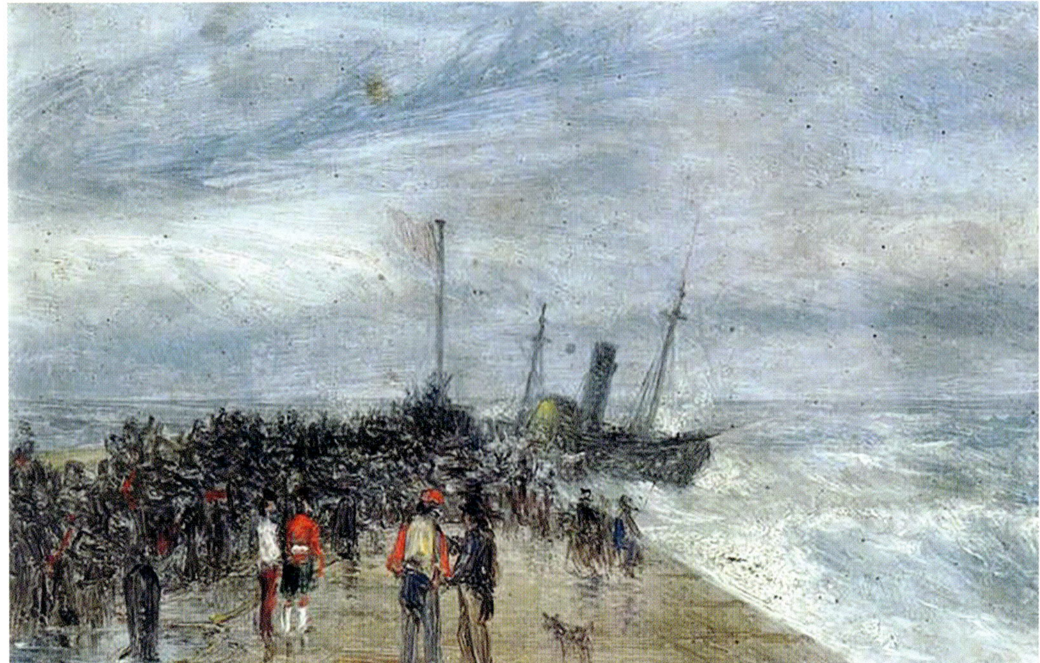

This 1863 painting by famed artist Sir George Reid is called *The Wreck of the Prince Consort*. (Courtesy of the Aberdeen Maritime Museum)

This shows the vessel wrecked at the North Breakwater in Aberdeen harbour. It had been trying to enter the port during very rough seas and was thrown onto a rock shelf in line with the breakwater. The vessel was stuck fast and continuing rough seas caused the steamer to part in the middle and it was considered a total loss. All passengers and crew and some parts of the cargo were safely landed using life-saving apparatus.

Although the vessel was broken in two, it was salvaged by being refloated using new technology in the form of pneumatic lifting bags. I have spent many years of my career in the subsea construction industry and we use airbags daily and it is interesting to see the press write-up of the marvellous new technological wonder – Airbags.

It was taken into Aberdeen harbour where it was rebuilt and later sold back to the Aberdeen, Leith & Clyde Shipping Co. and once again under the command of Captain Robert Parrott.

Robert Parrott is buried in Nellfield Cemetery in Aberdeen. Buried here also is his first wife, Annette Lewis; their stillborn child; Annette's sister Matilda Lewis; his adult son (also Robert); and his second wife, Margaret Milne.

This seems a very crowded lair with six people interred here. Nellfield Cemetery was the subject of a widely reported scandal in 1899 where the operators of the cemetery were re-selling used lairs and disposing of bodies and coffins in a gruesome manner – a morbid but fascinating subject that warrants further reading.

So after a very short but event-filled life, Captain Robert Parrott was laid to rest in Aberdeen. Although it seems like one catastrophe after another, this was a man who

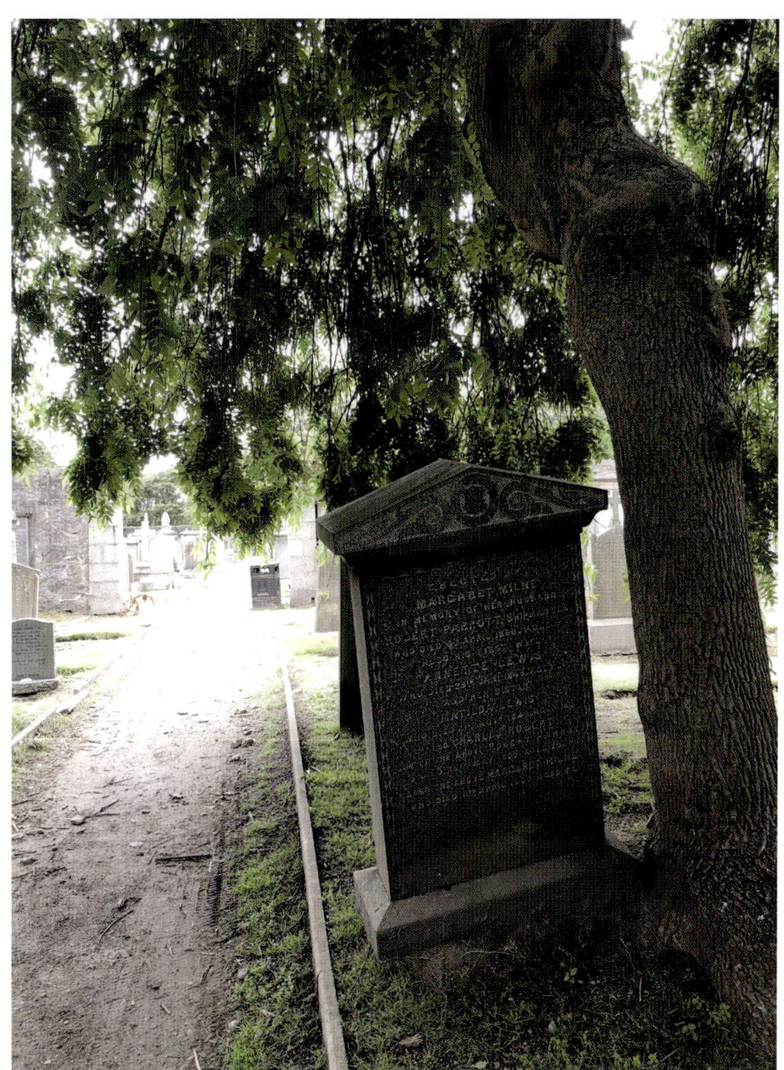

Captain Parrott's grave in Nellfield Cemetery in Aberdeen.

saved hundreds of passengers' and crew's lives by having coolness under pressure, a man respected and adored by his passengers. As any captain may tell you, if events happen on your ship, it may not be your fault but you are responsible.

I feel a close affinity with Captain Parrott, a seafaring man. He was shipwrecked near my village, he walked on my street and was held under guard in my neighbour's house. This chapter has only scratched the surface of a fascinating story. As with several other subjects in this book, he is worthy of further study.

The Burnbanks Trawlers

I have been able to find details of two trawlers called Burnbanks, both linked to the village by their owners. Although neither vessel would have been able to come into Burnbanks Haven, obviously a strong bond existed to their ancestors or place of birth.

The First Burnbanks Trawler

The first Burnbanks trawler was built in 1905, Ship No. 389, at the Hall Russell Shipyard in Aberdeen and was named *Strathisla* at launch. It was a very confusing ship to research. It was the second *Strathisla* built in the same shipyard to the same company and was skippered by the same captain. After the second one was launched, the first one was renamed *Strathisla II*.

During the First World War, it was requisitioned for war service and was converted to a minesweeper or mooring vessel AD 130 and operated from Inverness.

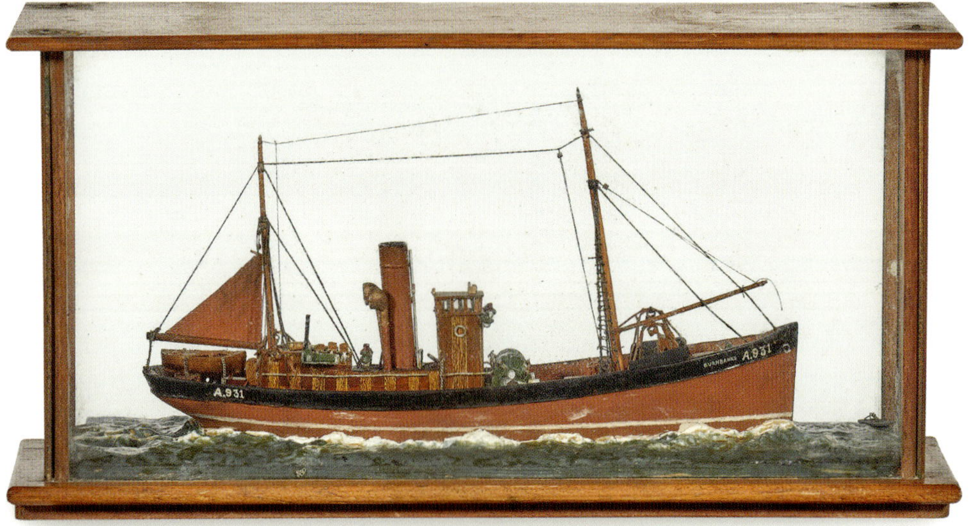

This is a model of the vessel that I purchased from Lyon & Turnbull auction house in Edinburgh. (Image courtesy of Lyon & Turnbull)

War duties ended and it was returned to the owners in 1919. In 1924, the vessel was renamed *Burnbanks*, registry number A931, and continued to fish out of Aberdeen for many years.

In 1926, it had a fortunate piece of salvage. Several large iron casks of proof whiskey were being found in the North Sea. It was unclear where they came from and was suspected they were from a vessel wrecked in the First World War and the cargo was only becoming dislodged several years later. Another suggestion was that they were jettisoned from 'Rum Runners': smuggler vessels sailing across the Atlantic during the prohibition years in America.

The cask that *Burnbanks* found was 52 gallons of proof whiskey – enough for over 400 bottles. Fortunate becomes unfortunate when they were not allowed to keep it or sell it and it had to be surrendered to Customs and Excise authorities in port.

I found a story about a man who went missing on his wedding day in 1938 and was dragged up in the nets by the first *Burnbanks*. The man's name was Stanley Watt of 19 Stranathro from Muchalls, south of Aberdeen.

It's a sad tale as his wedding guests were waiting for him in Inverurie and he was found at sea a month later by the trawler. They took some identifying items from the body but then buried him at sea. Bus tickets found on his body gave indications of his movements and intentions to travel to Keith Hall near Inverurie but it will never be known what happened to him.

During the Second World War, the vessel was still working as a trawler and was attacked by enemy aircraft in 1940. The newspapers gave a very one-sided view of the encounter in typical wartime journalistic style:

From the Western Morning News, 12 January 1940 for half an hour, two Nazi planes bombed and machine-gunned two Aberdeen Trawlers the Burnbanks and the Dandolo off the North East Coast yesterday.

Although at times the machines flew so low that they were mast high, their bombs failed to secure a single hit. After cutting away their gear, both trawlers escaped and returned safely to port. "They were good missers" said a member of crew. The crew of the Burnbanks tried to launch their small boat they were machine gunned and had to retreat to shelter in the galley. The planes returned to attack seven or eight times but neither trawler suffered any injuries.

The vessel survived the war but was scrapped in 1948 after forty-three years of service.

The Second Burnbanks Trawler

This vessel was built in Peterhead in 1959 and was called the *Lothian Leader*, registration number GN18. It fished out of Granton near Edinburgh. It is shown undergoing sea trials at Peterhead.

In 1972, it was sold to two brothers from Cullen, Skipper William and his brother Alex Mair. They renamed it *Burnbanks* for sentimental reasons because one of their relatives owned the previous version. They owned it for twelve years and sailed it out of Aberdeen.

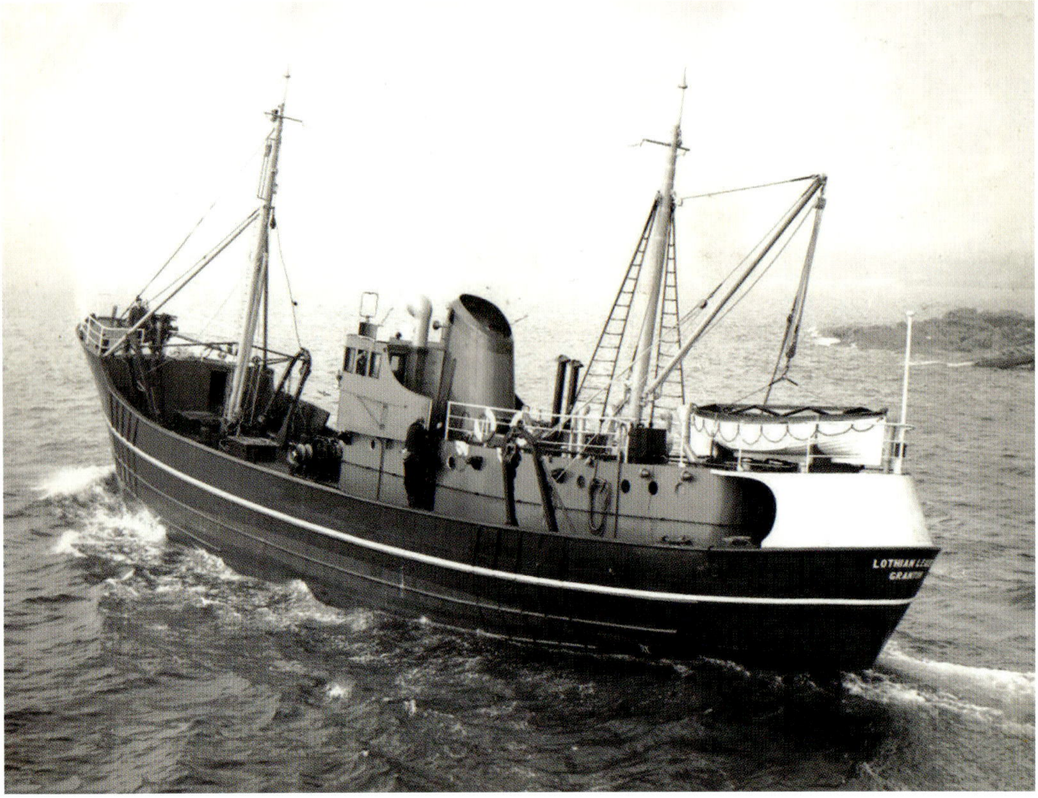

(From the Grantontrawlers.com website)

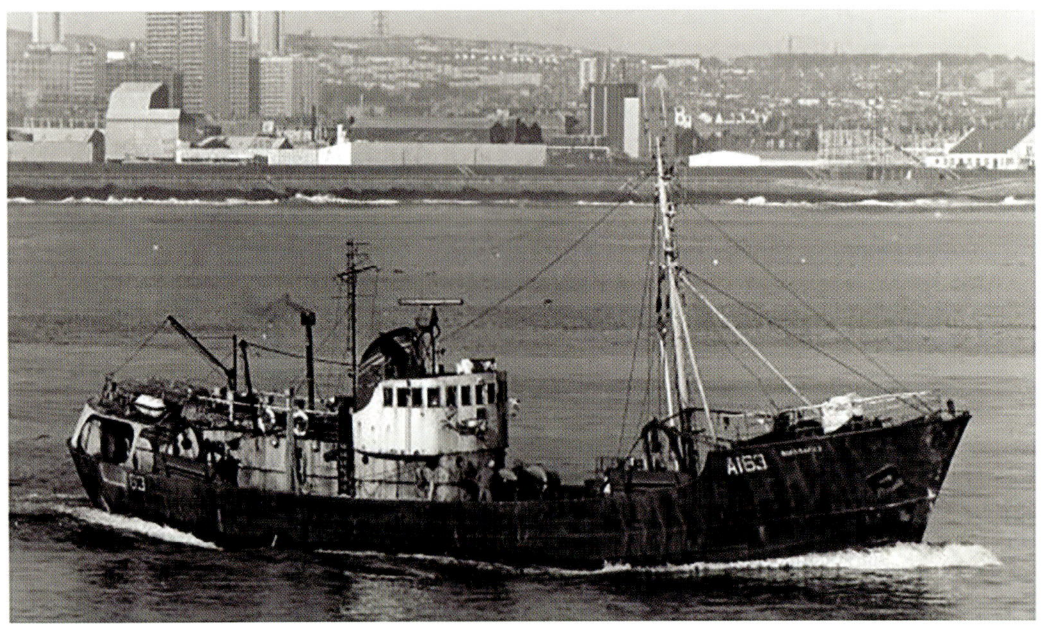

Here is the vessel leaving Aberdeen, date unknown.

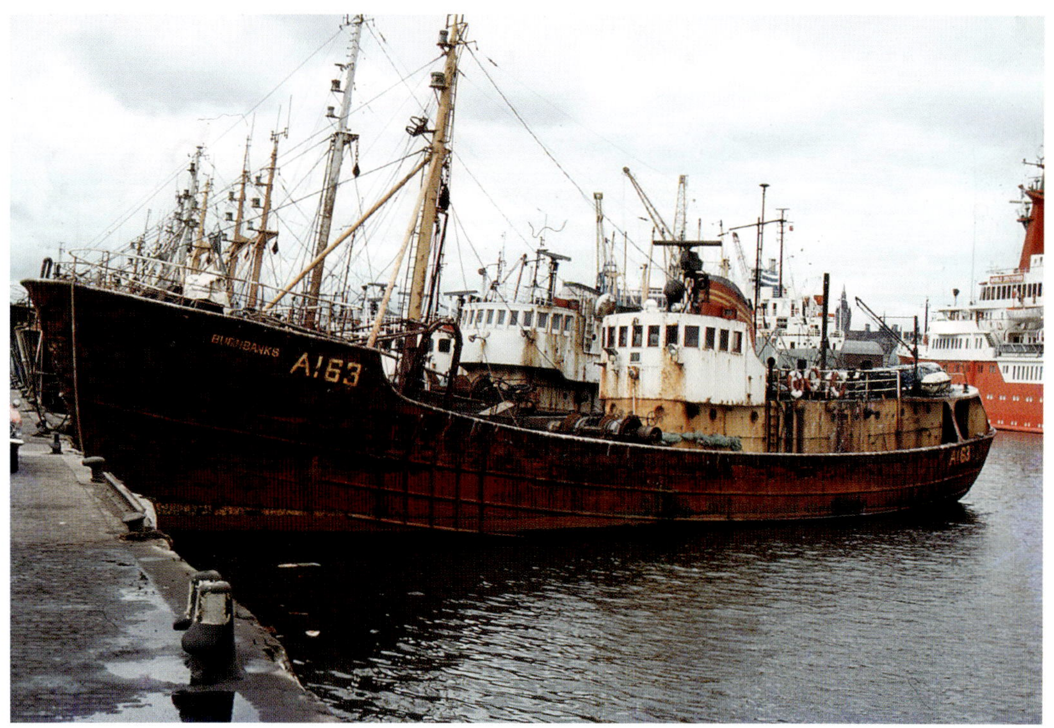

Burnbanks A163 in Aberdeen harbour, date unknown but it could be the early 1980s. (From the author's collection)

As a child, my father and grandfather often took me down the harbour in Fraserburgh to look at similar fishing boats. I know this is a hard-worked vessel and looks don't mean a thing, but the memories of my times in the Broch harbour come flooding back and I can smell it from here across the mists of time.

In 1984, it was sold and renamed *Culebra*. A conversion was started on it to become an oil supply and safety vessel but it was scrapped in 1985 at Gravesend before the conversion was completed.

17

The Cliffs

The coastline close to Burnbanks is a hard, unforgiving place – narrow paths, sheer-faced cliffs with drops up to 200 feet and exposed wind-swept approaches.

There have been many injuries and fatalities over the years right up to the present day. It's an area of great natural beauty but we must all be aware of the dangers that it presents. I won't discuss the incidents from recent times as many of the people involved or their families are still alive, so we must respect their privacy.

The following is a tragic story of a young girl who went to the cliffs to commit suicide and all she left behind was a humble pile of her possessions. She went missing on 8 August but was not found until 25 August. The Death Certificate Register of Corrected Entries states the cause of death was 'Drowning (suicidal)':

A strange discovery was made at Souter Heads, Burnbanks Nigg on Saturday. On a rock on the seashore a hat, a pair of gloves and a small sum of money were found with a note from a girl Alexandrina Knowles asking the finder to deliver the articles to Lawson 110 Union Grove, Aberdeen. The young woman is employed as a clerkess with a firm of wine merchants in the city and the address given is that of her brother-in-law with whom she resided. She left home on Friday and has not been seen since.

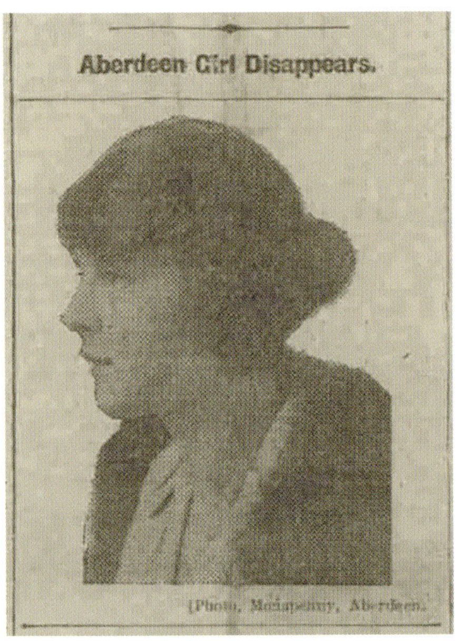

Alexandrina Knowles. (From the *Aberdeen Journal*, 15 August 1919. Used by kind permission of DC Thomson & Co. Ltd)

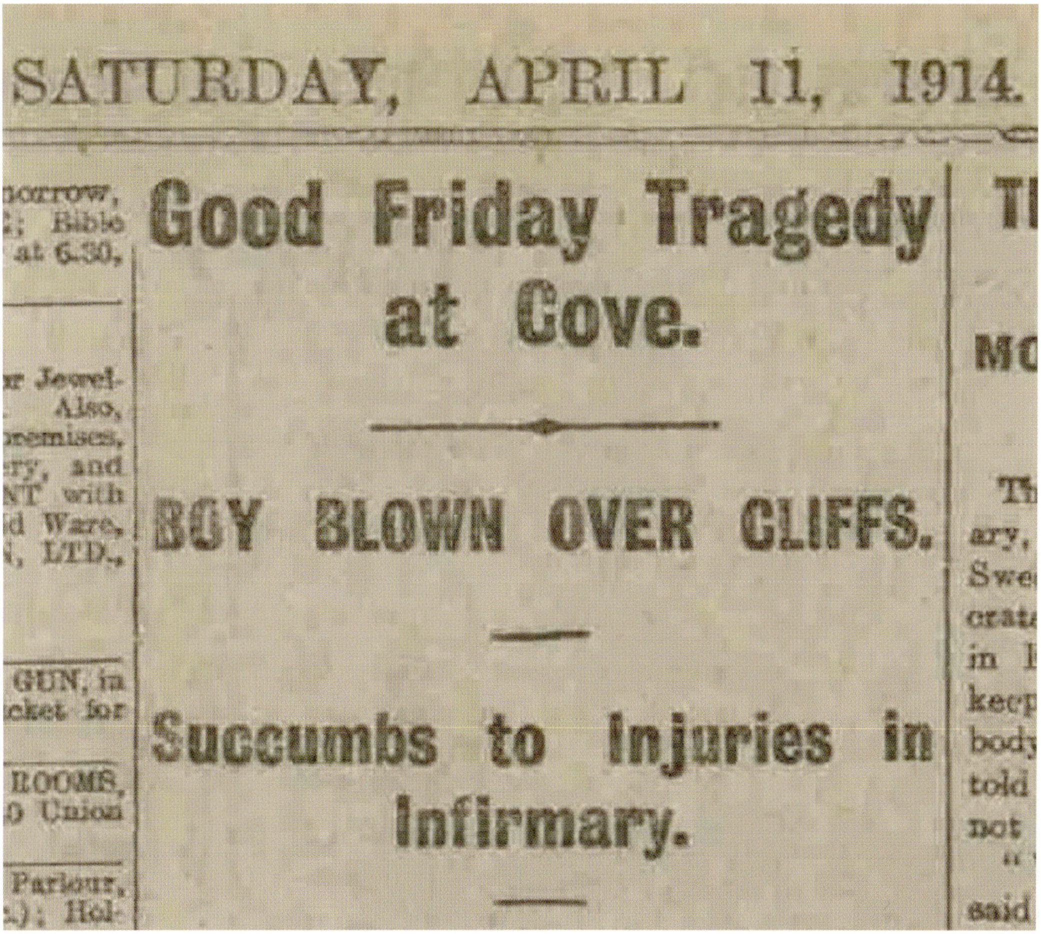

Good Friday Tragedy at Cove.

BOY BLOWN OVER CLIFFS.

Succumbs to Injuries in Infirmary.

Above and right: John Smith aged sixteen, 1914. (From the *Evening Express*, Friday 10 April 1914. (Used by kind permission of DC Thomson & Co. Ltd)

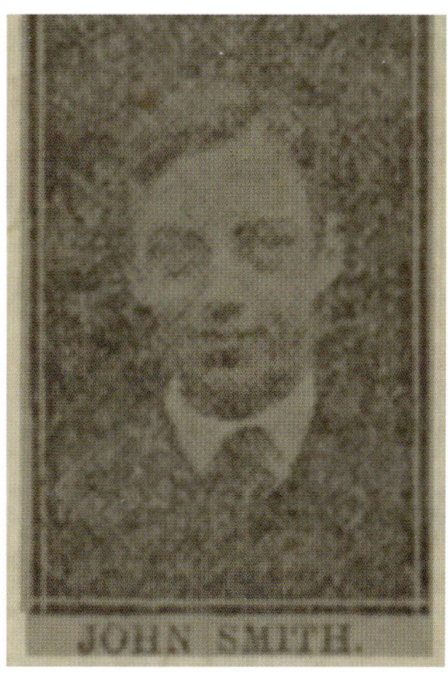

Between twelve and one o'clock today, a young man was blown over the cliffs at Burnbanks shore about a mile from Cove Bay.

When found by a Coastguard he was in a serious condition and Dr Milne conveyed him in his motor car to the Royal Infirmary, Aberdeen. The cliffs at that part are about 120ft high. The youth's name is John Smith, 52 Irvine Place. He is a schoolboy and had been spending the first day of his Easter holidays on the rocks at Cove.

This section of the cliffs is terrifying. The path is so close to the sheer face and during the seabird nesting season it is not a place to visit unless you are ready to fend off attacks. Poor William was looking for seagull's eggs and a simple stumble cost him his life.

Less than a year later, another fatality. Henry Nairn. This poor child was only seven years old.

All of the above stories are so tragic but the one that really strikes hard is the story of Frank Rennie Watson. Frank was a Burnbanks boy living with his grandparents in No. 6 Burnbanks, which is now No. 10 next door to us, and only ten when he died in 1935.

FALL OVER 200-FEET CLIFF.

ABERDEEN LAD KILLED NEAR COVE.

A thirteen-year-old boy named William Corwello, residing at Exchequer Row, Aberdeen, met his death yesterday afternoon by falling about 200 feet from a cliff on the Kincardineshire coast between Cove and the old fishing hamlet of Burnbanks, about a quarter of a mile from Cove Bay Station and some four miles from Aberdeen.

The boy left Aberdeen earlier in the day to go nesting for seagulls' eggs or gathering flowers on the high cliffs about Cove, and was seen about four o'clock in the afternoon.

He stumbled on the edge of the cliff, and fell headlong into the sea. The boy's companions ran for help, and workmen rowed from Cove in a small boat, and found the body being lagged against the side of the cliff by the inflowing tide.

Several bird-nesting fatalities have previously happened about this same part of the coast, the dangerous character of which has long been recognised.

In the evening an attempt to take the body up the cliffs by ropes proved unsuccessful, but it was subsequently taken to Cove and then to Aberdeen.

HOLIDAY TRAGEDY NEAR COVE.

City Boy's 50-Feet Fall.

As the result of severe injuries received by falling over the cliffs near Cove yesterday afternoon, Henry Nairn, the 7-year-old son of Mr Henry Nairn, watchmaker, 24 Esslemont Avenue, Aberdeen, died in the Sick Children's Hospital shortly before seven o'clock in the evening.

Nairn and another boy were playing on the top of the cliffs just outside Burnbank, which is about a mile north of Cove village. Nairn approached too near the edge of the cliff, and overbalancing, fell over the cliff on to the shingle beach, about 50 feet below.

BOY FOUND DROWNED IN SEA NEAR COVE.

Men Risk Lives in Recovering Body From Dangerous Gully.

PERILOUS CLIMB ALONG FACE OF ROCKS AT CLIFF FOOT.

The body of a ten-year-old boy, Frank Rennie Watson, who resided at Burnbanks, Nigg, Kincardineshire, was recovered from a gully near Cove yesterday afternoon.

Owing to the steepness of the cliff and the impractability of reaching the body by sea, great difficulty was experienced in recovering the remains.

Three men played a plucky part in the sad task.

Above left: William Corwello aged thirteen. (From the British Newspaper Archive, 16 July 1921. Used by kind permission of DC Thomson & Co. Ltd)

Above right: From the *Aberdeen Journal*, 2 May 1922. Courtesy of the British Newspaper Archive. Used by kind permission of DC Thomson & Co. Ltd)

Left: (From the *Aberdeen Journal*, 27 May 1935. Courtesy of the British Newspaper Archive. Used by kind permission of DC Thomson & Co. Ltd)

Edward Thomson of Torry was walking along the cliffs on Saturday afternoon when he saw a body at the water's edge. Constable William Bell from Nigg instituted a search by boat but failed to recover the body. The search was resumed the next day but recovery was impossible due to the severe swell.

Three men, James Maharey from Burnbanks, Andrew Henderson from Cove and an unnamed rockfisher, formed a plan to bring Frank home. After watching the poor child's body being dashed against the rocks for a day, the men had had enough. They made their way to the gully and recovered him from the water quite easily, but now faced the problem of hoisting him up the cliffs. A rope was secured to the remains and they were floated back out to a position where they could be hauled up the cliffs. After landing on a flat rock, Frank was transferred to a stretcher for hoisting to the top of the cliff.

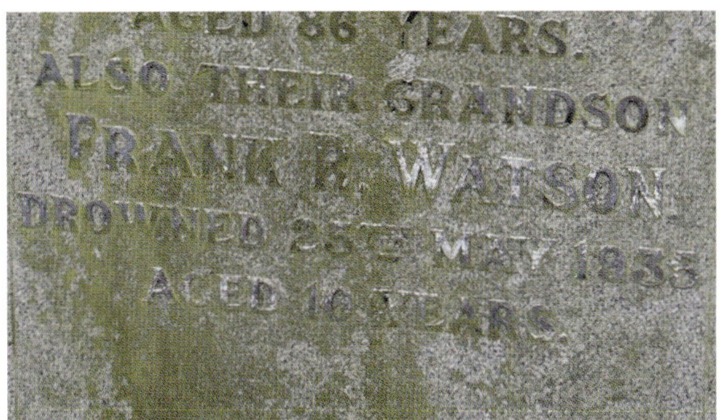

Above: Frank was buried in Nigg Kirkyard.

Right: His inscription reads, 'Their Grandson Frank R. Watson drowned 25th May 1935 aged 10 years.'

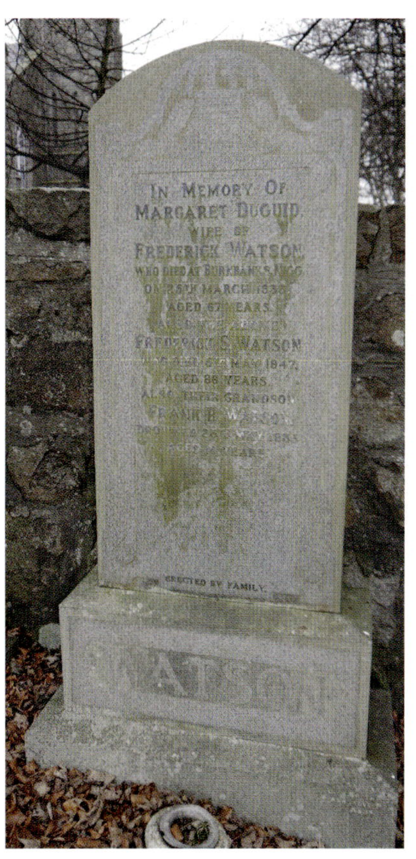

I've found stories of several cliff fatalities. I'm sure there are others but I don't want to read about them anymore. We have children of a similar age and it chills the blood to think about these poor unfortunates. If you go to the cliffs, please respect the dangers and hang on tightly to the children.

18

The Railway Line

The Main East Coast line from Edinburgh to Aberdeen passes within meters of the village. Although we are close to the line the noise is not a problem – a gentle whoosh as the newer trains pass; the daily freight train around 10.00 p.m. is a little noisier but not an issue.

On a passenger train journey south, you can see the village but only for a short time and it's gone in a flash.

The bridge that crosses the line next to the village is an access point for the clifftop walking routes. Most train drivers give a hoot on their horns if you give them a wave as they pass.

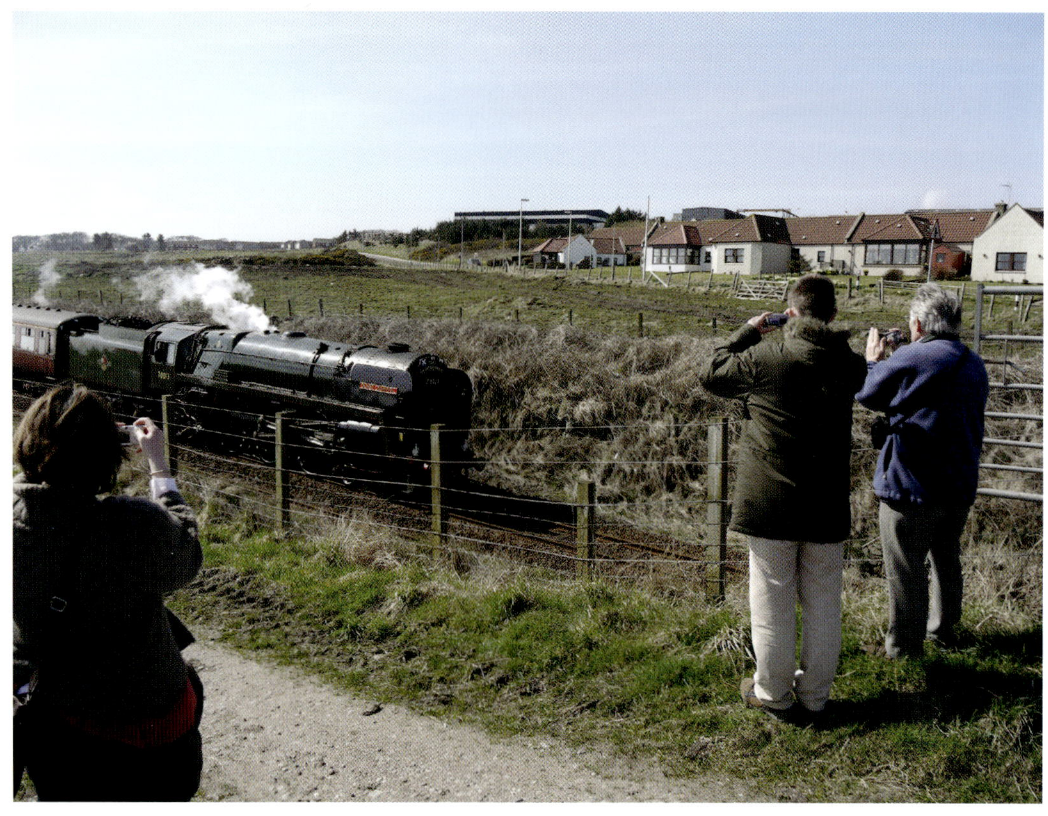

A rare visitor from modern times as a steam train passes Burnbanks en route to Aberdeen.

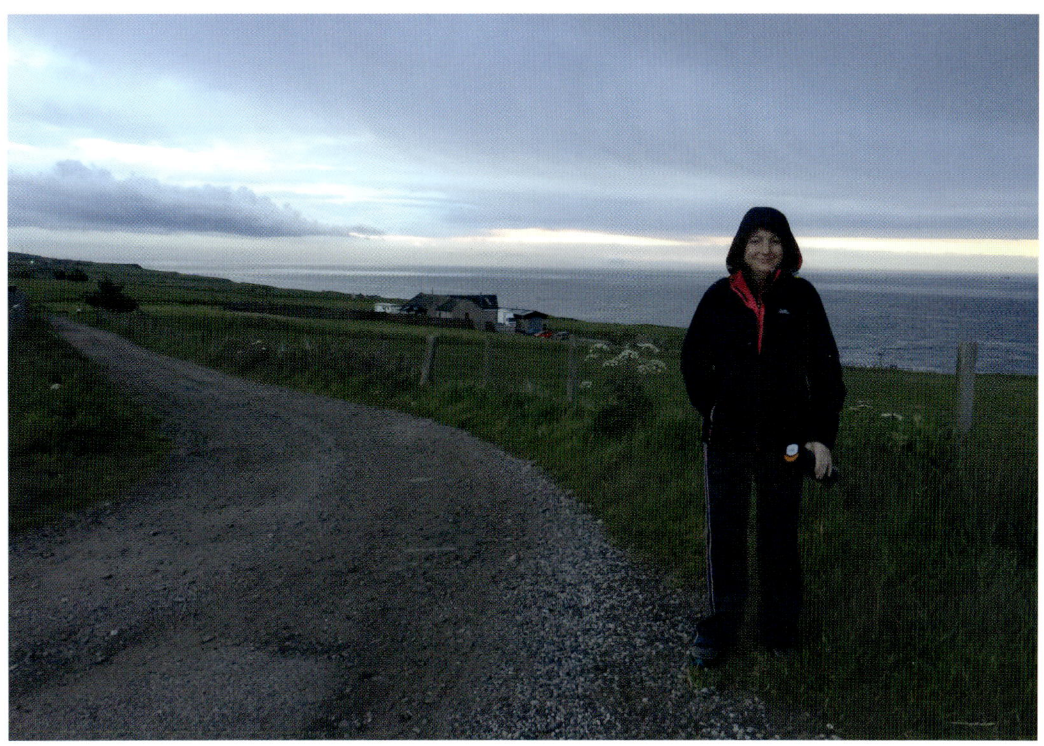

Rosa next to the railway bridge at sunrise on the summer solstice in 2016.

When I first started to send out messages in a bottle around the internet one of the first contacts returned was with ex-Burnbanks Loon Vic Garioch. Vic's family lived there in the 1930s and 1940s. One of his stories features in the section called 'Is The Village haunted?'.

Vic sent me this photograph of his father Albert Garioch who was a barber in Aberdeen city centre. Albert would take his bicycle to the railway station in Cove to catch a train into town. Money was tight and he would often not have the fare.

He would stand out of sight at the station and just as the whistle blew for the train to leave he would make a quick dash, hold up an old ticket and the station guards would hurry him onboard.

He got away with that stunt several times, likely because he was always in a nice suit and hat.

The railways came to the north-east of Scotland in the late 1840s. A tragic consequence of this has been the high number of fatalities, several suicides and many accidents.

The earliest casualty I found was in 1857. Joseph Leiper was on his way home from the Cove Bay Hotel. It's a very convenient, direct and flat route from the hotel to Burnbanks and this seems to have been the undoing of quite a few people.

There have been a number of suicides and it must have been horrendous for the villagers to come across these. In August 1897, James Rae came to Burnbanks, tucked a suicide note in his pocket, lay down on the line and was decapitated. Four months later, in December, Walter Gray became another casualty, leaving a wife and two children.

Other fatalities have occurred including George Craig in 1867 and Andrew Leiper in 1876. In 1910 William Meston was described as horribly mutilated and cut in two from

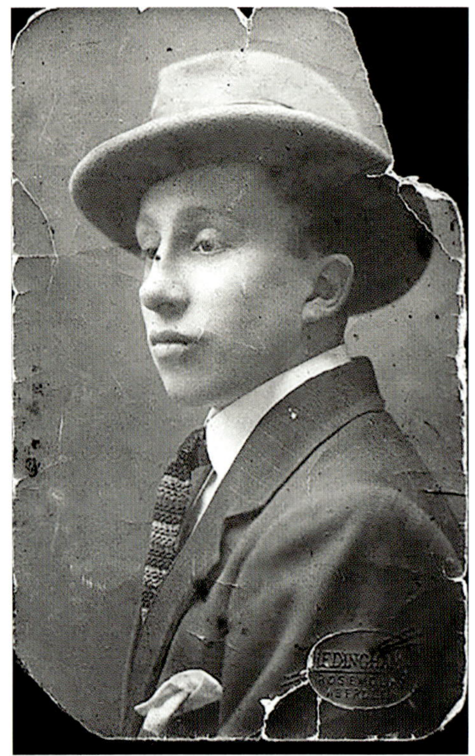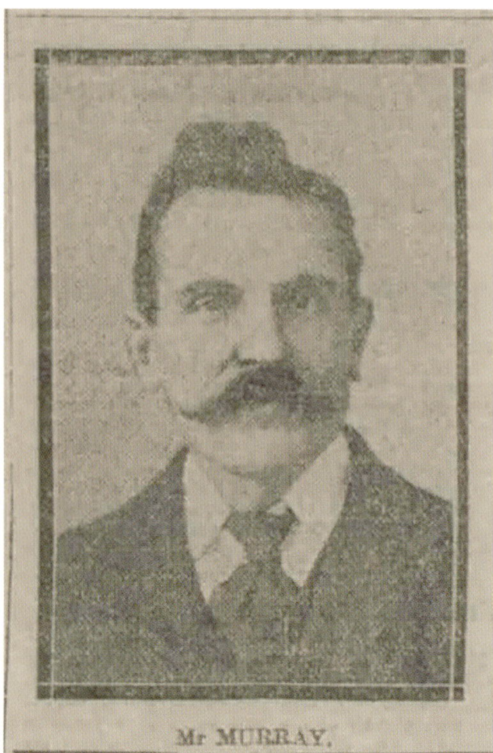

Above left: Albert Garioch. (Photograph courtesy of Victor Garioch, Albert's son)

Above right: (From the British Newspaper Archive. Used by kind permission of DC Thomson & Co. Ltd)

head to foot. In 1911 James Duncan also suffered a similar end. There seems to be a large gap with no injuries up until 1970 when Walter Anderson was killed.

I apologise for the grim descriptions but even though these incidents occurred over 120 years ago, it is still disturbing reading. Families were left shocked and heartbroken. Depression and mental illness are nothing new.

In early April, 1914 a train driver Edward Murray was killed at the Burnbanks bridge. The train was approaching Aberdeen and Edward went on top of the engine to move coal and conduct maintenance checks when he struck the overhead bridge with such force that masonry was dislodged. He was killed instantly. The fireman on the engine plate didn't hear anything but obviously knew something was wrong and realised his colleague was missing. He brought the train to a halt at the next junction and reported the incident. A light engine was sent from Aberdeen and found Murray in a ditch at the side of the line.

Only one month later, in May 1914, another fatality, that of Alexander Murray (no relation), occurred after he was struck by a train. His injuries included a fractured skull and a broken neck.

This was a very hard section to write; very troubling that so many sudden and violent deaths have occurred in our small area. Thankfully there have been none in modern times.

19

Crime

When looking back in history, we have a view that all people were God-fearing citizens, kept in place by the Church and by draconian laws with harsh punishments. This doesn't seem to be the case with Burnbanks Village – what a bunch of criminals!

Lots of minor crimes are reported in the newspapers of the day, details that wouldn't be bothered with now but back then newspapers needed filling.

Fight!

An early incident revolves around a prize fight in 1844. The fighters and the spectators were in a cat and mouse tussle with the authorities:

> From the *Aberdeen Herald and General Advertiser*, 6 July 1844
>
> Brutal Affair- We understand that the inhabitants of Nigg were alarmed at two o'clock in the morning by the incursion of a riotous mob, upwards of 500 of the dregs of the population of Aberdeen for the purpose of witnessing a prize fight got up between two noted characters well known to the authorities here.
>
> One of them a weaver and the other a Coal Carter. The whole of the mob entered and took possession of a pasture field on Mr Ferguson's property at Altens where having formed a ring, the two principal actors stripped themselves and mauled and cut and bruised each other for more than half an hour until the brutal work was put a stop to by the police.
>
> The whole affair has been put into the hands of the proper authorities and we trust that the result will be sufficient to prevent this quarter being disturbed by any such exhibitions of the exploded barbarism of times now happily passed away.

Sounds exciting. Get me a ticket!

Train!

A more recent crime was committed in the 1960s and was told to me by Dorothy Beattie. I'm sorry for airing this in public Dorothy but she was fined 11 shillings in the 1960s for crossing the nearby railway line. Her father had a potato field and they crossed the line to pick tatties.

(From *Aberdeen Evening Express*, 22 September 1954. Courtesy of the British Newspaper Archive. Used by kind permission of DC Thomson & Co. Ltd)

In the days of steam trains, it was a very common occurrence for engine drivers and firemen to shovel off a few large lumps of coal near to places where their families lived. After the trains passed, the family would go on the line and recover the coal.

An incident reported in the Aberdeen *Evening Express* resulted in a prosecution and a very hefty fine in 1954. Margaret Wood of Catto Crescent in Cove was fined £5 for stealing four shilling's worth of coal. It seems very harsh but this was her fifth conviction and the authorities were concerned because she was taking her children with her. It was hard times indeed and if it's a choice between keeping warm or risking another conviction, I would have done the same myself. Well done Margaret.

Fight! Again

Everyone has been to a wedding where an argument or a fight breaks out – nothing different back then.

In 1874, two criminals from Burnbanks were convicted of assaulting an elderly man because they were arguing over how a song should be sung.

The court prosecutor noted that it was the custom for everyone to get 'fou' at fisher-folks' weddings. 'Mighty' Joseph Craig was arguing with 'Stucco' John Main and they came to blows. Sixty-year-old George Main intervened to try and get them to stop and they turned on him.

The poor man was so severely assaulted that although the incident happened on 22 November, he was not able to appear as a witness until 28 January.

In the meantime, the fighters were remanded in custody for over two months. They were found guilty and given the option of a further thirty days of imprisonment or a

£5 fine each. The fines were paid. What? You didn't enjoy the jail lads? You two must have been brave beating up the old man.

Breaking Windows

Two boys named George Walker and Alexander Main from nearby Torry were charged with breaking four windows at an unoccupied house in Burnbanks. The sheriff said that cases of juvenile crime had been too frequent of late and he was afraid it was due to the leniency shown by the court in such cases.

This sounds like a modern story with the authorities lamenting the falling standards of the youth of today but this happened in 1887. The boys were ordered to pay a fine of seven shillings and sixpence or go to prison for twenty-four hours.

Stop, Thief!

In 1880, James Chapman was before the crown for several thefts from washing lines between Cove, Burnbanks and Torry. Several shirts, trousers, and vests were stolen. Chapman was sentenced to sixty days in prison.

Oooya Ma Heid!

In 1885, Charles Stephen of Cove was convicted of assaulting James Beattie of Burnbanks and causing malicious damage. He struck him on the mouth and held a knife to his throat threatening to stab him. Tables and chairs were overturned and smashed. Sounds like a Wild West brawl. The penalty was ten shillings or a week in prison.

Burnbanks Men Like Drinking and Swimming

In August 1876 *The Aberdeen Journal* reported that Alexander Wilson of Burnbanks Village fell into Aberdeen harbour whilst in a state of intoxication. He was promptly rescued by the crew of a hopper barge and was little the worse for his involuntary bath.

While this seems a funny story, it's the sad truth that many people lose their lives falling into harbours or falling off vessels even to this day. This was in the summer months but if it had been winter he'd have been dead in minutes. Nothing changes.

Travel the World, Meet New People, Start a Fight

Born in 1888, ex-resident of Burnbanks William Bruce Main emigrated to Australia in 1912. His wife Louisa intended to follow him with the children but she sadly died before she could make the trip.

He returned to Scotland to collect the children and lived in Australia for many years until he passed away in 1959 after being a resident of New South Wales for forty-seven years.

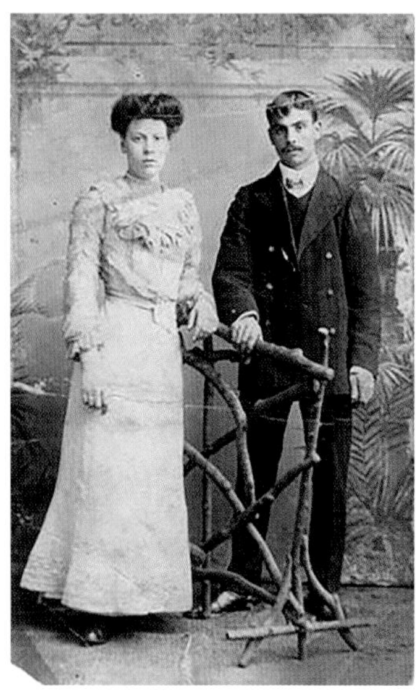

William Bruce Main and Louisa Main.

On 1 September 1939 the Second World War breaks out in Europe, soon to spread across the world. In Sydney Australia only two weeks later William is arrested at a government building for trying to take a rifle away from a sentry. What was he thinking? The world was in a nervous state, and anyone with a gun had an itchy trigger finger, so trying to show a sentry 'how to guard his weapon' by snatching it away from him was a dangerous move.

Although he had a point because he did manage to take the weapon off the man, it was still very unsafe to attempt that. Battered, then fined £5.

The Bigamist – The Man with Four Names

In 1916 the Great War was into its second year. A soldier called Alexander McPherson came to Burnbanks and left a trail of destruction behind him.

He claimed he was in the 4th Battalion Canadian Highlanders in France, owned large areas of land in Canada, and was due large sums of money. He claimed he was twenty-seven years old but his age wanders as high as thirty-five on various documents and reports.

He came to London and fell in with evil company. He was afraid to return to the Canadian battalion, so he deserted and joined the Gordon Highlanders and ended up in Aberdeen. This is where he comes into contact with Burnbanks.

He met Roselina Will, twenty-four years old, and she was attracted to him. He told her that he knew her brothers in Vancouver and promised to take Roselina and her mother to Canada.

He convinces her to marry him but even by the day of the wedding, he's already in trouble for falsifying signatures of the two witnesses in the marriage licence and theft of articles from a boarding house.

He borrowed a tweed suit to get married in, from Donald Bruce who lived in my house, the excuse being his uniform was covered in blood. They were married in

Nigg Manse on 14 May 1916 but the day after the wedding, he rose early and went into town. That was the last Donald saw of his suit, the last anyone saw of their money they loaned to him and that was the last Roselina saw of her groom.

Then the family discovered that more money was missing – £4 from the mother and twenty-five shillings from the sister.

Can you imagine the atmosphere in Burnbanks as they slowly realised they had been swindled? Roselina would have been furious and hurt. 'He stole my money, my brother-in-law's suit, my dignity and my heart.'

The police were informed and the next time the family heard of him, he was convicted of theft, falsifying the marriage licence and desertion from the British Army. He was jailed in Craiginches Prison in Aberdeen for ten months. He promised that he would sort everything out when he finished his sentence but when he did get out, soldiers from the Canadian Army were waiting for him.

Less than a year later, he moved to Mossblown in Ayrshire and was about to get married again. His name was now Robert Steele. His bride to be, Jeanie Duff Scott, aged twenty-one, had heard a rumour that he was married but he denied it and convinced her such that the wedding went ahead on Christmas Day 1917.

He did the same thing again: disappeared the day after the wedding.

Roselina Will had to put notices in several newspapers to try and find her husband to bring a divorce action in 1922.

This is where it began to unravel for the bigamist, as a divorce was granted based upon his desertion from Roselina and the second wedding was no longer recognised because of the bigamy.

This is where his aliases were discovered: Alexander MacPherson, Robert Steele, Robert Crawford and George Irvine. His real name is still unknown.

He appears in a police gazette from 1922 under the name of Robert Crawford having faced a charge of larceny in Chelmsford, England. He has four aliases listed. His previous convictions are given as theft, fraud and a minor offence at Stonehaven. Bigamy?! Minor?! Poor Roselina would argue that it was no minor offence.

He returned to Mossblown a few years later on 31 July 1925 and was swiftly arrested. On 18 August, he was up in court and was found guilty of bigamy and sentenced to six months in prison.

So after this, he disappears. If he's known to have used four names it's likely he did it again. Who knows how many times he changed names, stole from friends and then disappeared again.

One of the genealogy sites I use is Scotland's People, where you can find birth, marriage and death certificates. It is a favourite site however, it is not a subscription site, allowing unlimited views and downloads; it is currently a pay-per-page site. While looking for the bigamist I spent a lot of time and money on that site but his trail goes cold. He's even managing one final scam, one final robbery from beyond the grave that cost me £60 in credits – and I got nowhere.

Both of the known bigamy victims remarried and had a (hopefully) more happy life. Roselina remarried in 1922 and died in 1973 at the age of eighty-one in Aberdeen. Second wife Jeanie Duff Scott remarried sometime later.

I couldn't find any further trace of Robert – nor Alexander nor George or whatever name he was using at the end of his life. Did he do any further time in jail? Did he leave the country, or did he return to Canada? Surely no more marriage …

20

Cholera, 1866

An outbreak of Asiatic cholera occurred in the village in 1866. Outbreaks were common across the country throughout the 1800s. The symptoms include severe stomach cramps, diarrhoea and dehydration, which can cause death if left untreated. The causes are drinking contaminated water or eating contaminated food. Unsanitary living conditions and overcrowding helps the disease spread.

From 14 September to 26 October 1866, seven people died in Burnbanks. The table below collates some of the information regarding their deaths. A father and son died within a day of each other and one man, William Main, lost an uncle, his wife and daughter in a little over three weeks.

Casualty Name	Age	Date of Death	Length of Illness	Comments
Margaret Craig	68	14 Sept 1866	28 hours	
James Craig	3	27 Sept 1866	9 hours	Father and son
Andrew Craig	34	28 Sept 1866	12 hours	
George Main	55	3 Oct 1866	45 hours	Uncle, wife and daughter of William Main
Margaret Main	31	17 Oct 1866	5 days	
Jean Masson Main	5	26 Oct 1866	6 days	
William Main	2	26 October 1866	22 hours	Not a sibling but died the same day as Jean Masson Main

will not be lost upon others.

THE CHOLERA.—Several cases, of what appears to be Asiatic cholera, have occurred in the small fishing village of Burnbank, Nigg, during the past eight days. The deaths include an elderly woman; a fisherman in the prime of life who was ill for only ten or twelve hours, and died on Thursday; and one or two children. On Thursday, we learn that another death occurred, and that several persons were ill. A nurse has been obtained from the town here, as no person could be got in the village to enter the affected houses.

From the *Dundee Courier*, 6 October 1866. (Used by kind permission of DC Thomson & Co. Ltd)

When the outbreak occurred the village closed down, neighbour avoided neighbour and a doctor, nurse and constable had to be sent from the city as no one in the village would enter the affected houses.

Two of the deaths were registered by Constable John Bremner from the Bridge of Don area as none of the surviving family members were well enough to travel to the city to complete the registration.

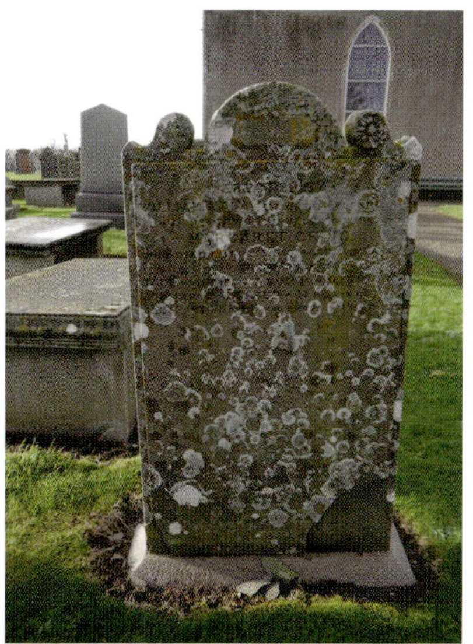

Right: Five of the casualties are buried in Portlethen Cemetery 5 miles south of Burnbanks. This is the gravestone of Margaret Main (née Craig) and Jane Masson Main.

Below: The lichen on the gravestone makes the inscription difficult to read.

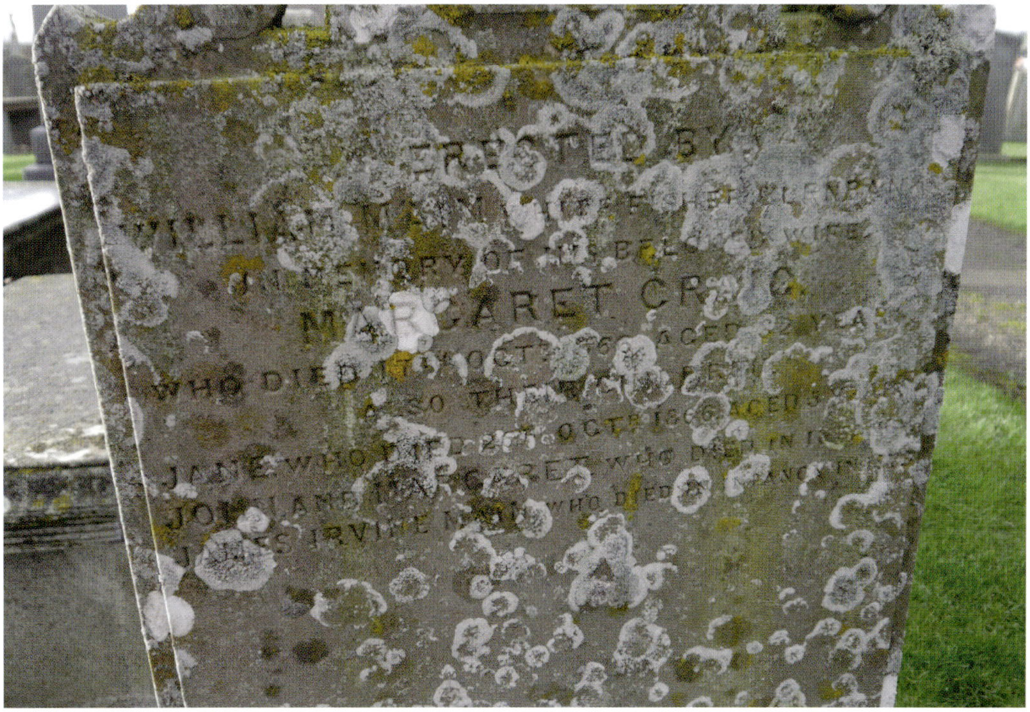

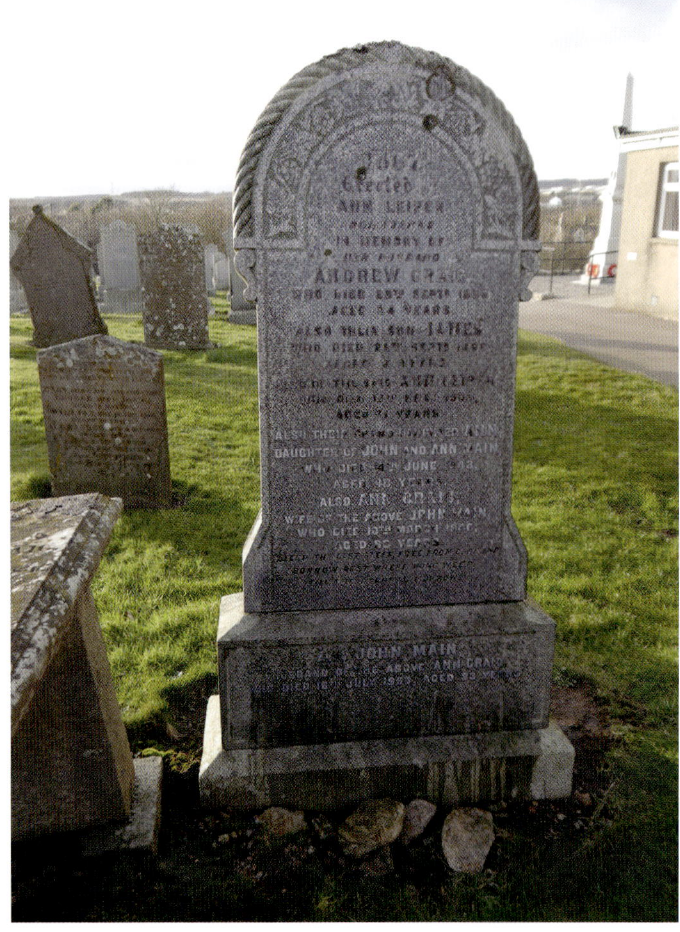

The grave of Andrew Craig,
also in Portlethen Cemetery.

The police were commended for their swift action in dealing with the cases of cholera.

In William Leiper's article in the 1929 *Deeside Field*, it stated that when death visited the village, no man went to sea and all took turns to watch the dead by night as well as by day.

On this occasion, the authorities insisted that bodies had to be dealt with immediately; no funerals were allowed, no gathering for wakes.

A rapid burial was required to prevent the disease spreading with the bodies being treated with pitch and quicklime. The pitch was a rudimentary sealing of contaminated bodies and the lime ensured rapid decomposition.

This is another story that affected me whilst carrying out the research. These grim instances didn't happen in some far-flung corner of the world; these happened right outside our door. The fear that the villagers felt, the sadness at the deaths and the rapidity that the cases were dealt with must have been truly shocking.

The last two casualties were children under the age of five and they died within an hour of each other.

Look around your own communities and try to imagine the horror of two children dying in your street within an hour.

21

Artist James Cassie

Whilst researching for this book, I became very interested in the life and works of the artist James Cassie (1819–79). As with several subjects in this book, he is worthy of further study.

He was very highly regarded for his works during his lifetime and enjoyed some success. Aberdeen Art Gallery have several of his pieces and many others are scattered worldwide. His works regularly come up for auction and command very reasonable prices, which means that collecting can be affordable.

He was born in 1819 in the Keith Hall area near Inverurie, Aberdeenshire, and hoped for a career at sea. He had an accident when he was a child which resulted in a leg being amputated. He moved to Aberdeen and became a pupil of James Giles of the Royal Scottish Academy. He specialised in portraits in his early career but then concentrated on landscapes and seascapes for which he became better known.

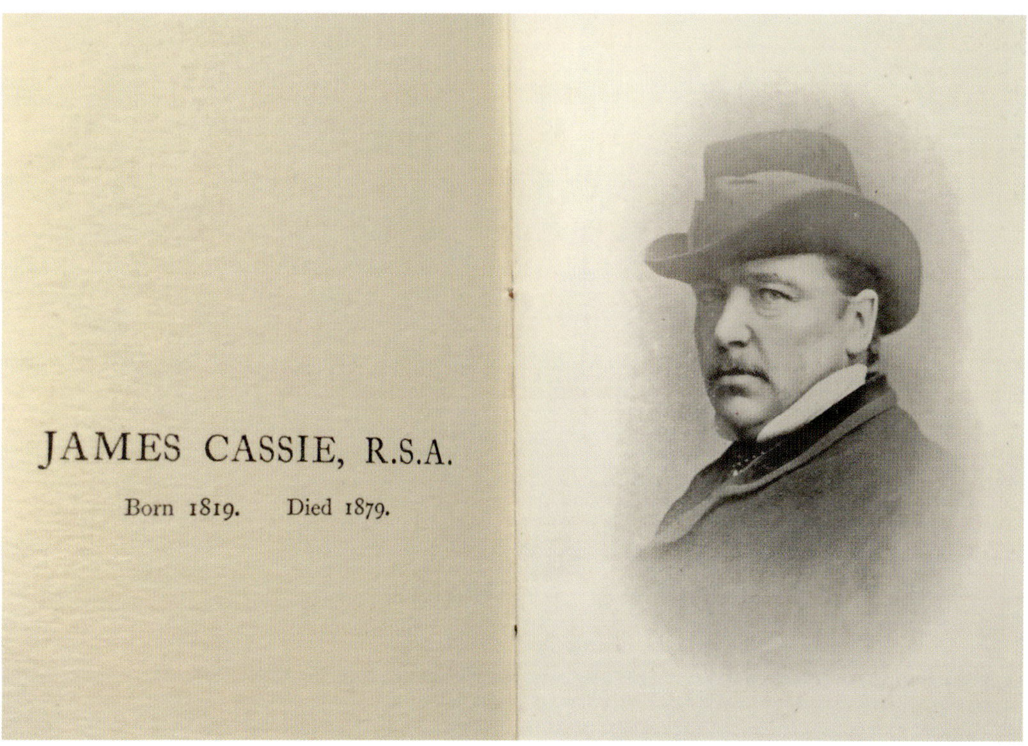

(Photograph by the author, from Aberdeen University Special Collections)

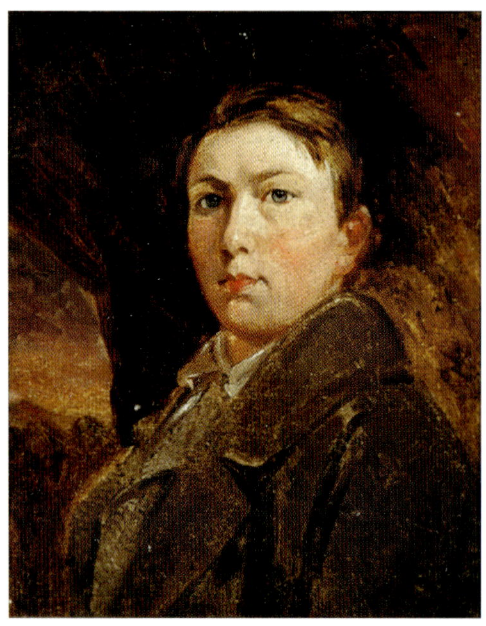

An early self-portrait. (Aberdeen Art Gallery Collection)

His connection to Burnbanks came about as he regularly travelled along the coast from Aberdeen to Stonehaven painting landscapes and seascapes. He became very well known to the villagers, who showed great friendship, and they were rewarded with being used as subjects and models for his works.

One of his paintings was called *Sunrise, Burnbanks, Aberdeen* and featured in an exhibition of paintings in the Royal Scottish Academy in Edinburgh in 1866. The *Dumfries and Galloway Standard* printed an article on the exhibition and discussed Cassie:

'Sunrise, Burnbanks, Aberdeen', by James Cassie is a very beautiful painting, worthy of that rising artist. This artist is universally regarded as one of the most promising of our younger aspirants, and will certainly, if spared, become an Academician.

Unfortunately, I cannot find a more recent mention of the painting. It may be in a private collection, forgotten up someone's attic or perhaps has ended up on a bonfire. I hope it has survived and it would be fantastic to be able to see it.

In 1904, twenty-five years after he died, there was an exhibition of his paintings in Hay & Lyall's Fine Art Gallery on Union Street in Aberdeen. The Aberdeen University Special Collections have an exhibition catalogue which contains a list of oils and watercolours exhibited.

An excerpt from the concise biography text is reproduced below:

James Cassie RSA

Few more lovable men have ever handled palette and brush than James Cassie.

His out-of-door professional endeavours were mainly spent along the Aberdeen and Kincardineshire coast from the Bay of Nigg to Stonehaven; and it may be said that he almost made his home amongst the fishers of Cove, Findon, Portlethen and Downies. The hardy dwellers in those villages, every one of them, young and old – the Woods, the Leipers, the

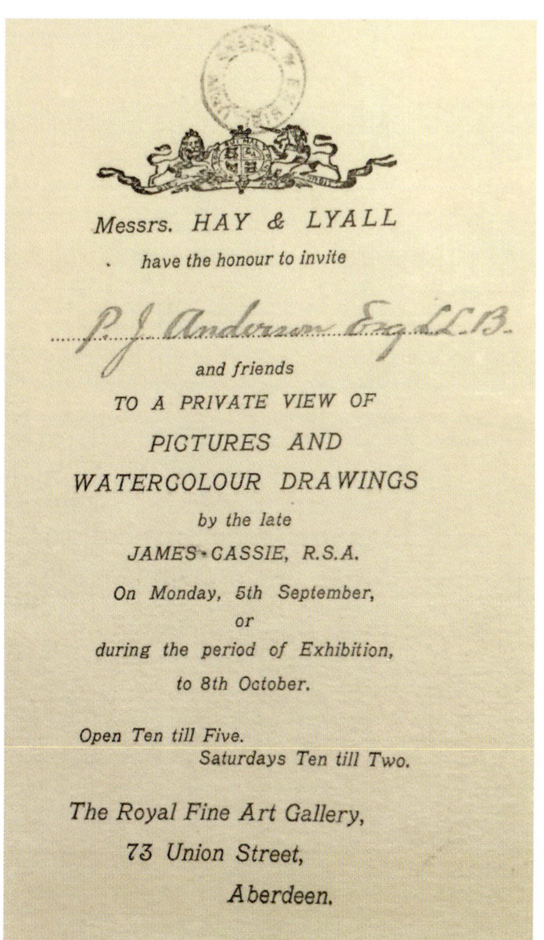

The front page of the 1904 Catalogue.
(Photograph by the author, from Aberdeen
University Special Collections)

Craigs – knew him, and with joy hailed his arrival. The best of his paintings 'breathe of the brine', shore, and silent wave.

Mr Cassie's reputation was now such that in 1869 he removed from his well-loved 'Silver City by the sea' and took up his abode in Edinburgh. Here success followed him. His pictures found favourable hanging space in the Royal Scottish Academy.

Apart from his professional genius, James Cassie was a fascinating raconteur, and found congenial company in other gifted brethren of brush and chisel. John Phillip, R.A., and James Cassie were life-long friends, and spent many happy hours together at the great painter's summer retreat in Glen Urquhart.

Mr Cassie never married and died at 7 Castle Terrace, Edinburgh, in 1879, on the morning of the 11th May, in his 61st year.

His death was registered by his sister Katherine (Kate) and she was listed as the executor of his estate. A sale was conducted of all his belongings, from finished works to sketchbooks to brushes. A painting came to auction in late 2015 showing his sister.

He was buried in Dean Cemetery in Edinburgh and his friends arranged for a striking monument to be erected over his grave.

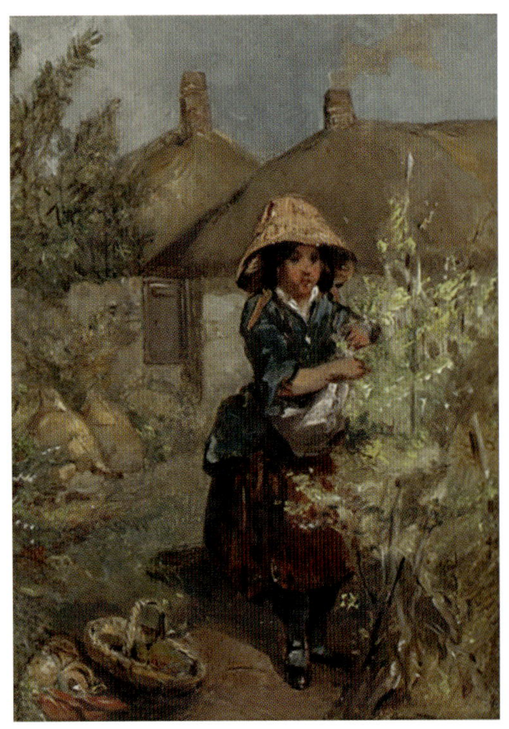

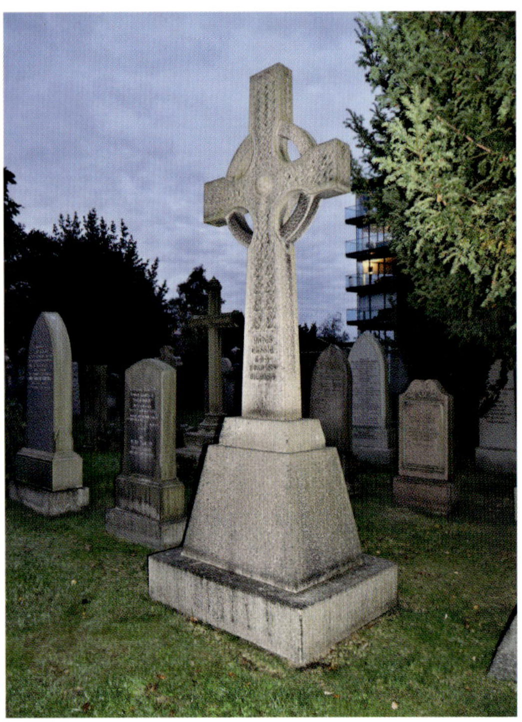

Above left: Cassie's sister Kate.

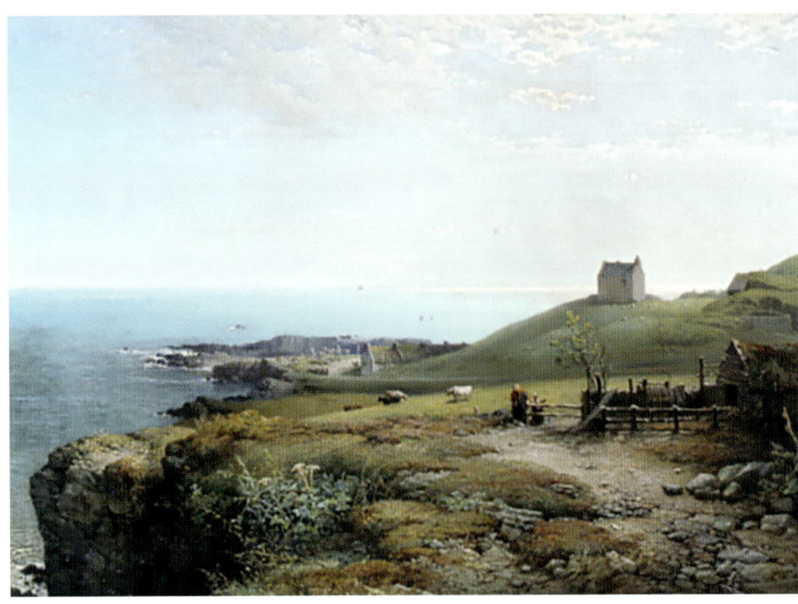

At Cove.
(Aberdeen
Art Gallery
Collection)

Several other examples have interesting connections to the area around Burnbanks. The example above is called *At Cove*. The view shows the white house on a small hillock near to Cove harbour which is still there and recognisable as you leave Burnbanks.

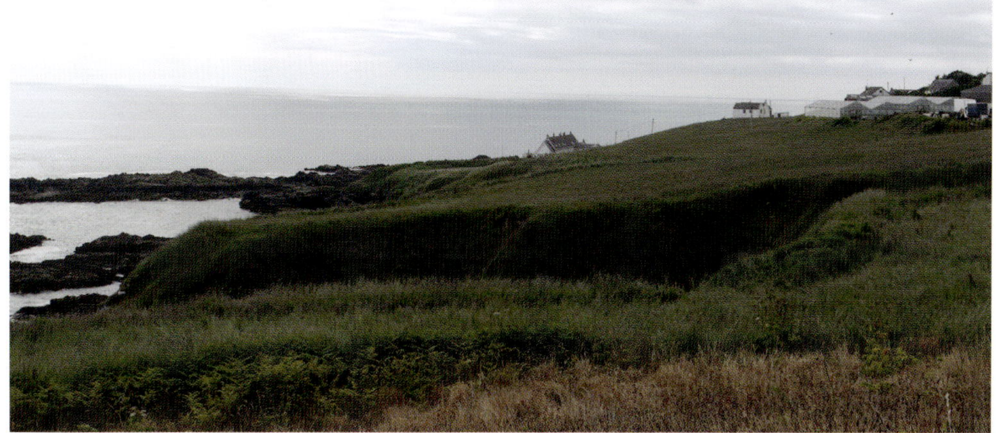

My own photograph of the same view.

The painting that really excites me is called *Fisherman's Tales* and I was fortunate to purchase this one at an auction in Edinburgh. It poses an unanswerable question: 'Are we looking at the faces of our villagers?' The houses are a similar construction to many of the small villages along the Kincardine coast and the references made in the 1904 Exhibition Catalogue states that he befriended the fisherfolk and used them as models.

We love this painting and the scans do not do it justice. I had the frame repaired by Belvedere Galleries in Aberdeen and the owner made a comment that gave me a lot of thought as it's something that never really occurred to me. He said, 'You have something special here. For me, a painting stands out if the hands are done well.'

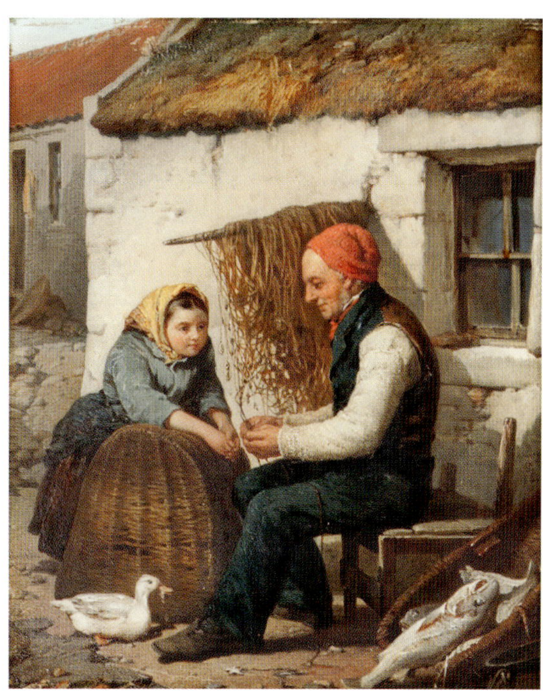

Fisherman's Tales, 1869.

115

Who Lived in Our House?

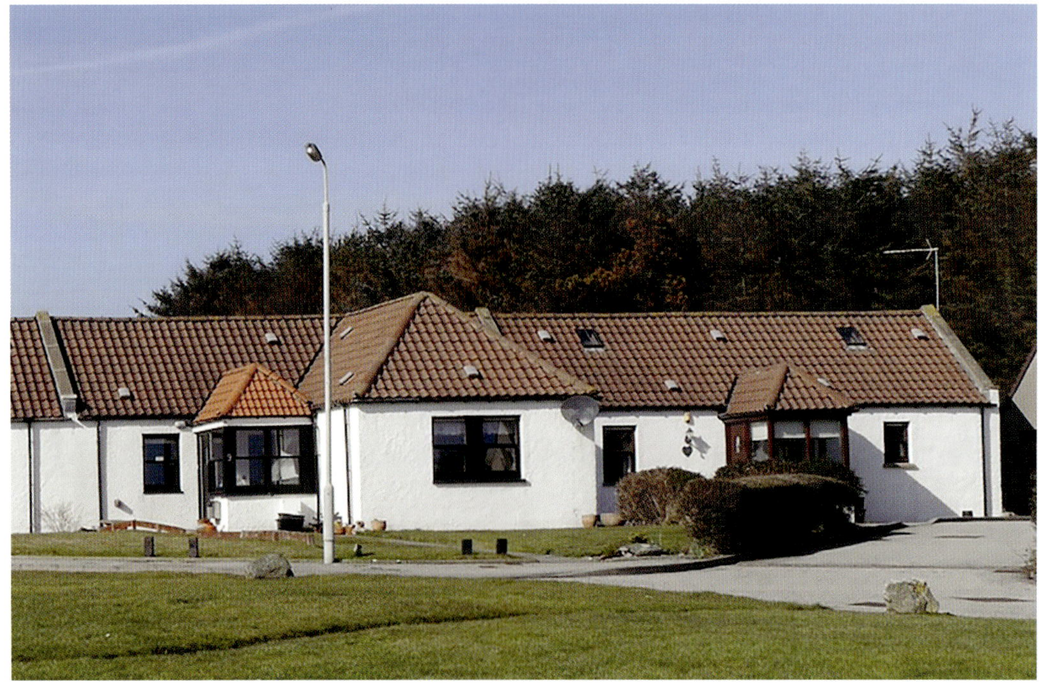

Nos 9 and 10 Burnbanks Village. The old numbers were Nos 5 and 6.

We have lived in Burnbanks Village since the rebuild in 1991–92 and through researching valuation rolls, census returns and electoral registers I have been able to piece together who lived and died in our house.

The earliest confirmed resident is George Main from the 1881 census and 1885 valuation rolls. The 1881 census lists nine people in total from two families living in the house, ranging in age from eighty-four-year-old Joseph Craig to one-year-olds William and George Main.

The valuation rolls before 1875 become unclear about which house is being referred to. The numbering in census returns also shows inconsistency, so for the sake of accuracy I shall only deal with our house from 1900 onwards.

Donald Petrie Bruce

When I did the walking tour in Nigg Kirkyard in 2018, just as I was leaving, my eye was drawn to the gravestone pictured, which is very weather-beaten and difficult to read.

I'm not in any way a believer in any spooky stuff but this whole project seems to be one creepy coincidence after another. I don't know why I was drawn to their grave. I know there are dozens of others buried there who have links to Burnbanks.

The inscription details Donald Petrie Bruce and family. Something was stirring, so I went home and found him and his family on www.scotlandspeople.gov.uk. It turns out he lived in my house at the 1901 census and several of his children were born here.

He married a Burnbanks girl, Helen Will, in 1896 and her witness, Elspet Barron, the mother of Freddie Beattie on the war memorial, was one of the graves we visited during the walking tour. Helen was the sister of Roselina Will who married the bigamist discussed in the Crime chapter. Everyone seems to be connected.

Bruce's daughters Nellie and Barbara died within six days of one another in 1918, one from influenza and the other from pneumonia (probably linked to influenza). This was during the Spanish influenza pandemic that killed millions of people across the world from 1918 to 1920.

They'd moved on from my house by that time, but still lived near Burnbanks.

The photograph below shows Donald Petrie Bruce and his wife, Helen Will, seated, holding the babies Ernest and Brian. The man standing on the right is James Mackie

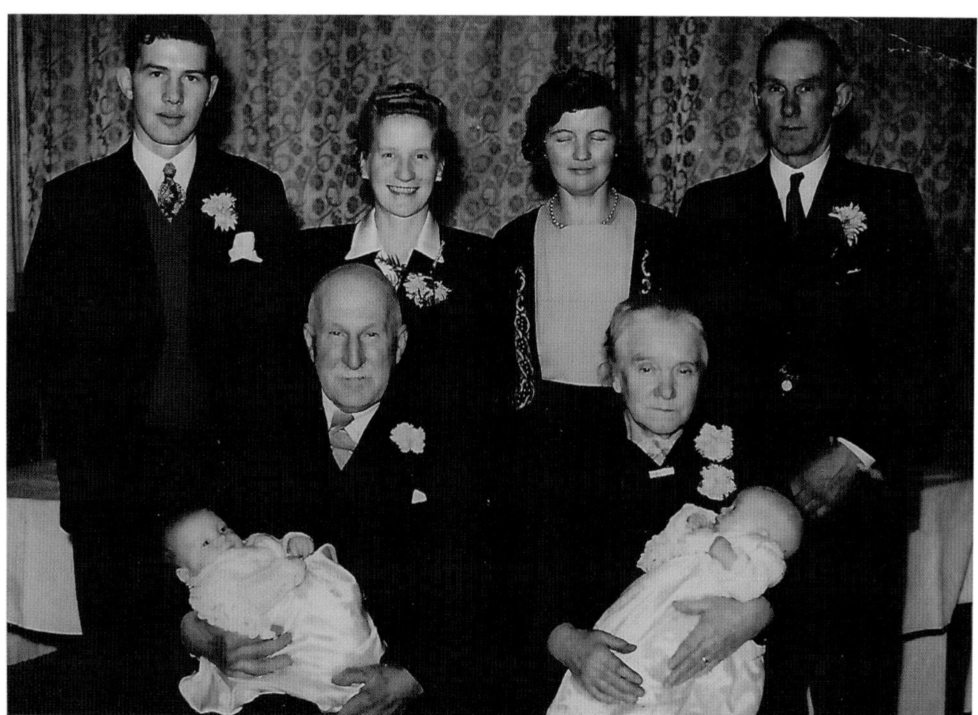

The Bruce family at their Golden Wedding celebrations and the christening of twins Ernest and Brian Bruce in 1946.

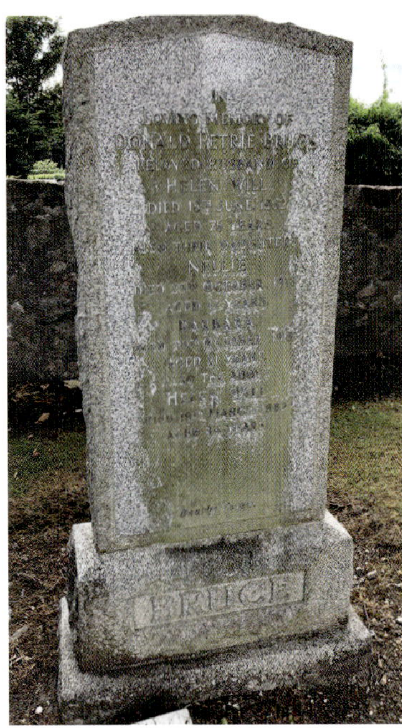

Bruce who was born in our house next to his wife, Annie. The couple on the left, the parents of the babies, are James Bruce Jnr and his wife Nellie. The photograph is courtesy of Louisa Low, granddaughter of Donald and Helen.

Other Residents

The 1905 valuation rolls show Henry Duncan as the occupier. Henry was an ex-military man having served in the Boer War and was a long-term resident right up until his death in 1956. He moved around several houses in the village and ended up in old No. 9, which is on the site of the current No. 17. Henry and his family feature in other chapters.

The 1915 valuation rolls show the occupier as farm servant George Bruce with the tenant as Charles Catto. Charles Catto was very well known in the area and was works manager at the Cove Oil Works. He was known for his generosity to all and on the event of his death in 1921, it was stated that Cove had never seen such a large funeral. Catto Crescent in Cove is named after him. He seems to have been the tenant but not occupier of several Burnbanks houses and even after his death, he is still listed as tenant of three houses in the 1925 valuation rolls.

In 1925, the house was occupied by labourer James Will.

1930 shows the occupier as William Barron, a railway porter.

In the late 1930s and 1940s, our house was occupied by James Milton. His wife Elizabeth died at home in 1936 at the age of sixty-two and James followed in 1947. They are both buried in Nigg Kirkyard.

William Wood and his family lived in Nos 5 and 6 from the late 1940s onwards until 1963. They operated a blacksmith workshop in the house that is currently No. 1.

As the village declined, our house was no longer occupied from 1963 until the rebuild.

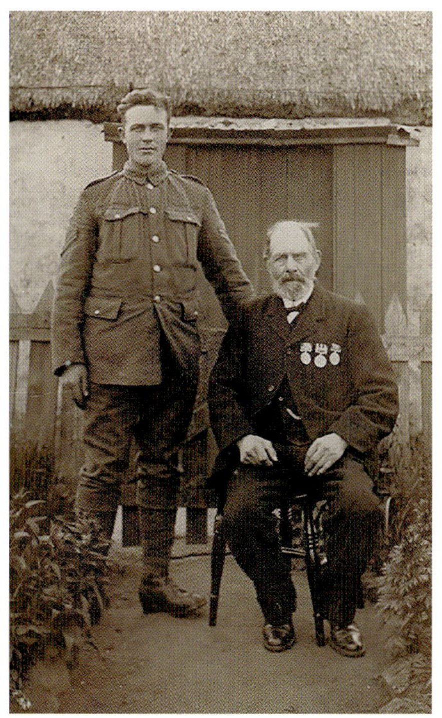
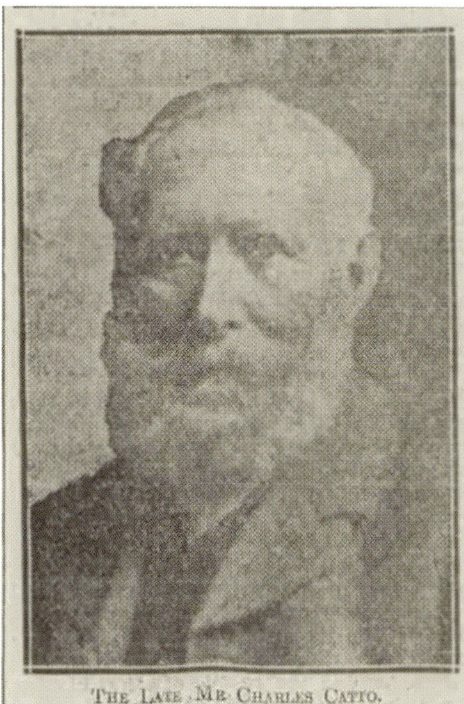

Above left: Henry Duncan on the left with Sam Duncan.

Above right: (From Aberdeen Press & Journal, 15 February 1921. Used by kind permission of DC Thomson & Co. Ltd)

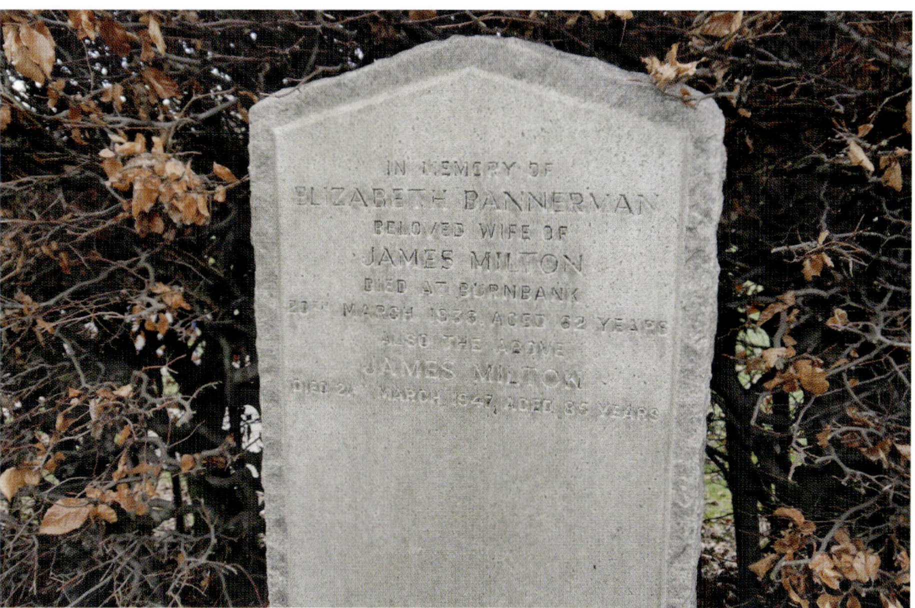

Gravestone of Elizabeth Bannerman and James Milton.

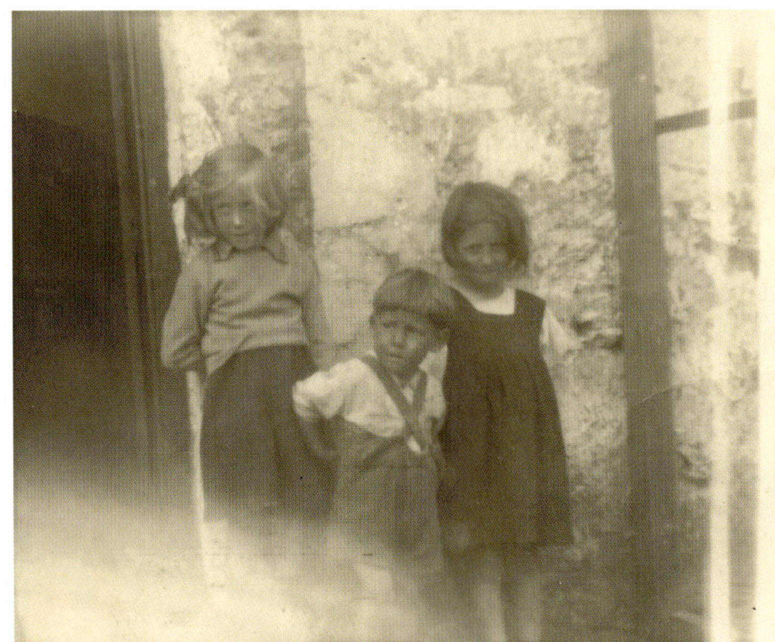

This photograph from Dorothy Beattie shows (left to right) Dorothy Beattie, Billy Wood and Mary Wood outside our front door.

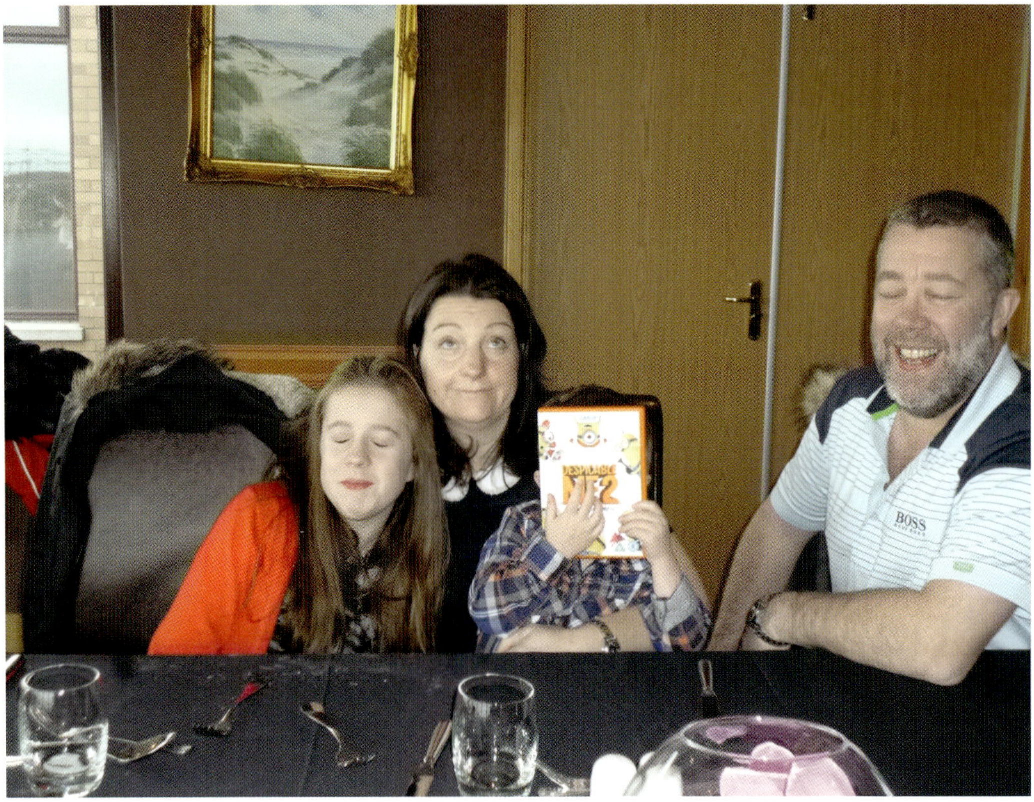

And then we arrived … Not a staged photograph; we honestly look that daft!

23

The End of the Old Village

Valuation rolls show the gradual reduction in the number of inhabited properties. In 1895, there were seventeen houses listed and two were uninhabitable. Up to the 1940s there was a steady amount of inhabited properties, but we begin to see the decline from the 1950s onwards. In 1951 only ten properties are listed. In 1970 we are down to four, occupied by David and William Webster in No. 7, George Robbie in No. 8, James Maharey in No. 9 and Robert Sim in No. 10.

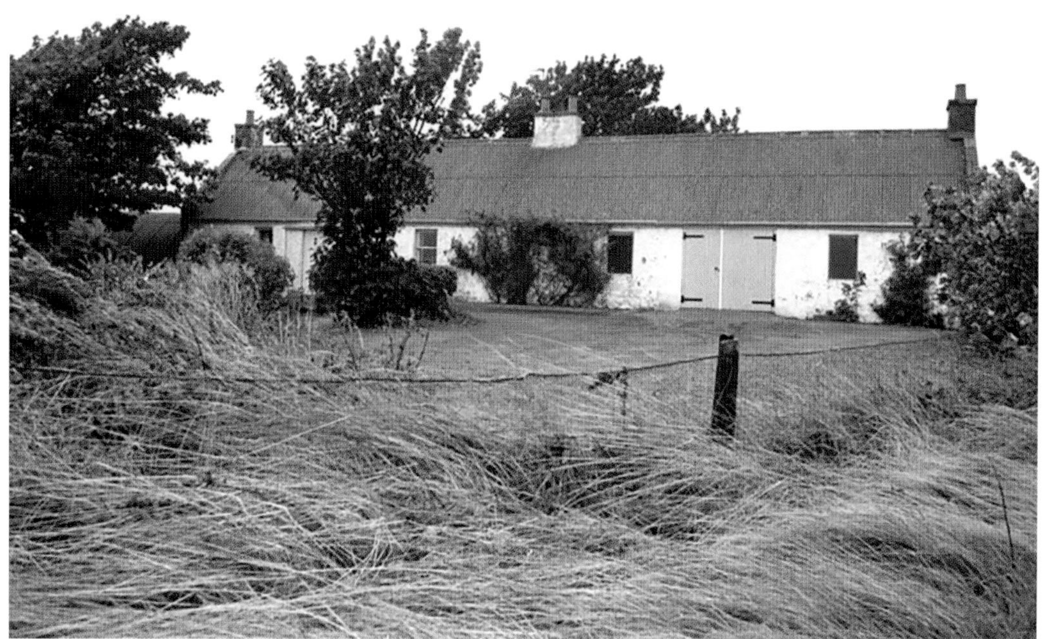

After 1977, we are now down to three occupied houses and by 1979–80, we have one last occupant, William Webster, in old No. 7. This is now Nos 5 and 6. Other villagers note that George Robbie was the last inhabitant in No. 8.

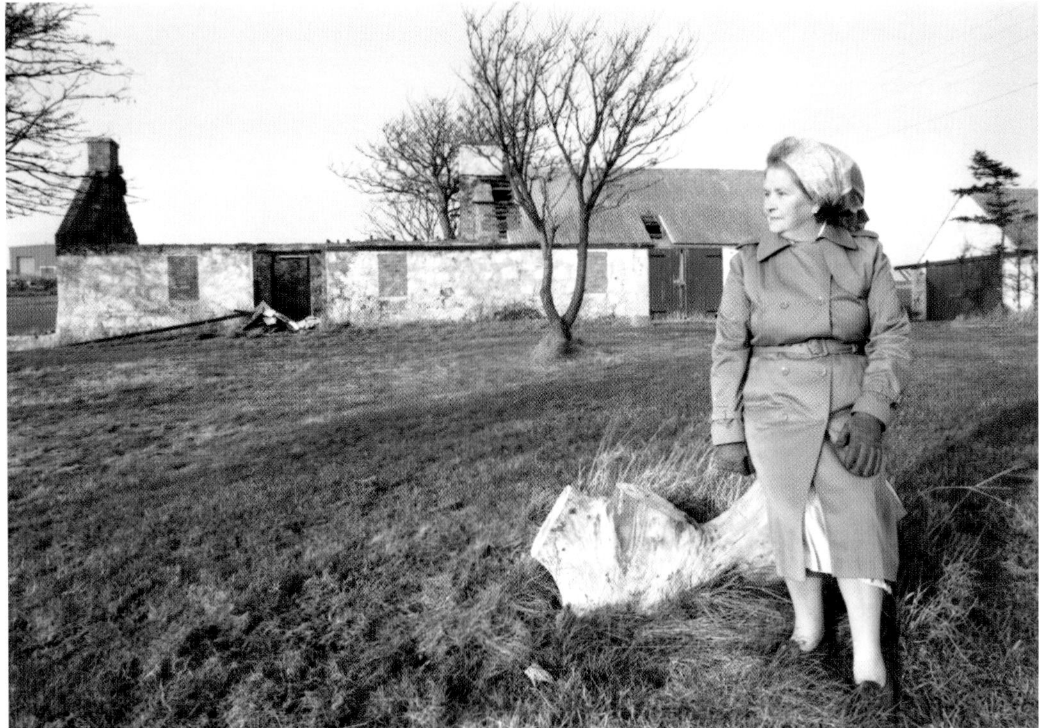

The same building only four years later. (Photograph courtesy of Aberdeen Journals Ltd. Used by kind permission of DC Thomson & Co. Ltd)

Ex-resident Mina King visited the remnants in 1984 for an article in the local paper and the pictures by Aberdeen Journals photographer show a desolate place. She was born Jemima Penny Bruce in the village in 1915 and the article covered her early family life.

Dereliction

One of the reasons behind the abandonment was typical discordant landowner versus tenant relationships. There was no running water, drains or sewerage right up to 1980 and very late installation of electricity in the mid-1960s – this is in a location only 4 miles from the city centre.

The houses were owned for many generations by the Sinclair family, who operated Altens Farm close to the village and rented out to the residents.

Ownership was transferred to Aberdeen District Council Housing Department in 1966 and they decreed that the houses were unfit for human habitation. The residents of the time would strongly disagree.

Although no one was evicted, families were offered alternative accommodation elsewhere and other families moved on or people died and the houses were not re-let.

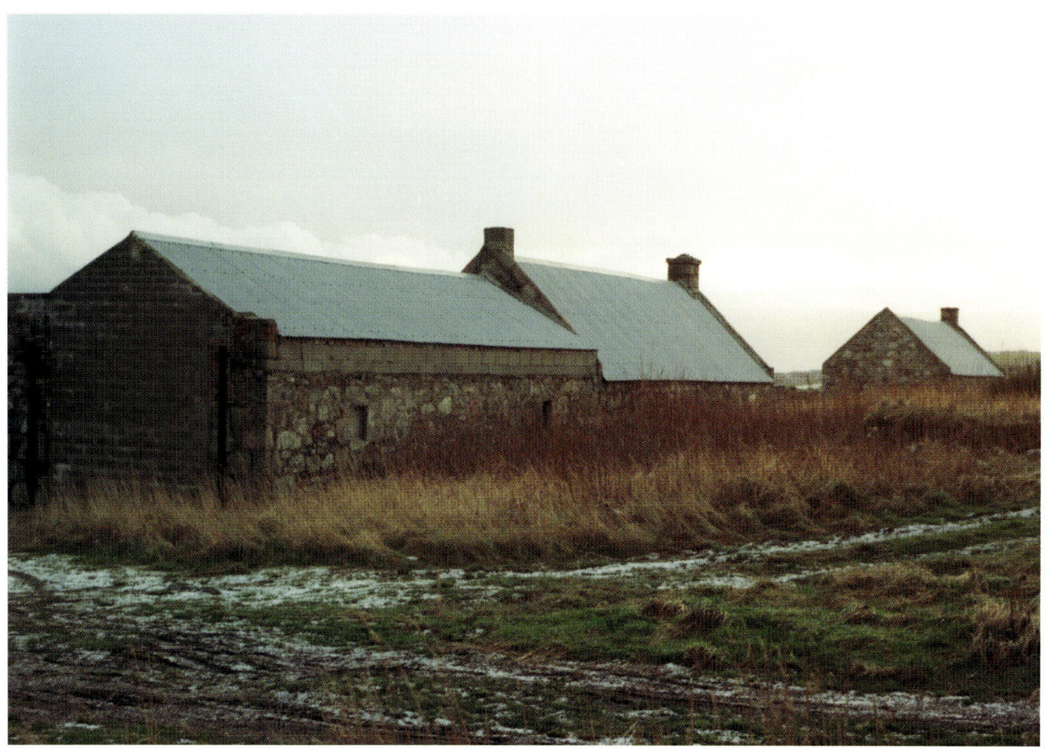

This is the bricked-up building used by Jim Maharey's haulage business which closed after his sudden death in 1970, the location of modern Nos 18 and 19. (Photograph courtesy of Aberdeen Journals Ltd. Used by kind permission of DC Thomson & Co. Ltd)

The villagers viewed their final days with mixed feelings. Some were relieved to be moving to better accommodation but others were sad at the end of days in the village.

Moira Riddler's family were one of the last with school-age children in the village and said it was a very lonely existence. She was ten when her family moved on around 1962–63.

Both Dorothy Beattie and Moira Riddler told me that the families struggled with changes to their living style after moving out. Electric lights were a novelty but welcome. After being brought up with outside dry toilets/latrines, which were obviously well ventilated due to Burnbanks' exposed windy location, they now had indoor toilets. Moira commented 'who's the barbarian now, shitting *inside* the hoose?!'.

An agricultural museum and store was short-lived. Some buildings had been used as stores by salmon fishers.

A couple of hundred metres away, Altens Industrial Estate was beginning to expand. Aberdeen's boom years with the oil industry meant that new premises were being rapidly erected, so who would want an area with no water, no sewerage and limited electrical supplies?

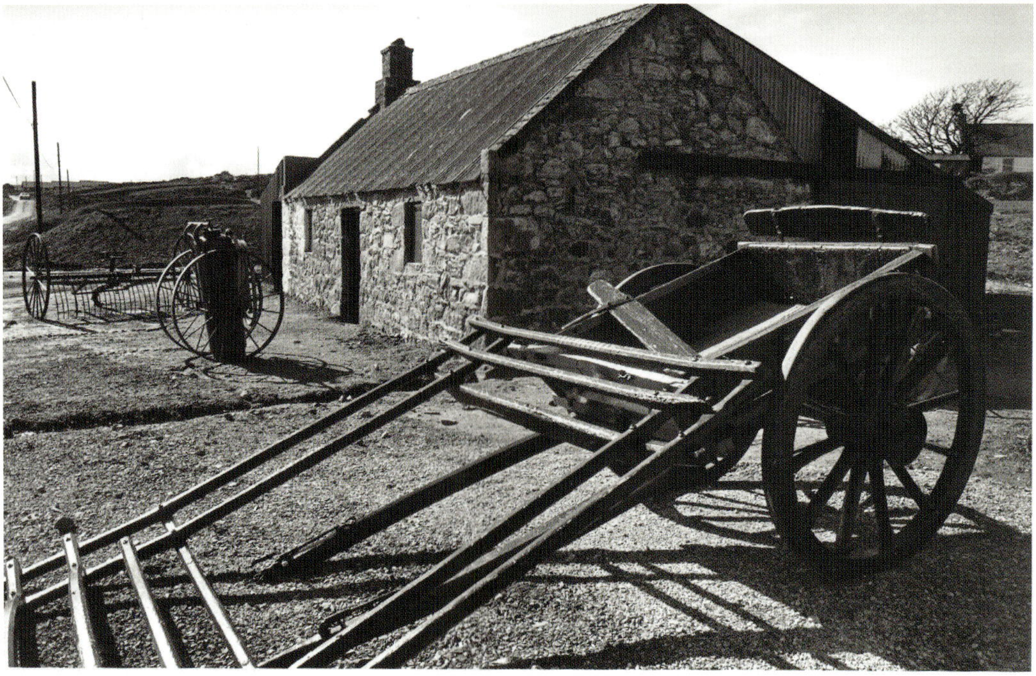

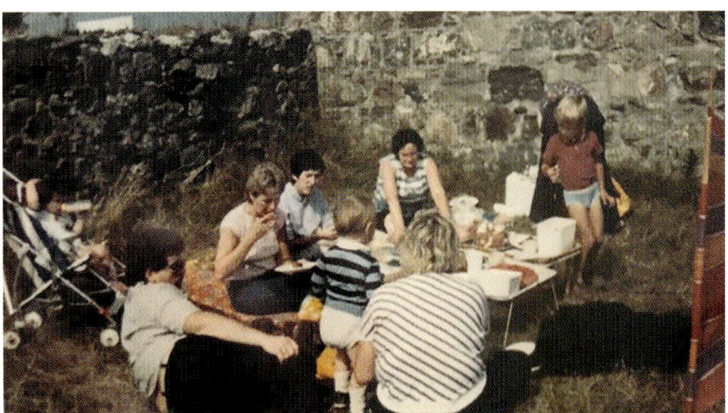

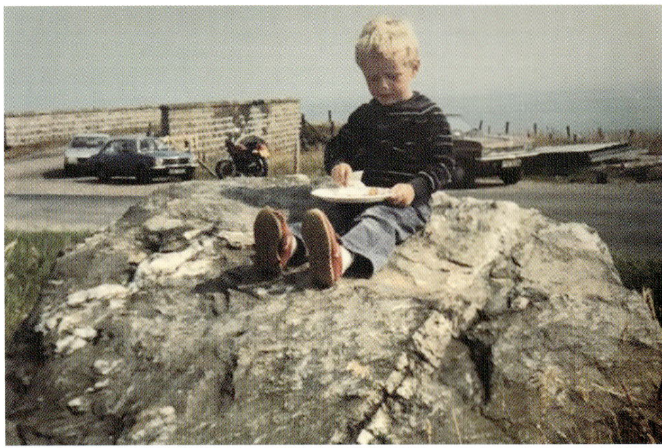

This is looking towards the
railway bridge and shows Lee's
cousin Craig Milne.

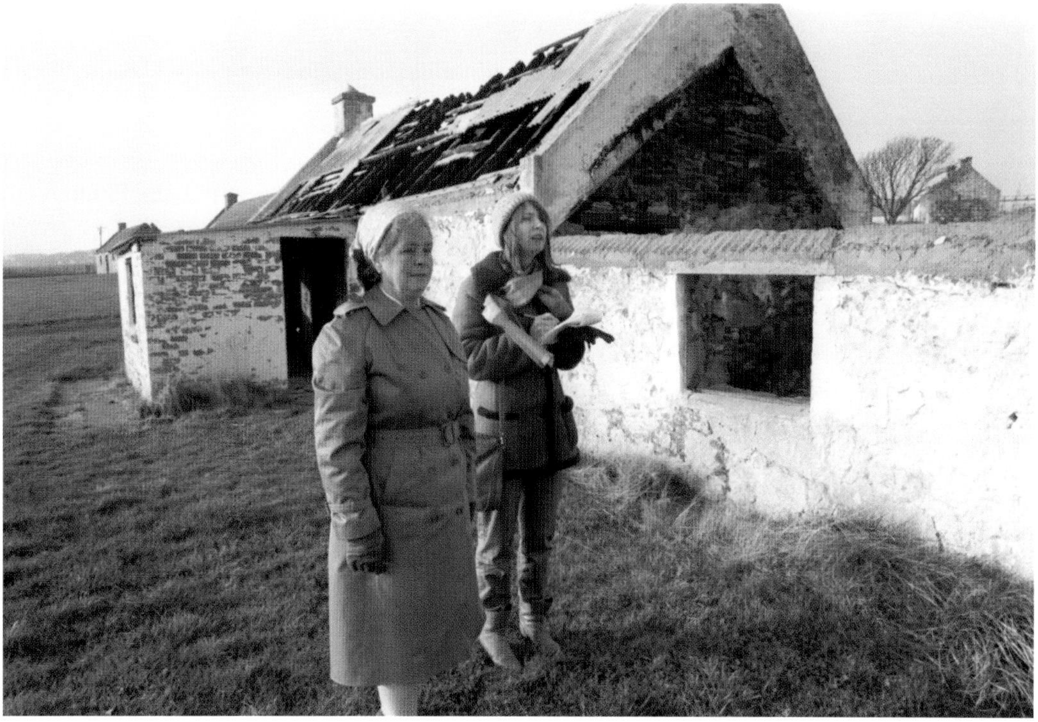

Mina King is accompanied by journalist Sheila Hamilton looking at old No. 9, the site of the Maharey home, now in the garden of No. 17. (Photograph courtesy of Aberdeen Journals Ltd. Used by kind permission of DC Thomson & Co. Ltd)

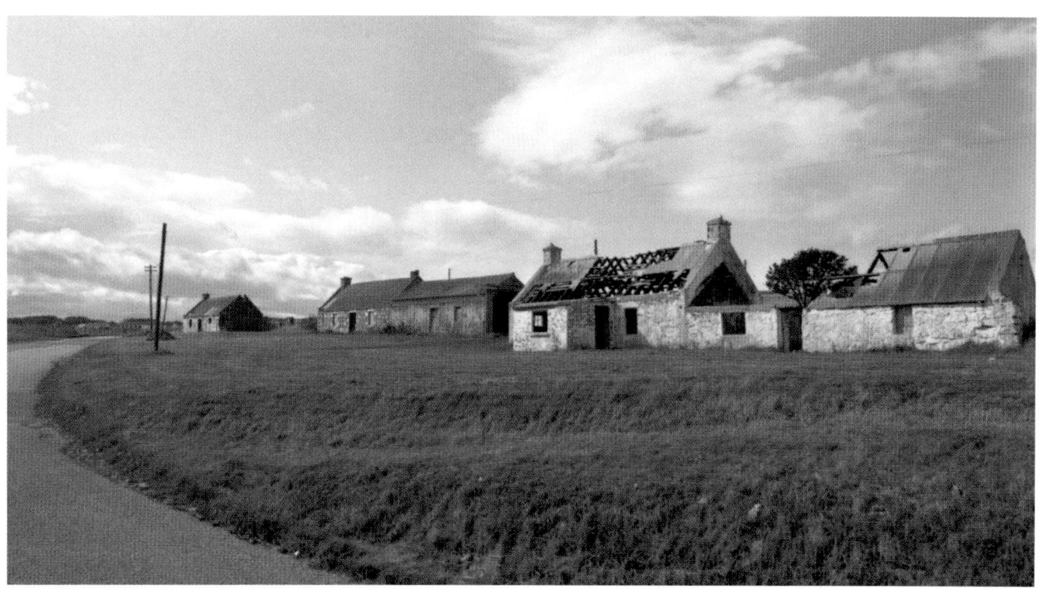

This is the view from the main road. (Photograph courtesy of Aberdeen Journals Ltd. Used by kind permission of DC Thomson & Co. Ltd)

So the decline of the village was hastened. Roofs fell in and the buildings were opened to the elements. Other times the area was used as a drinking den for youngsters, motocross practice, susceptible to vandalism and it became abandoned and derelict.

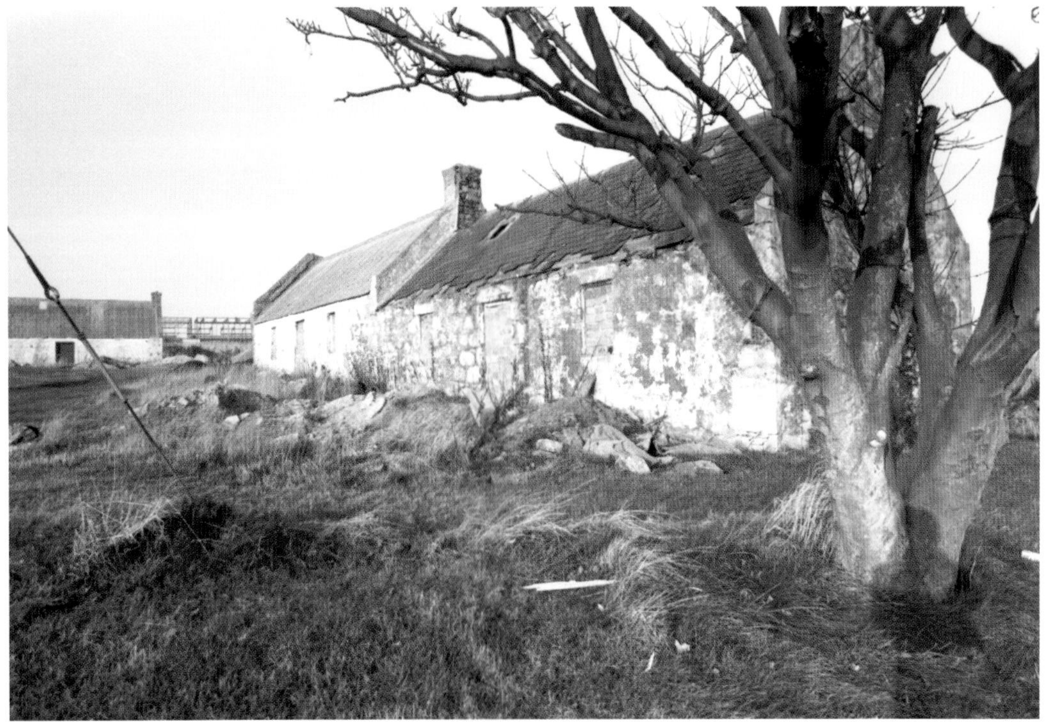

The house with the slate roof, deserted and dilapidated. (Photograph courtesy of Aberdeen Journals Ltd. Used by kind permission of DC Thomson & Co. Ltd)

24

Rebuild and Rebirth

Over time, various attempts were made to resurrect Burnbanks and Aberdeen City Council hold records of at least two attempts at Planning Applications. The council placed local adverts for development opportunities in 1987.

Real progress was made in 1988 when Scotia Homes of Ellon submitted a planning application for the restoration of the twelve surviving houses and ten new-build homes. By this time, only roofless shells remained of the buildings but it was a condition of the planning application that the original buildings should be retained if possible, even if only part of the structure, like gable ends, remained.

Scotia Homes worked on through 1991 and 1992 to complete the development and it created a bit of local excitement.

At the official opening of the show house, ex-residents were invited to attend and the local newspapers the *Press & Journal* and *the Evening Express* printed several stories.

There was an air of excitement on the day and arguments erupted over who was next in the queue. The newspapers reported that nine houses sold in an hour.

All houses had two bedrooms and were quite compact but there have been many extensions since the rebuild, which has improved the available living space.

The modern house No. 1 was the show house and I must admit, I wasn't that keen on the arrangement or the available space and was prepared to walk away when the

City of Aberdeen

DEVELOPMENT OPPORTUNITY

BURNBANKS VILLAGE, COVE

This site comprises the now derelict Burnbanks Village situated on the coastal road between Cove and Nigg Bay. The site on offer extends to 3.20 acres or thereby and includes the remaining 13 cottages which are suitable for reconstruction, with possible modest extensions, for residential or institutional purposes. The cottages are category 'C' Listed buildings and the retention of the character and layout of the existing buildings is of importance. The site and buildings offer a unique development opportunity for the re-creation of a traditional village environment.

Further particulars and a Development Brief prepared by the Director of Planning and Building Control and approved by the Council may be obtained from

The Director of Estates,
St Nicholas House,
Broad Street, Aberdeen, AB9 1EZ.
Telephone Aberdeen (0224) 642121, Ext. 829.

(From Aberdeen Journals Ltd. Used by kind permission of DC Thomson & Co. Ltd)

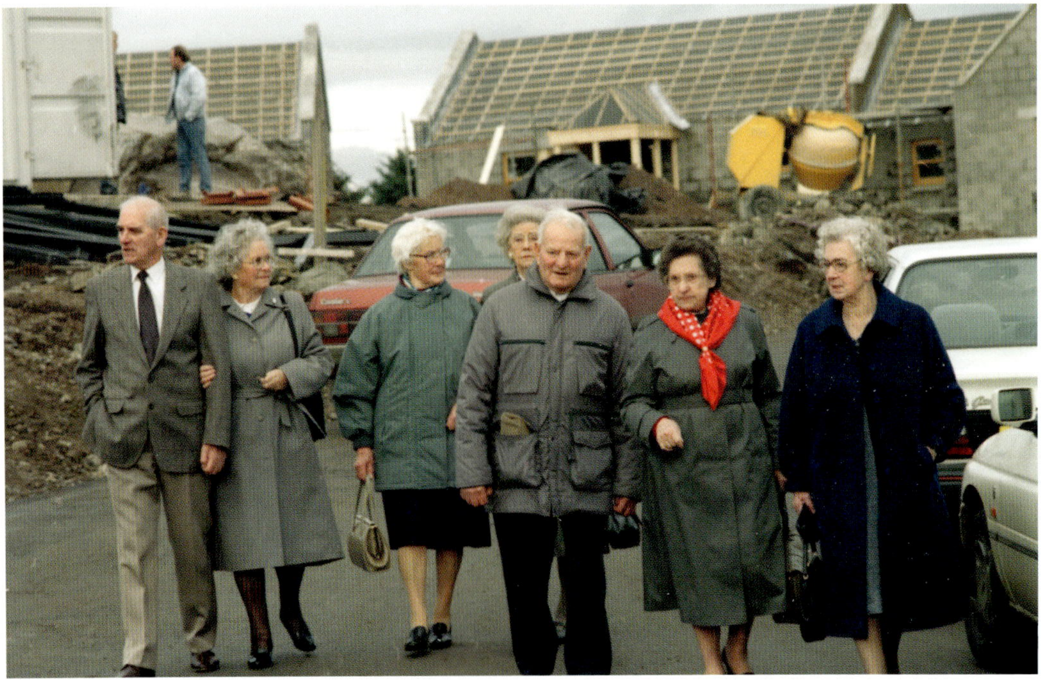

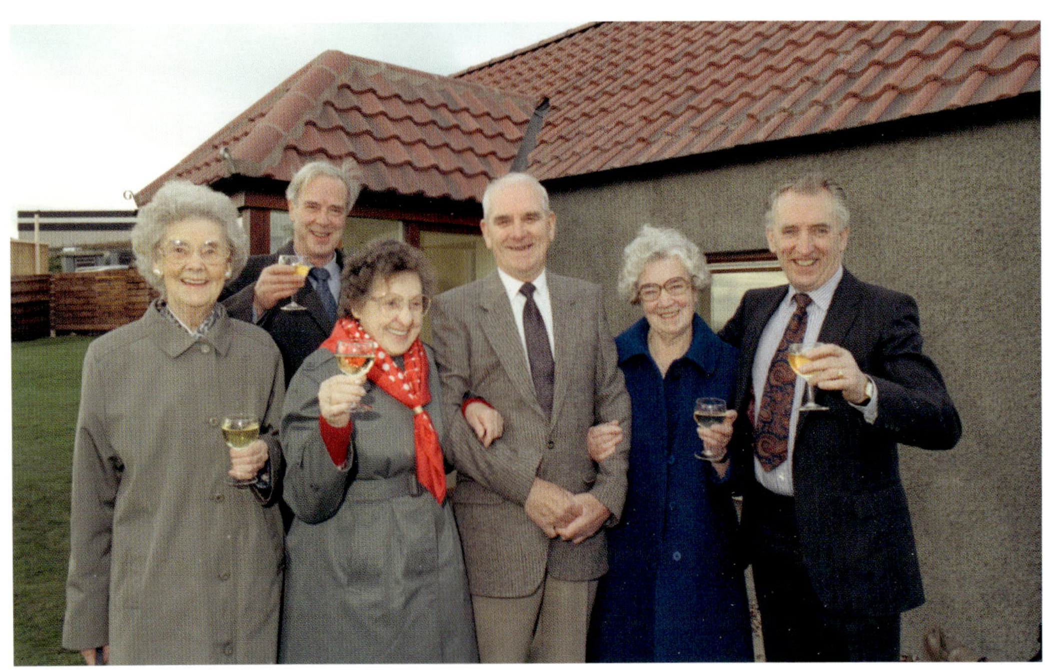

Photograph courtesy of Aberdeen Journals Ltd. Used by kind permission of DC Thomson & Co. Ltd)

Outside the showhouse, No 1. Left to right: Ida Robertson David Paton (Chairman of North East Scotland Preservation Trust), Jessie Robertson (Maharey), Harry Morrison, Jean Ingram and Bill Bruce (Chairman of Scotia Homes). (Photograph courtesy of Aberdeen Journals Ltd. Used by kind permission of DC Thomson & Co. Ltd)

owner of No. 21 called us over. His house was nearing completion at that time and he offered us a look around. That was a much better layout, so we trotted back into the show house office to lay down the £300 deposit. The sale price was only £57,000 – what a bargain.

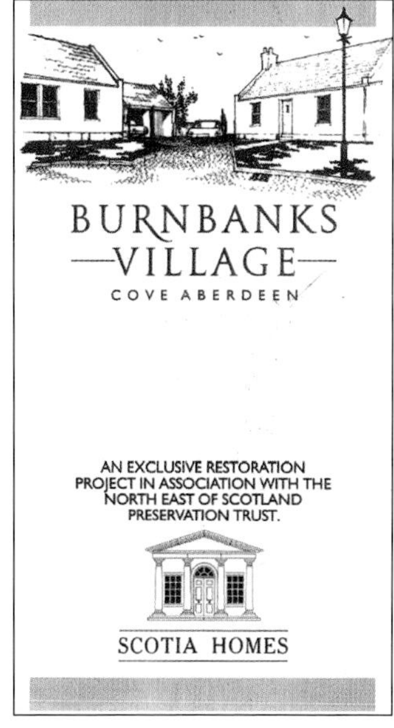

Right: (From the original prospectus)

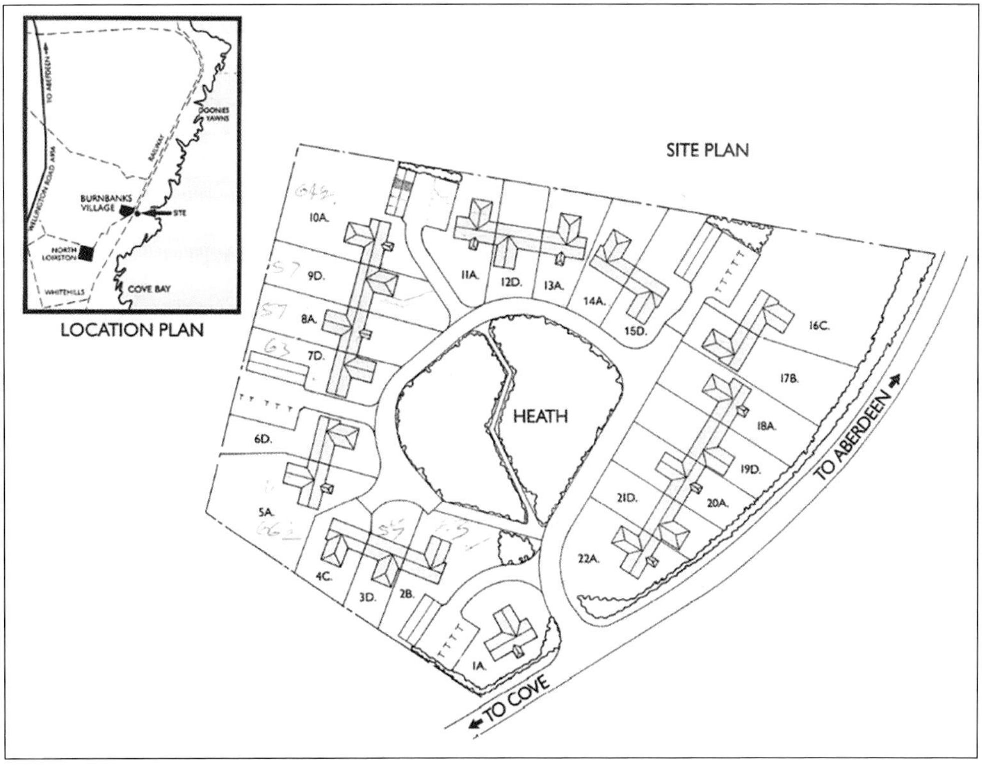

I lived in Cove at the time, which was less than a mile away, so I was at the building site a lot following the progress and the house was ready for occupation in early 1992.

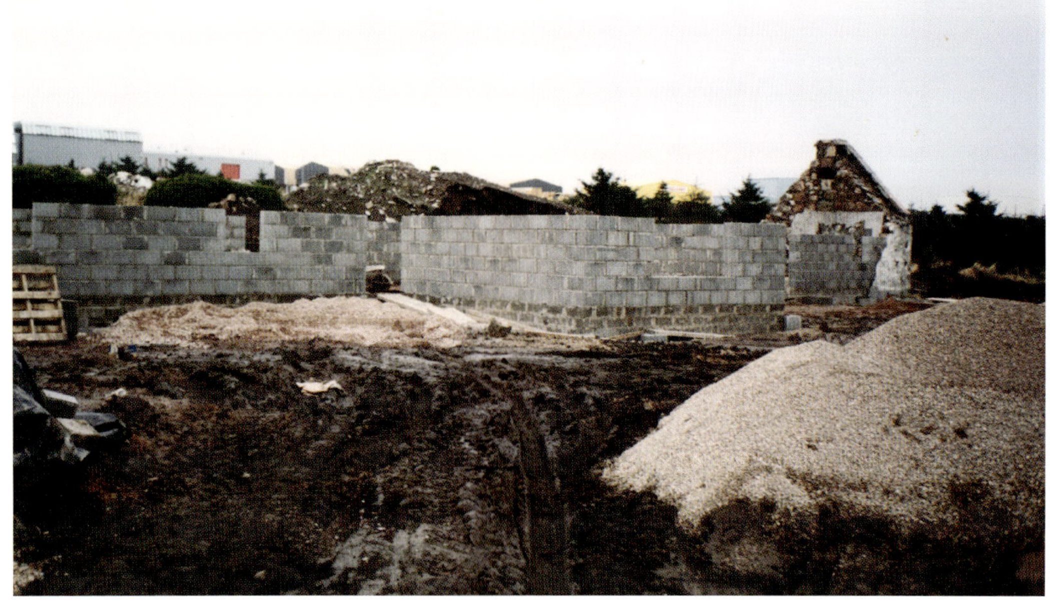

Building underway, looking towards our house.

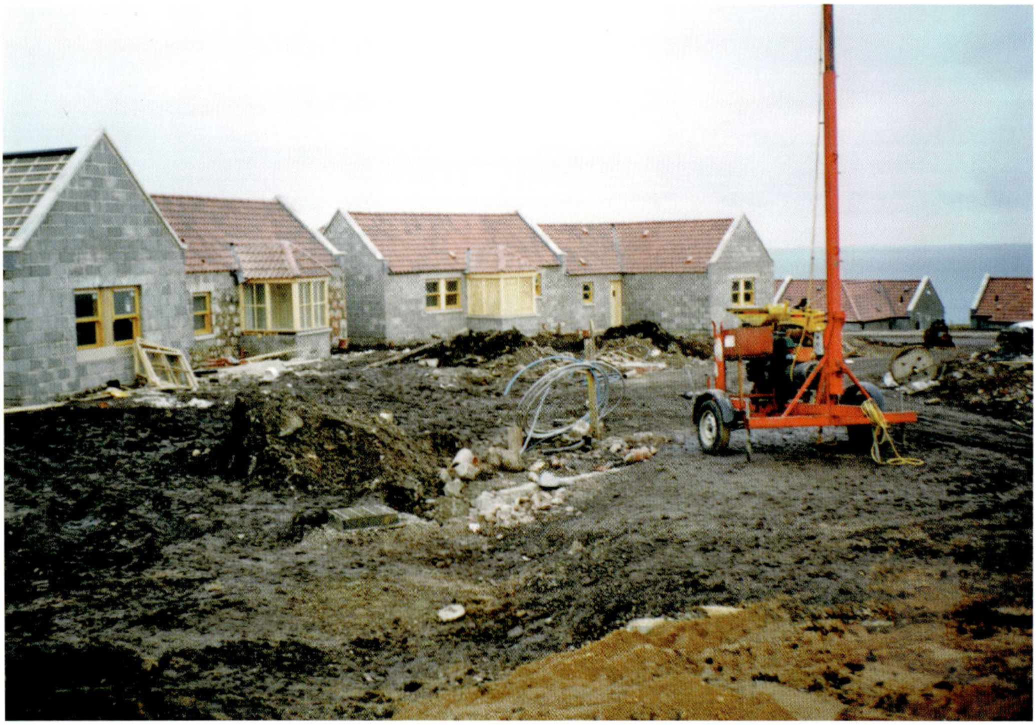

Looking towards Nos 12–15.

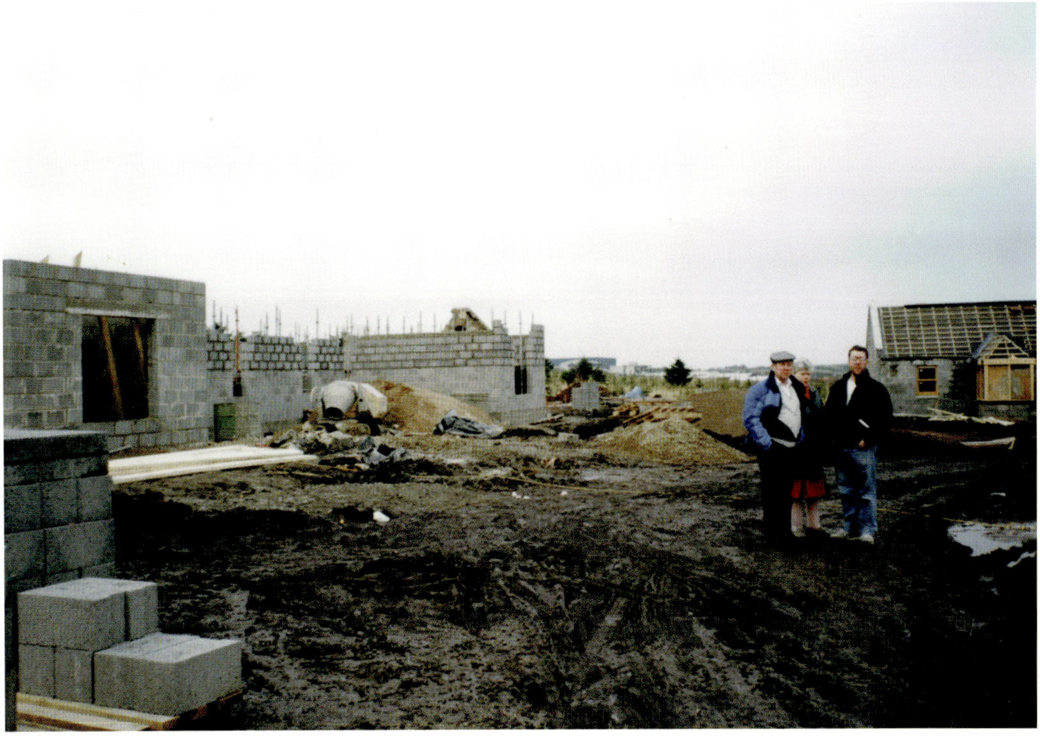

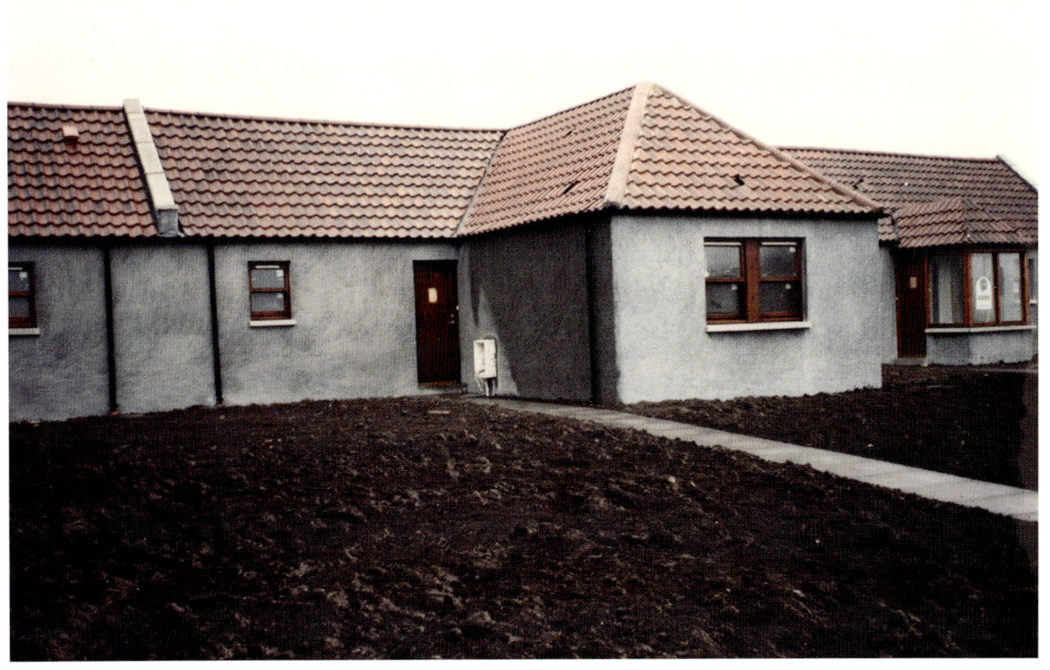

Standing outside our house with my mum and dad in late 1991.

Our house completed in April 1992.

Kathleen and Denny Baxter

The first to move into the village after rebuild were Kathleen and Denny Baxter. As of 2021, they are one of only three houses who still have the original occupiers. They were first by a matter of two days in November 1991, just as the show house was open for the final sales day.

They saw an article in the local paper about Scotia Homes in 1990, so they came to see the site. Their concern was noise from the railway line, so they stood on the centre of the heath and waited for trains to pass. The gentle whoosh of the train allayed any fears and the decision was made.

Their row was completed first but with no paths, no roads and no street lights. The other houses weren't even started.

I interviewed them and asked what is the best thing about living here: 'Well it's the view, and we have always had lovely neighbours in fact everyone in the village. We have always enjoyed our yearly BBQ and missed it very much this year. With the countryside and town within easy reach, I think we are very lucky. I know we have been very happy here. Who would want to live anywhere else!?!'

Well said neighbour.

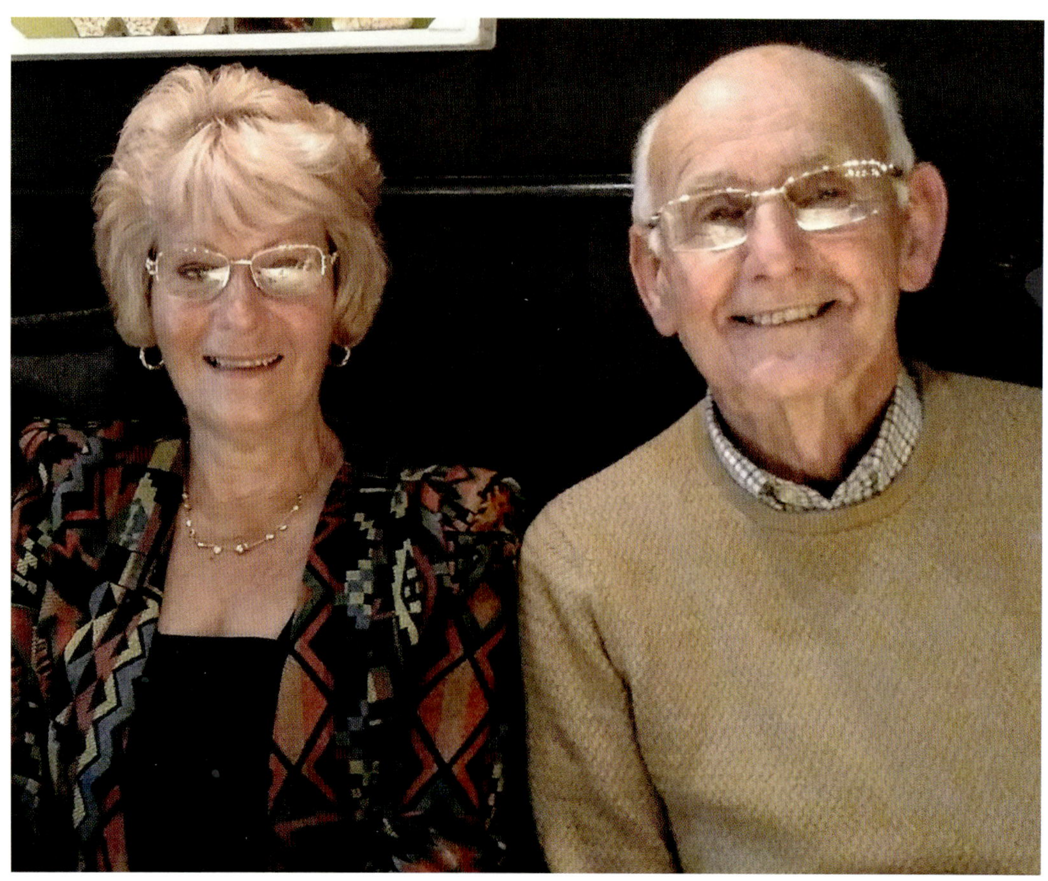

Kathleen and Denny Baxter in 2020.

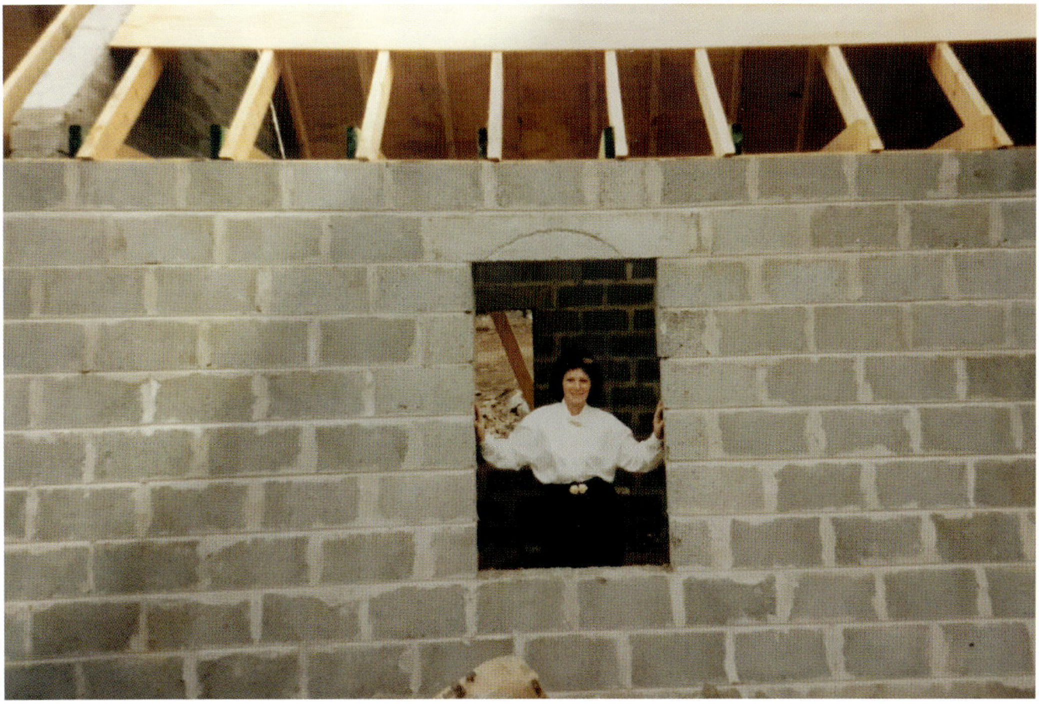

Kathleen Baxter in 1991.

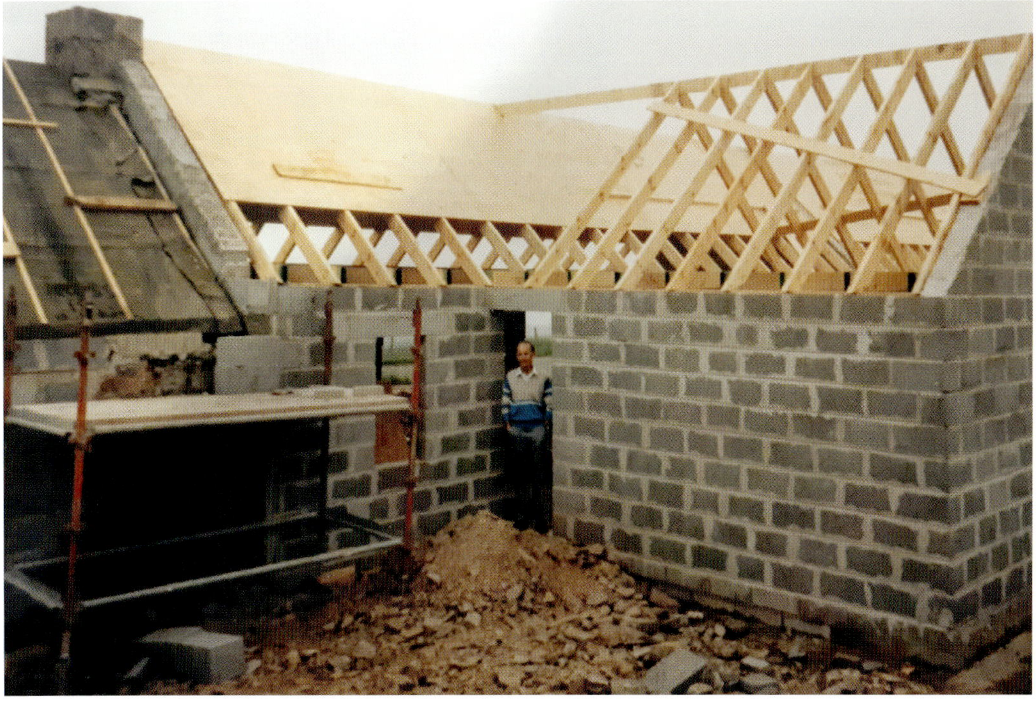

Denny Baxter in 1991.

25

Current Life

At the time of writing, I have lived here for twenty-nine years and have seen quite a few families come and go.

Sure, it's windy in the winter and quite often fog-bound in the summer, but we have a clear view of the sea which outweighs any negative points and for me; that alone is worth the price of the house.

Not all villagers have enjoyed living here and several have had very short stays, but for those who do enjoy it, they are full of pride and praise for Burnbanks. Some have left with broken hearts, but the need to move on is understandable as families grow up and need more space.

If you want to become involved in the community, it is open to all, but if you want a quiet existence with minimal contact with others then that is fine as well.

Socially there are a few groups of friends who frequent each other's houses for coffee, chats, and possibly some drinkies on a weekend. There have been holidays overseas together. Everyone gives a wave.

One of the highlights of the year is the summer barbeque on the heath. Starting around midday, it goes on for a long time and last man standing occurs in the early hours of the next day. We sometimes have bouncy castles for children, karaoke and one

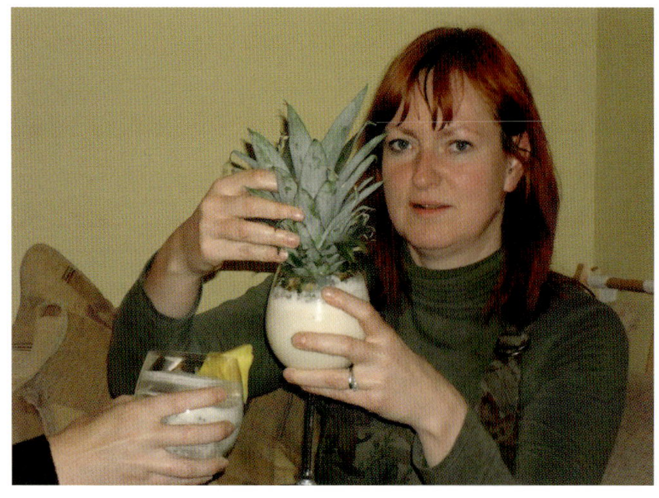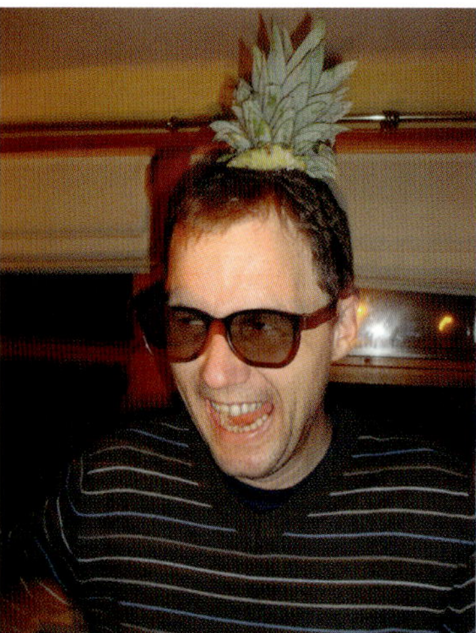

Above left: Hey Mel – you'd pay twenty quid for that in a real bar.

Above right: Ian Duncan – Oh dear! One of those nights.

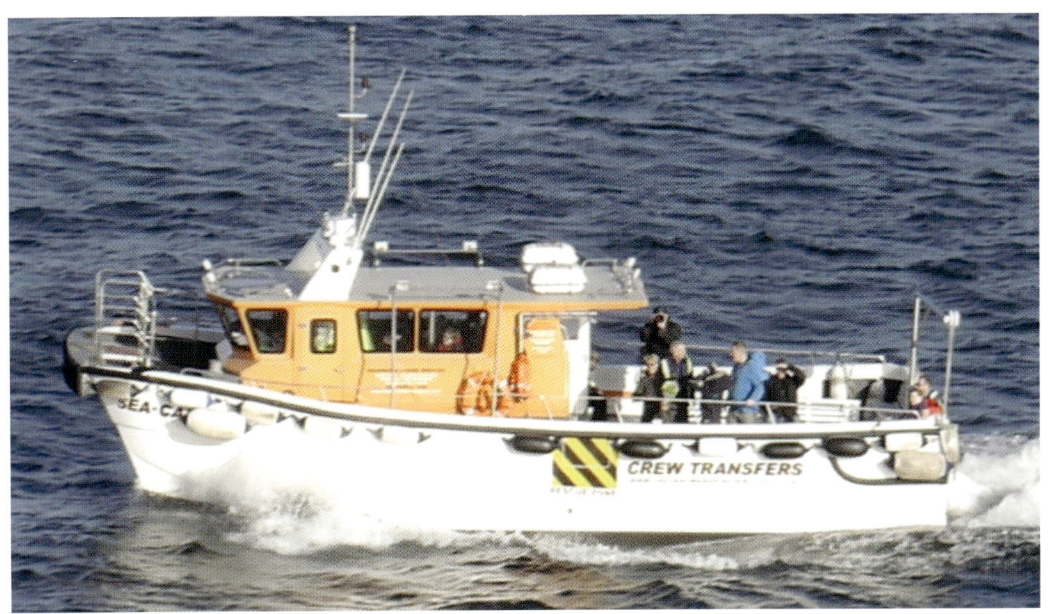

A Burnbanks residents outing along the coast.

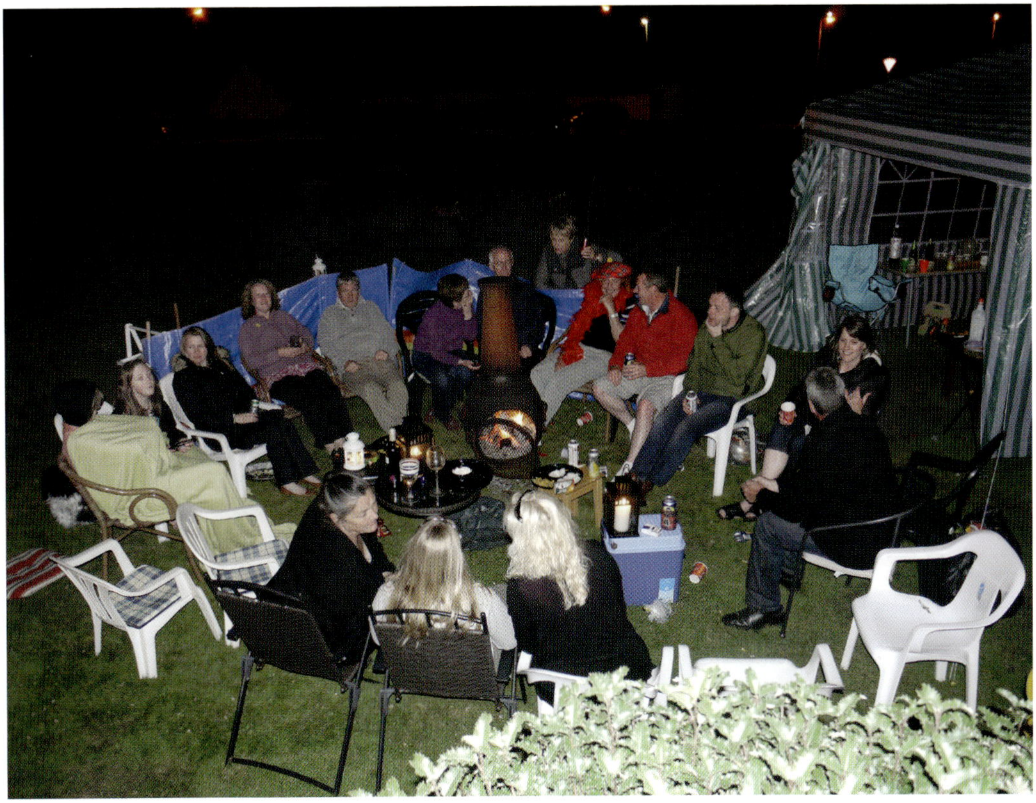

The annual BBQ.

of the most crooked raffles you will ever witness. It's strange how the children, then the women win the best prizes and the blokes receive junk prizes …

On New Year's Eve as the clock approaches midnight, a number of villagers will creep out to the centre of the heath to see in the New Year with the neighbours. As we are close to Aberdeen harbour, the ships in port can often be heard blasting their horns at the stroke of midnight.

Then it's back to a few houses for old-fashioned Scottish 'First Footing', where you visit a house with a small gift, usually chocolates or biscuits, and have a few drinks, then move on to another one. If you don't want visitors, put your lights out!

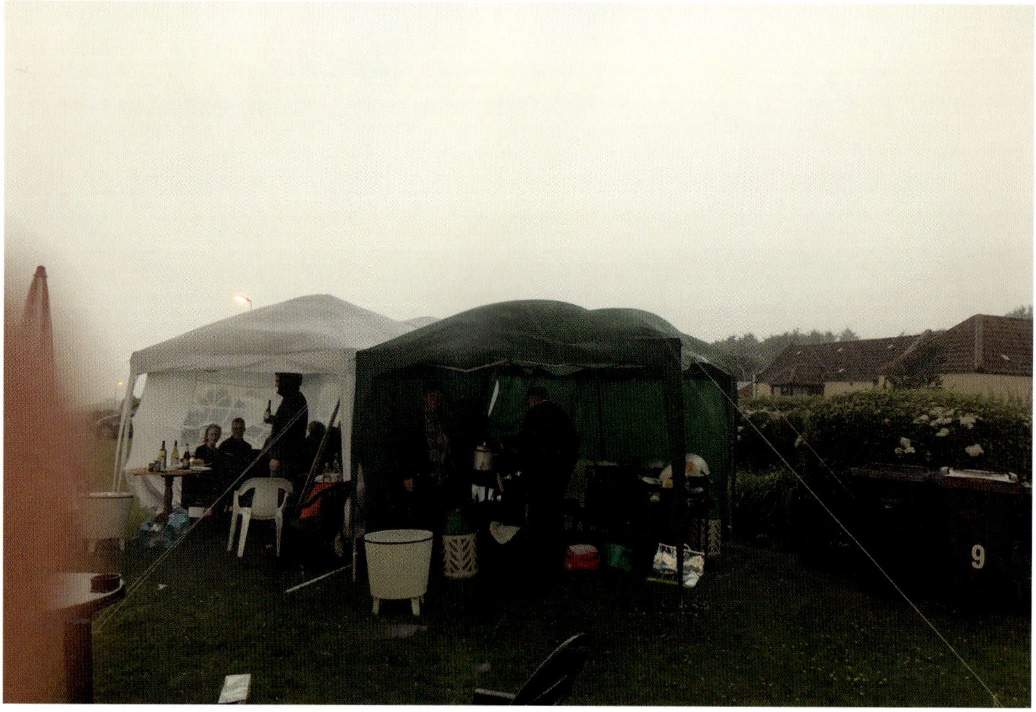

Above: Some years are better than others.

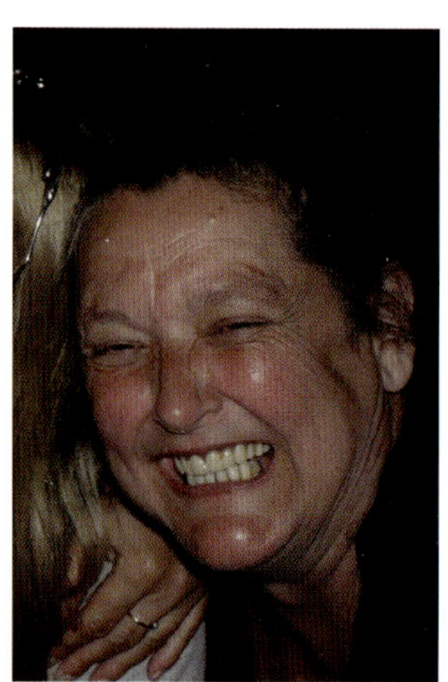

Left: Moira Rapley – one of Burnbanks' Ancient Monuments and raffle organiser – up to nae good.

There are currently three houses that have had only one occupant since the rebuild. I'm one of them and it was my first house that I bought.

To be frank, I didn't appreciate what I had back then: my grass was never cut, I was always late paying the annual village dues and I had a stream of undesirables coming round to visit.

There is a resident's committee which meets regularly to discuss various items. The discussions can be lively sometimes but their hearts are always in the right place and it shows that we care about the village.

The grass heath in the centre is always well maintained and communal areas are well tended with flowers, shrubs and bushes.

We are so fortunate to be so close to nature. Deer and foxes regularly come into the gardens and we've had red squirrels in the car park. Bats are very common. Mind you, there's too many seagulls and I saw a rat once. A big hairy thing … One of our neighbours, Iris, thought we had bought one of those large garden ornaments of a deer sitting down but the thing was real, got up and ran away when she came closer. That was in our front garden in broad daylight!

What would we change about Burnbanks if we could? Certainly the excessive speed of drivers on the main road next to us is terrifying. One house has been hit twice when vehicles fail to take the bend. Other than that, very little as we now appreciate what we have here.

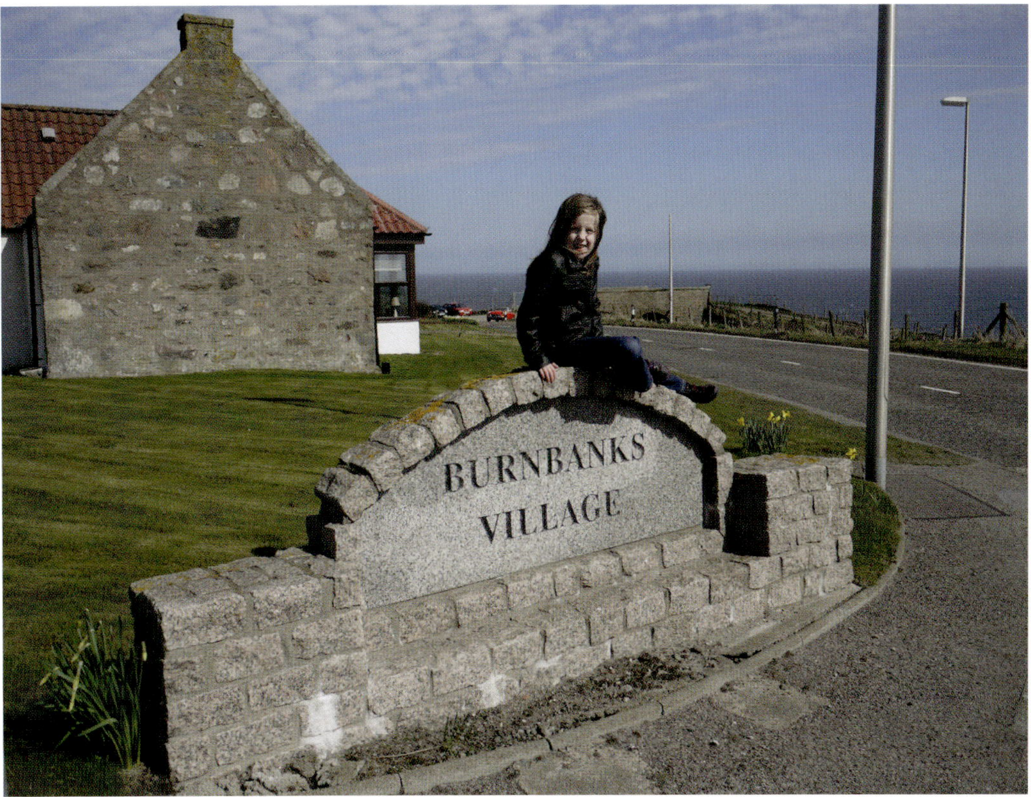

Our daughter Christina.

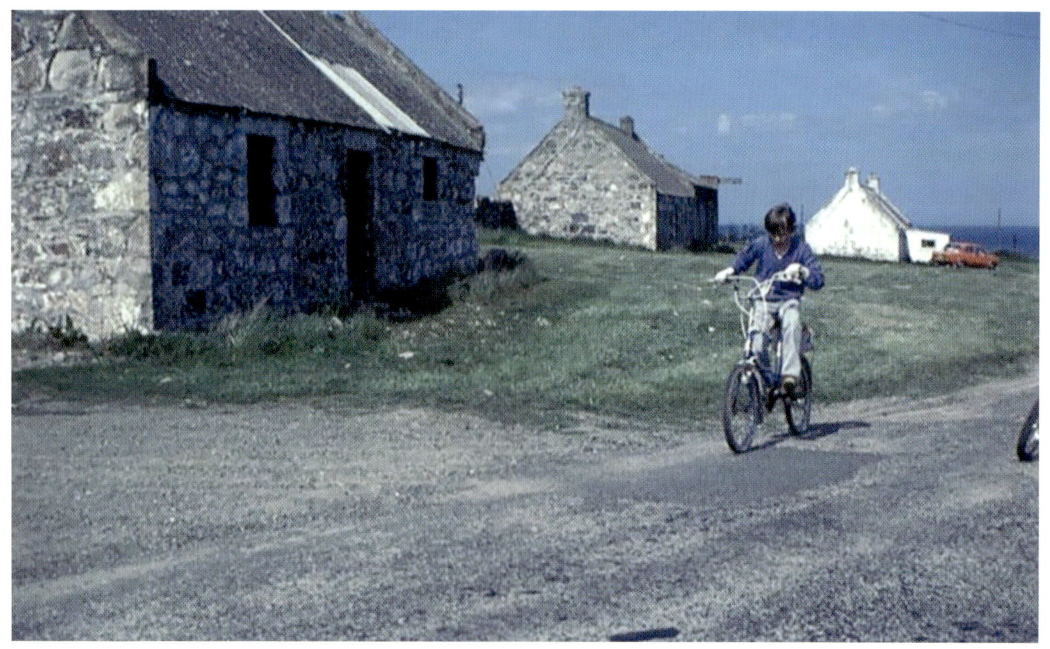

Cycling past in 1981. (Photograph from www.scran.ac.uk)

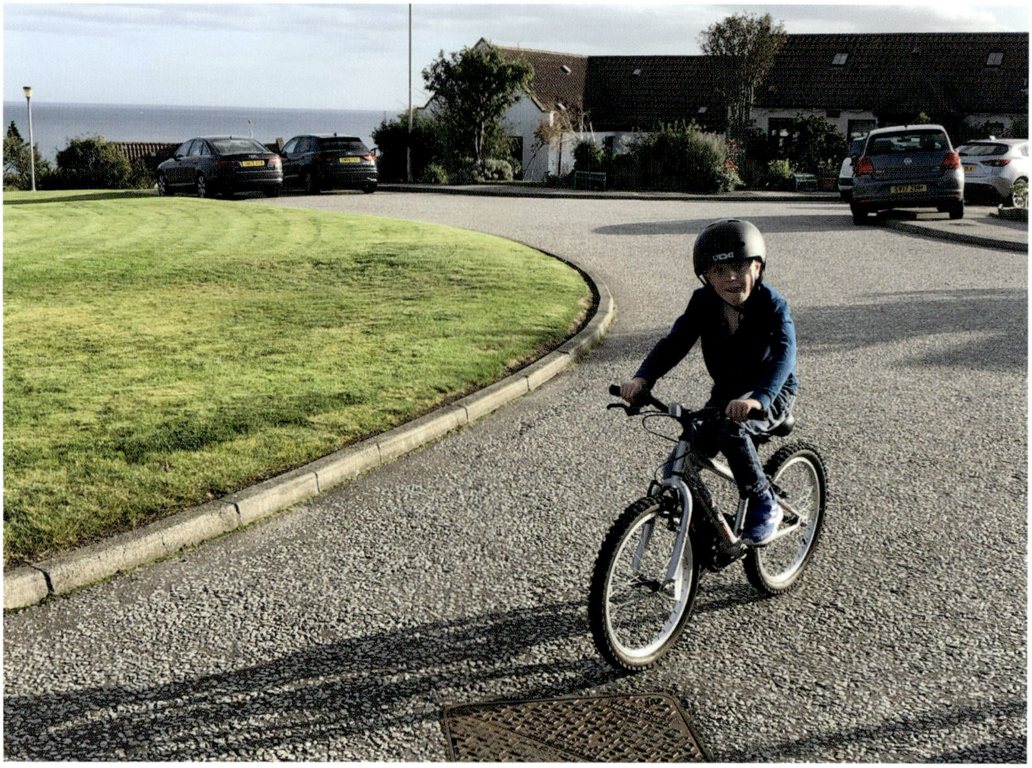

Our son Marco thirty-eight years later in 2019.

26

Is the Village Haunted?

I have never been a believer in the supernatural; I've always viewed any stories with scepticism but I enjoy a good ghost story or film.

If the dead are indeed among us, I have no fear. Why would they want to hurt the living? So why am I bothering to include a section that is obviously nonsense?

Burnbanks was referred to as 'The Ghost Village' in several newspaper articles around the time of the rebuild. The first story concerns Vic Garioch who lived in the village as a child in the 1930s and 1940s. A tale his brother Jack and sister Doreen used to tell him to scare the living daylights out of him was the Glaring Eye'd Mannie fae Burnbanks, a spirit of a long-dead man with a serious limp who dragged his dead leg around the village and groaned loudly about trying to find his house and why was someone else living there? He could be seen looking into windows (with his glaring eye) if there was a light on. Remember that there were no street lamps, no electricity at this time and the village would be jet black.

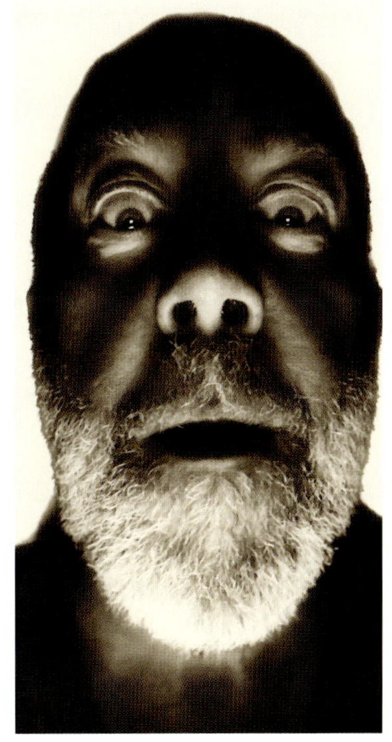

A reconstruction of a Glarin' Eye'd Mannie fae Burnbanks.

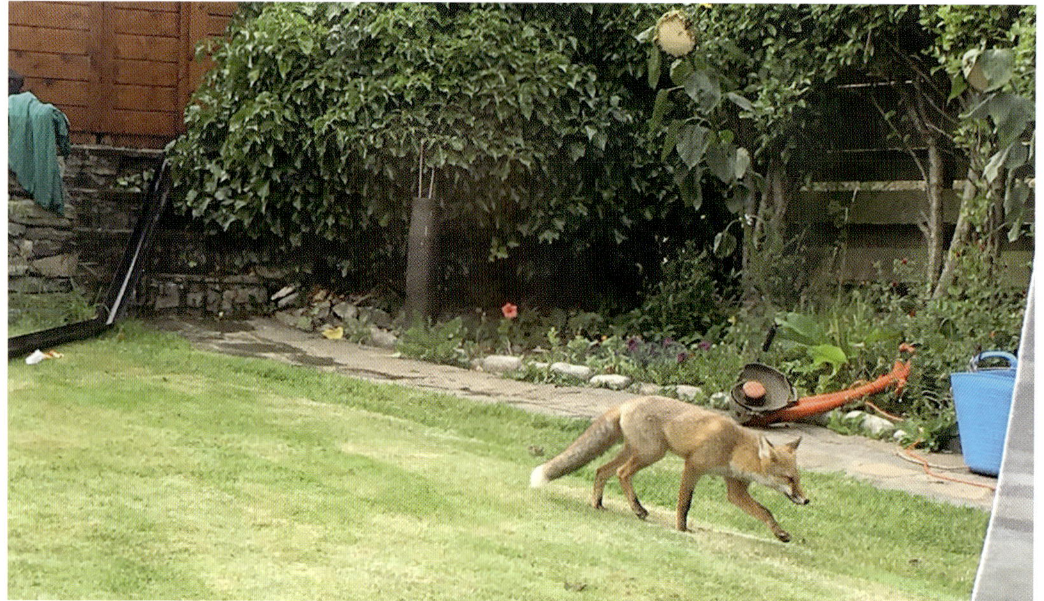

Vic was told that if he didn't go to sleep, he might see the face of the Glaring Eye'd Mannie. What a great story.

Several people who claim to be receptive to the spirit world have made comments that the place has a supernatural aura. One villager claims to have regularly seen a ghost. Others have asked me during the research if anything bad had happened in their house. Of course, it has; no matter where you live, someone has lived and died there before you. All the Burnbanks houses have witnessed childbirth, life and death.

So much death and heartbreak has happened in the village, so if spirit presences do exist, surely an imprint would be left. Have you ever felt someone close to you when you know you are alone, have you ever heard an unusual knock, creak or groan?

We have a small log cabin in the garden and in the summer months, we love to sleep out in it. Perhaps I'm having vivid dreams but now and again, I hear noises that seem so real and so close, so explain to me why does it sounds like someone is talking directly into my ear? And there is no one there.

I know Mr Fox comes past regularly. Here he is in our garden brazenly walking through in broad daylight. He can only bark or growl; he can't speak words, he can't say your name.

When I was looking at the cholera cases, I couldn't find where they were buried and I had a chill thinking 'They're STILL here!' Buried in a communal grave and dealt with so quickly to prevent the spread of infection. Thankfully that turned out to be false and they are mostly in Portlethen Kirkyard.

Many of the deaths have been so sudden, for example the instantaneous deaths on the railway line. Are spirits aware that they have died? So many children have died and one has great pity for wandering spirits of children looking for their parents or siblings.

So many coincidences have happened during this research and sometimes I feel my hand is being guided to find the stories to tell about the people and to remember them.

So, for a non-believer to write this section, one has to ask: Am I really a non-believer or do I just deny what we *all* experience here?

27

Red Herrings

During research for this book I came upon several stories that were not quite true but interesting anyway.

Film Star Cary Grant's Mother Came from Burnbanks Village – No She Didn't

Cary grant was a huge film star in Hollywood's golden era from the 1930s onwards and starred in many successful films including *The Philadelphia Story*, *Bringing Up Baby*, *North by Northwest* and many others.

He was born Archibald Alexander Leach in Bristol, England. On his birth and death certificates, his mother is listed as Elsie Maria Kingdon, who was born in Clifton near Bristol. She had quite a troubled life which has been covered in various biographies.

His parents lost a baby a few years before Archie was born and this affected her greatly. She suffered from depression and mental illness for a great part of her life.

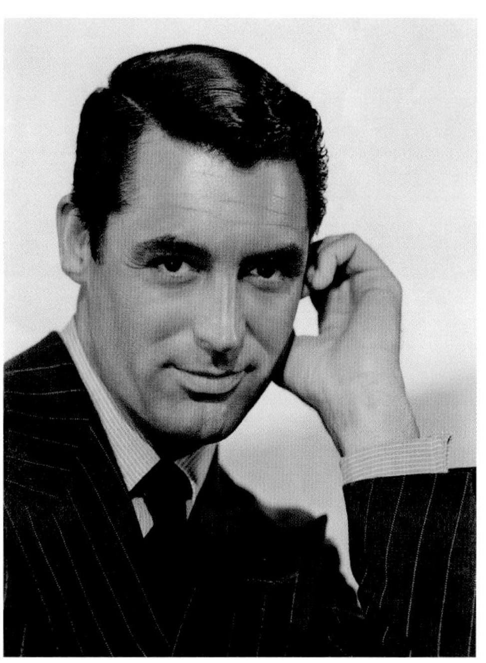

Cary Grant.

She was sectioned when Archie was nine and that was the last he saw of her for a great many years.

His father was noted as a drinker and womaniser and took the opportunity to follow both of these hobbies. He told Archie his mother had gone on a long holiday and was never to return. He was later told that she had died.

Archie didn't find out until he was an adult that she was still alive in a psychiatric hospital 5 miles up the road from the family home. He did his best to look after her but she refused to come to America with him. He provided for her for the rest of her life. She lived until she was ninety-six years old and died in 1973.

A sad story but no links to Burnbanks.

Granny Sim's Brother Was Lost on the *Titanic*

A whole week of searching proved this story was not true but it's a good story anyway. There has never been any other vessel with so much study, and this helped debunk the story. There are published passenger and crew lists, survivors and casualties, crew who joined but left, and people who were booked on but for one reason or another didn't make it.

There are few known links to the north-east of Scotland. The ones I could find were an engineer from the Nairn area, the gymnasium instructor Thomas McCawley (born in Aberdeen), and Quartermaster Hitchens, who was at the helm at the time of the collision and survived the sinking. He's buried in a communal grave in the Trinity Cemetery in Aberdeen after suffering a heart attack aboard a ship close to port in 1940.

So how did this story come about? Chinese whispers, repeated family anecdotes being incorrectly told over time. Dod Sim hurt his arm on a boat and before you know it, the story expanded to him being lost on the *Titanic*.

Again, no links to Burnbanks.

Legendary Celtic Football Club and Scotland Manager Jock Stein Was Born in Burnbanks

No, he wasn't; he was born in Burnbank without an 'S' in South Lanarkshire. Close but once more, no links to Burnbanks.

Witchcraft Rituals Were Performed in Burnbanks

We had a local tradesman, Steve, doing some work on our house and he told us stories of when he was a youngster in the 1980s, hanging around the ruined buildings with his motorbikes and beer. The buildings were empty shells by that time.

Steve's dad then told him to steer clear of Burnbanks Village as there were rumours of witchcraft rituals being performed there – witches and their followers running about in the nuddy and attempting to summon demons. No street lights meant that it would have been a very dark and foreboding place.

There seems to have been no truth to this story; probably just Steve's dad trying to scare some sense into him, but if anyone knows better, please let me know.

28

Burnbanks People

This section covers various short stories.

I feel a close link to the man photographed below. His name is John Main and he served an apprenticeship in the same shipyard as myself, Hall, Russell & Co. of Aberdeen. He went to sea at twenty years old and sailed for many years as a marine engineer, a similar career path to myself. Later in life he was a marine surveyor. He died in 1936 aged seventy-four.

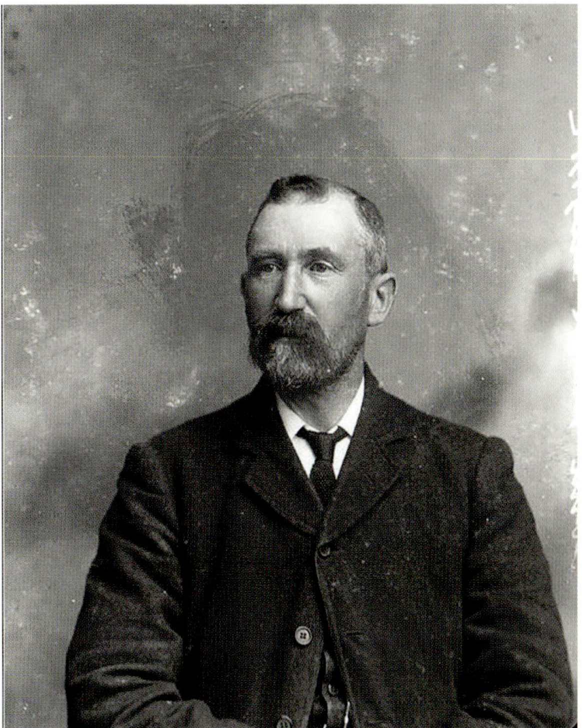

MARINE SURVEYOR
DEAD

Mr John Main: Well Known in Aberdeen Circles

Mr John Main, who was for many years well known in Aberdeen shipping circles, died at his home, 7 Chestnut Row, yesterday, after being ill for some time. He was seventy-four years of age.

Mr Main was born at Burnbanks, near Cove, and was educated at Aberdeen Grammar School. After serving his apprenticeship as an engineer with Messrs Hall, Russell and Co., Ltd., he went to sea when he was twenty years old, in the service of the Newcastle and Hull Steamship Company. In four years' time he had taken his chief's ticket.

The late Mr J. Main

Above left: (Photograph from the Wick Archive)

Above right: (From the Aberdeen Press & Journal, 11 June 1936. Used by kind permission of DC Thomson & Co. Ltd)

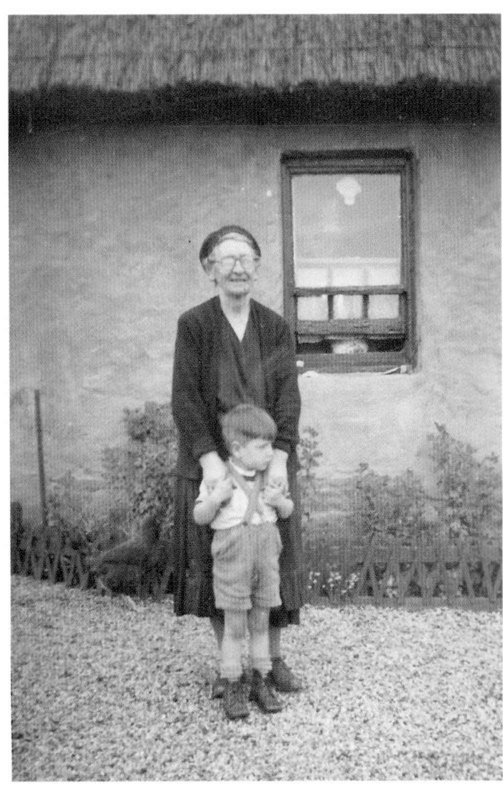

(Photograph courtesy of Moira Ritchie)

This photograph shows Mrs Elizabeth Sim, known as Granny Sim, standing next to John Riddler. She lived in two houses knocked together – one part was the only house in the village with a slate roof, and this helped identify houses from the older photographs.

All other houses were thatched roofs and later ones were just corrugated iron sheets. Another unusual feature about her house was that the outside was painted shocking fluorescent pink. She had a very vicious parrot that terrorised children with screams and a sharp nip. This is now modern Nos 12 and 13. She died in 1958 at the age of seventy-six. She was widowed many years previously in 1921 when her husband Robert died at the age of only forty-one.

The top photograph on the next page shows Mrs Jane Webster with the first TV in the village. At the time this photograph was taken the village didn't have electricity and the TV was supplied by a wind-powered dynamo. The village children would peer into the windows hoping to catch a glimpse of the programmes being shown.

The items in the background are quite interesting: a valve radio and what looks like a family photograph of a large group. I wonder who they were. Mrs Webster lived at No. 7, which is the modern No. 5. Her son was one of the last residents in the village before abandonment in the late 1970s.

The woman on the left is Mrs May Black who lived in the house next door to ours. Her daughter Dorothy Hughes is on the right. The family featured in several adverts over the years selling everything from cars, chickens and what would now be regarded as a classic motorbike, a BSA Empire Star. Her husband Henry was a fish-worker. He died in 1964 at the age of sixty-two. May died in 1970.

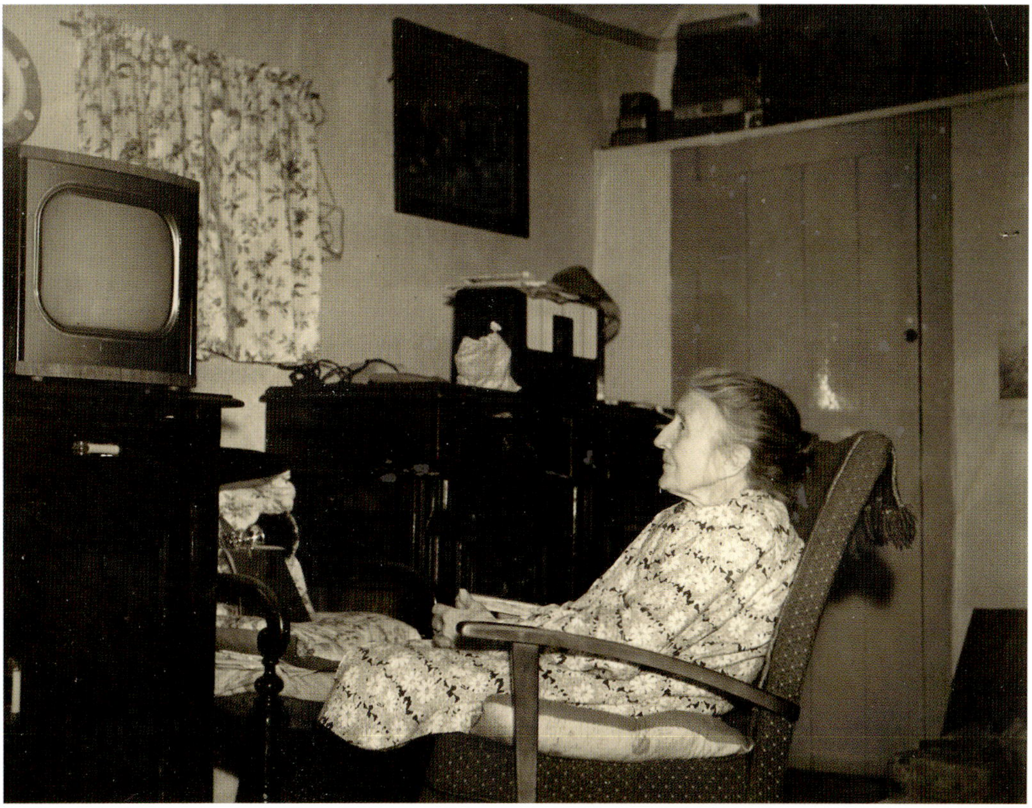

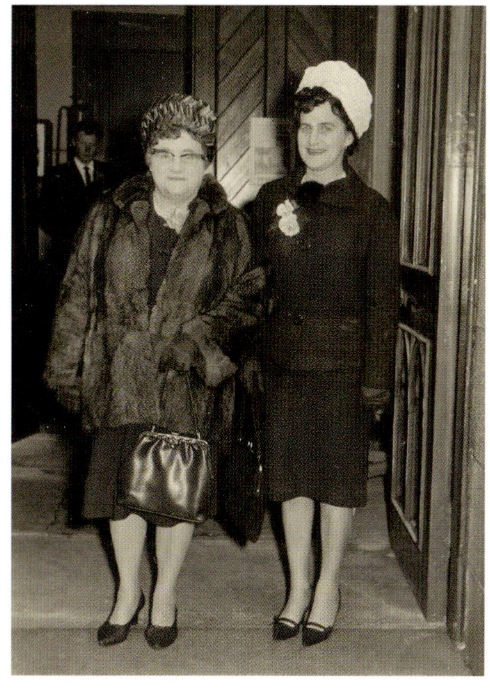

Above: (Photograph courtesy of Dorothy Kirton)

Right: (Photograph courtesy of Dorothy Kirton)

HMS *Clyde* and Cutlass Practice

In Aberdeen harbour an old warship, HMS *Clyde*, was used as a training base for the Royal Naval Reserve. In the 1870s, Burnbanks man George Craig attended four times a year for cutlass practice and was given a retainer of twelve shilling and sixpence each time.

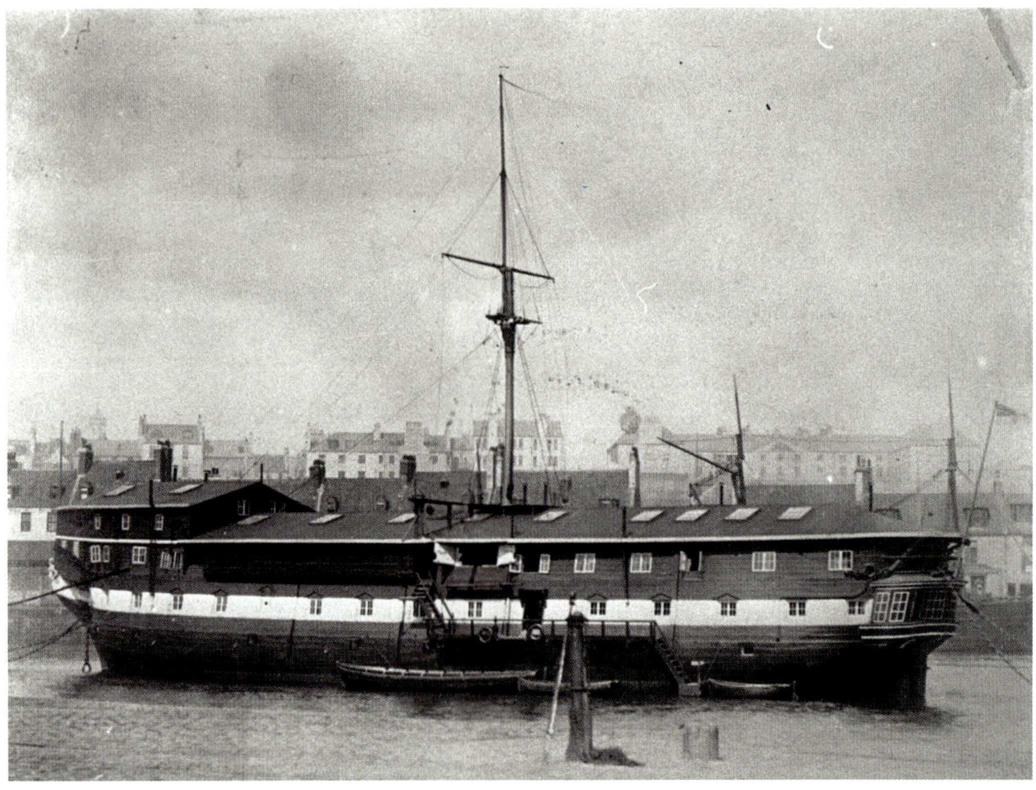

HMS *Clyde*. (Photograph courtesy of Aberdeen City Library)

(From the National Archives)

146

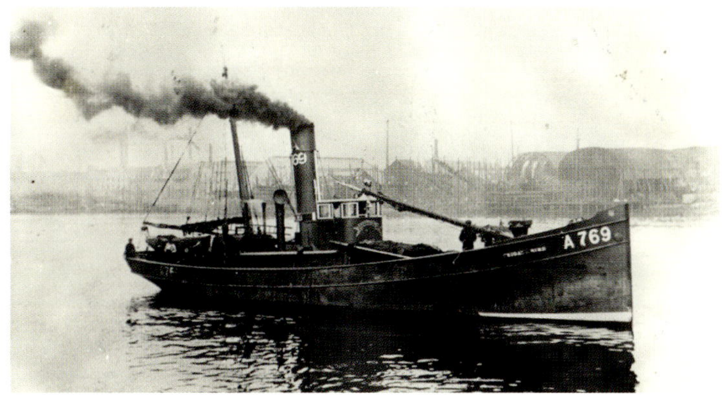

This is the *Frigate Bird* from the Wilfred Dodds collection. (Courtesy of Lancashire County Council's Red Rose Collections)

The vessel shown above was built in the Hall Russell shipyard in Aberdeen and was an identical vessel to the first Burnbanks trawler discussed in another chapter.

Old Sailors

During the First World War, many fishing vessels were taken up by the Royal Navy to perform patrol duties or be converted to minesweepers. The National Maritime Museum lists SEVEN men born in Burnbanks who became skippers of these vessels:

John Leiper, skipper of *Phalarope*
George Craig, skipper of *Premier* and *Betty Inglis*
George Main, *Frigate Bird*
Joseph Main, *Craigievar*
Andrew Craig, *Volunteer*
Alexander Main, *Strathban*
Robert Craig, *Chancellor*

Skipper George Main (1859–1938)

Skipper George Main was born in Burnbanks. His family lived in No. 11, which is modern No. 13. His wife Mary Main (1860–1928) was also born in Burnbanks and they were married in 1882.

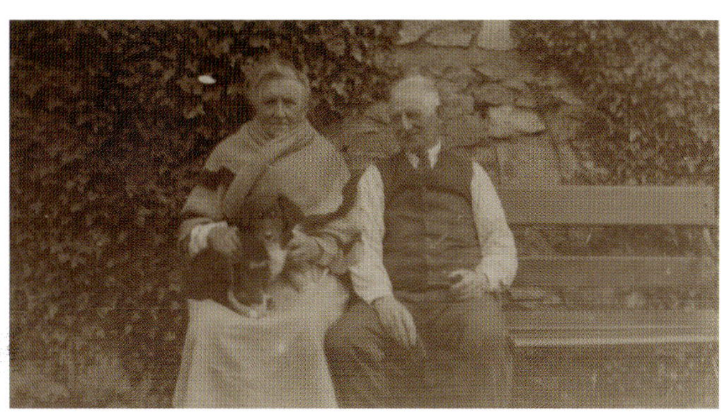

George Main and Mary Main. (Photograph courtesy of John King)

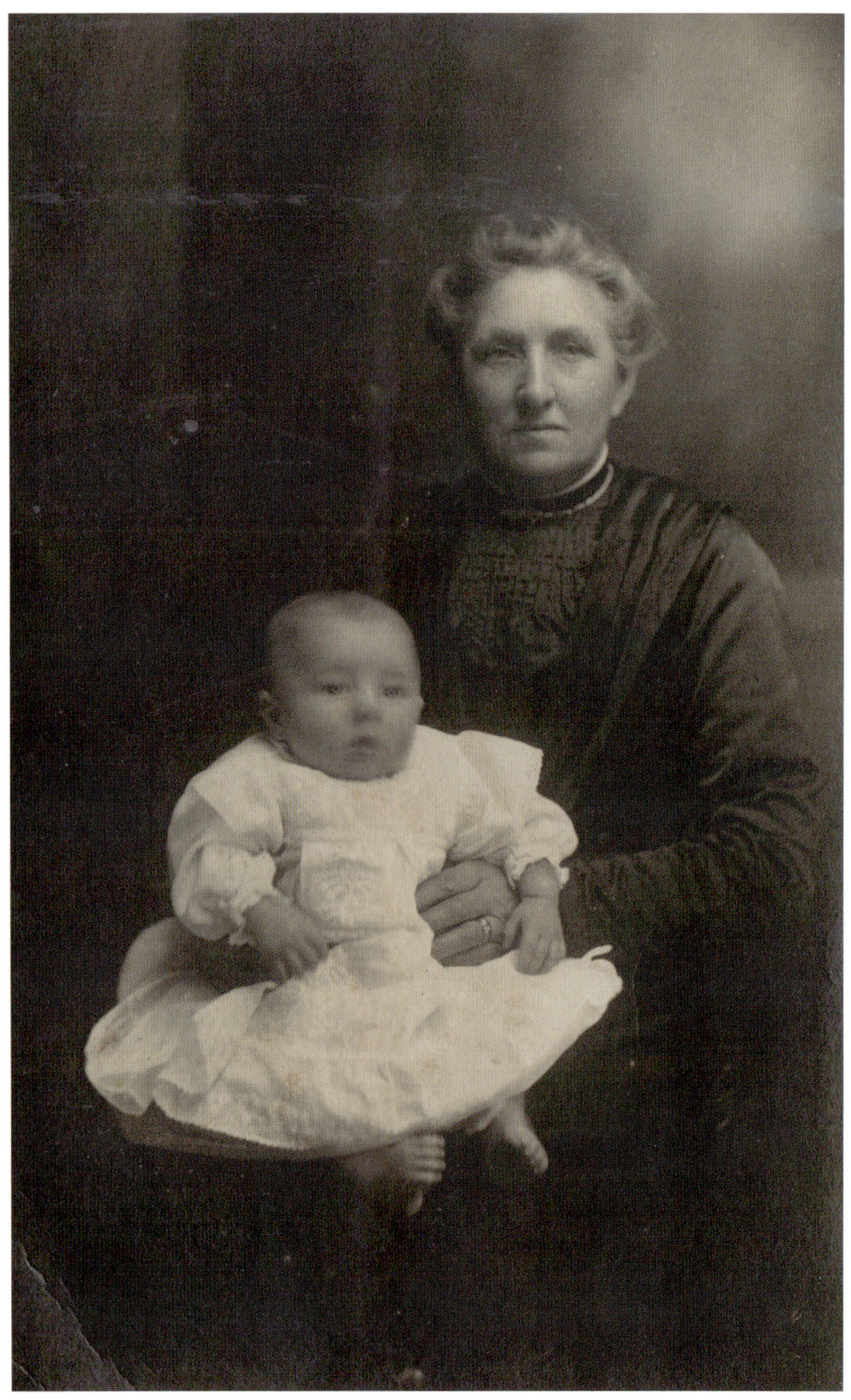

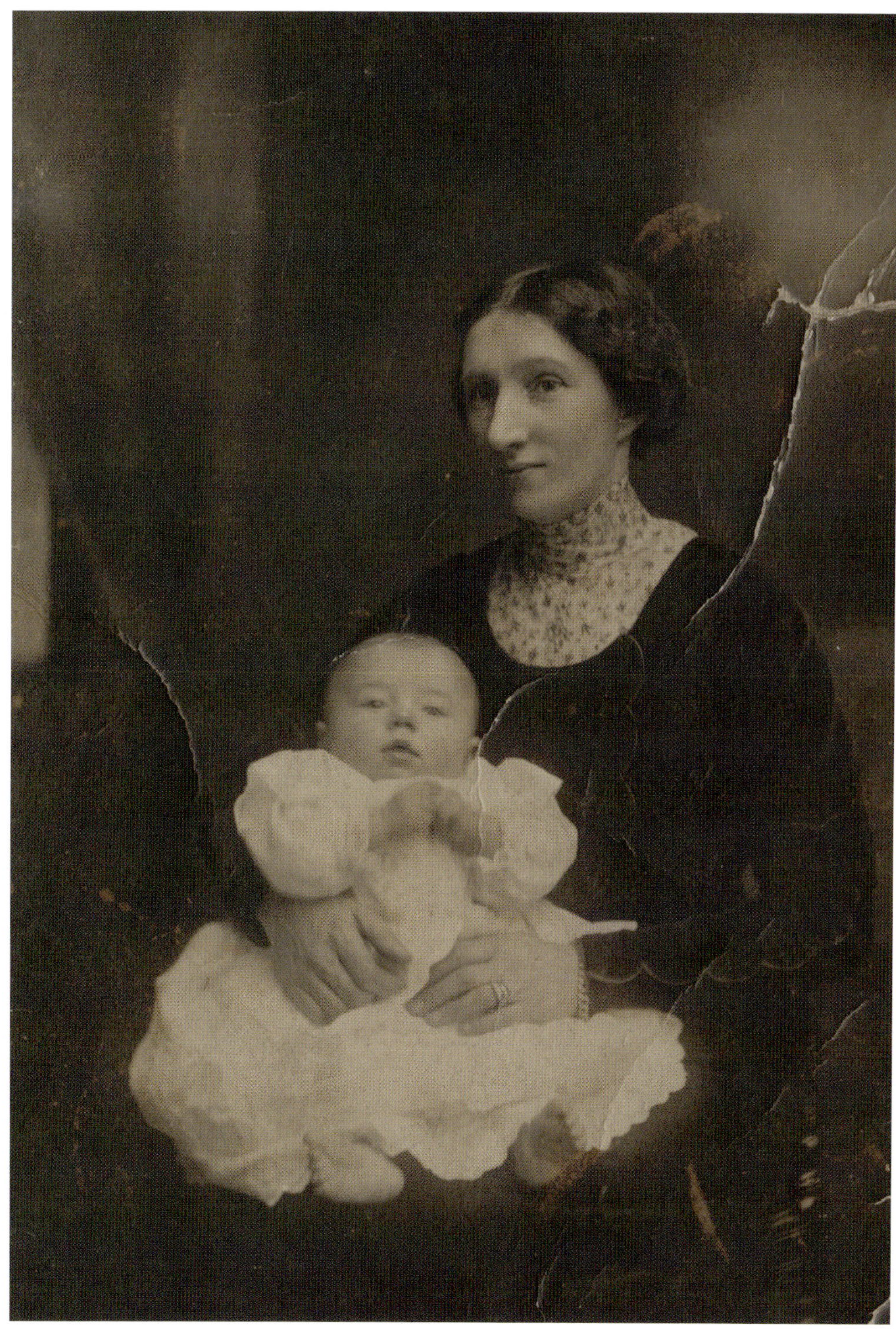

These photographs show Mary Main and daughter Jane, with her son John George Main King. Jane was born in the village in 1884. (Both courtesy of John King, the son of the child in the picture)

Old Soldiers

Alexander Campbell

Alexander passed away at the age of ninety-eight in 1930 and was buried in Nigg Kirkyard. He lived in Burnbanks for twenty-three years and was well known locally.

He had a distinguished military career which began when he ran away at seventeen years old. He seems to have had an alias of William Rogers when he was in the army, perhaps to try and avoid being taken back by his family. He was the last surviving member of the Highland Light Infantry that was involved in the Indian Mutiny.

During the Crimean War of 1853–56 he witnessed the famous Charge of the Light Brigade at Balaclava. He was wounded at the Siege of Sebastopol when a Cossack sabered him in the hand.

When the Aberdeen City War Memorial was opened at the Cowdray Hall in 1925, he was part of the guard of honour at ninety-two years old. He was presented to King George V who complimented him on looking so well. Film footage exists of the King inspecting the guard of honour, but I'm unable to identify Alexander.

The local press commented that he was always first to vote on election days, walking 2 miles from Burnbanks to the polling station.

Heartbreak visited his home many times: one grandchild, Henry Nairn, was killed after falling off the Burnbanks cliffs; another, Jeanie Deans, died at three years old of diphtheria.

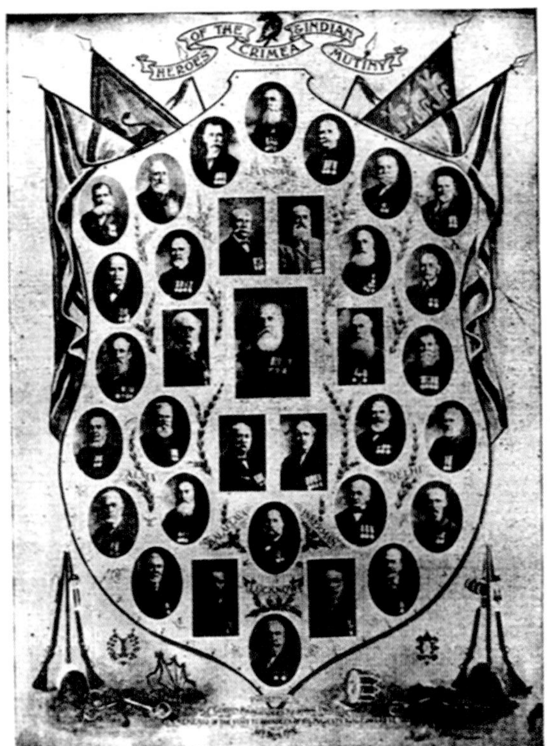

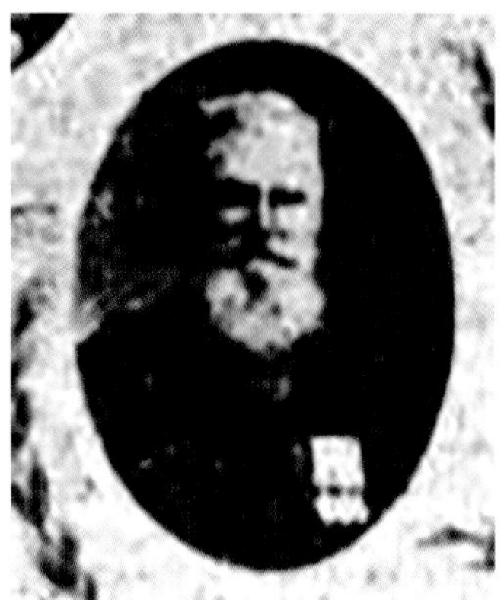

Above: A blurred photograph taken from a commemorative shield for the Crimean War.

Left: Shield from the British Newspaper Archive. (Used by kind permission of DC Thomson & Co. Ltd)

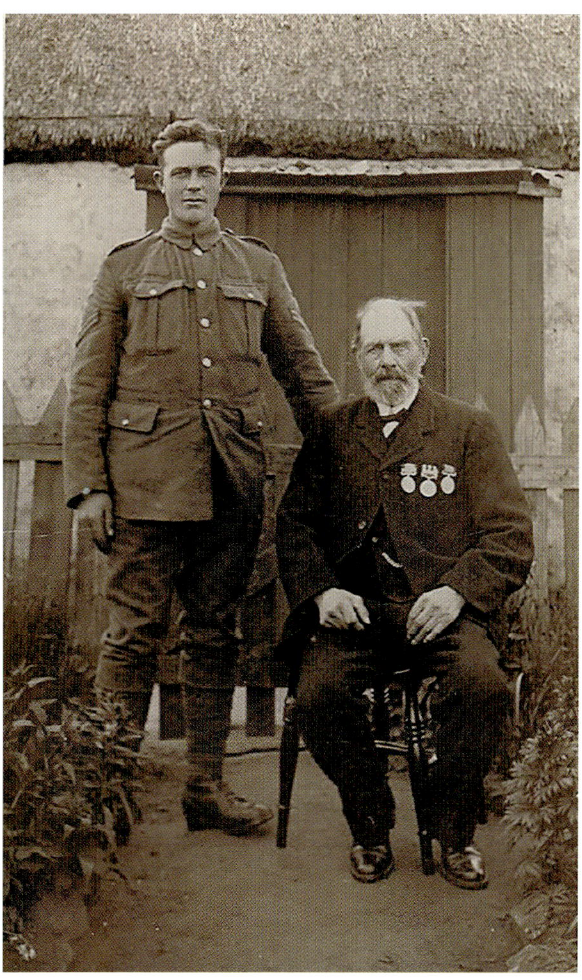

Henry Duncan and Sam Duncan.

His daughter Helen married James Coutts who was lost on the *Norwood*.

This photograph is listed as being Henry Duncan on the left and Sam Duncan but I have a feeling this may be Alexander Campbell. The wounded hand and three medals with five clasps seems to fit.

First Day at School

There are currently two primary schools that serve the Cove area: Charleston School and Loirston School.

Before the 1980s the Cove School was in a different building which is now used as a community building and there is an After School Club which our son Marco attended.

Aberdeen City Archives hold school enrolment records dating back to 1870s and they are a great resource that give so much data. Seeing names of people that are covered in stories in this book and noting that one day, many years ago they were the same as our

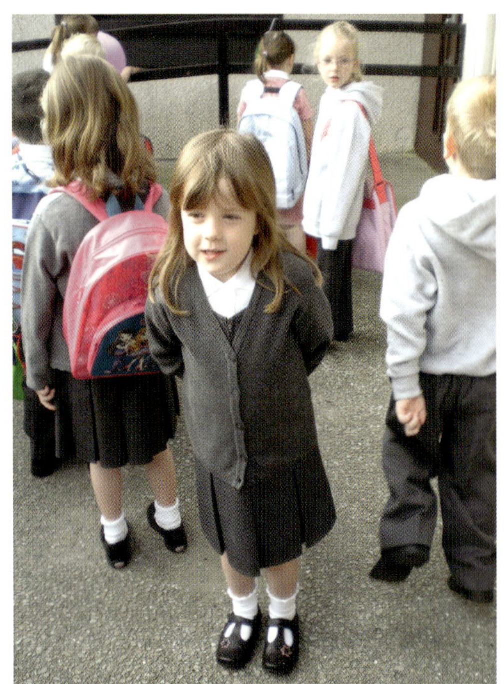

Left: Here's a photo of our daughter Christina on her first day at Loirston School August 2007.

Below: Comparing shoes with our neighbour Chiaran Duncan.

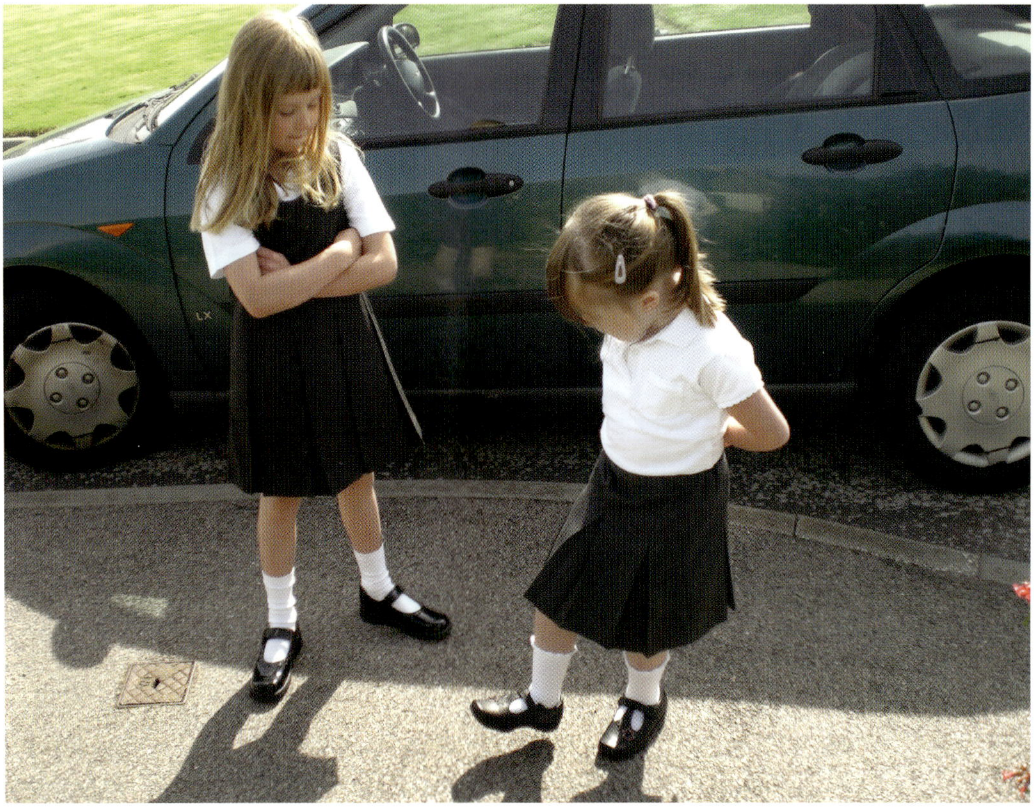

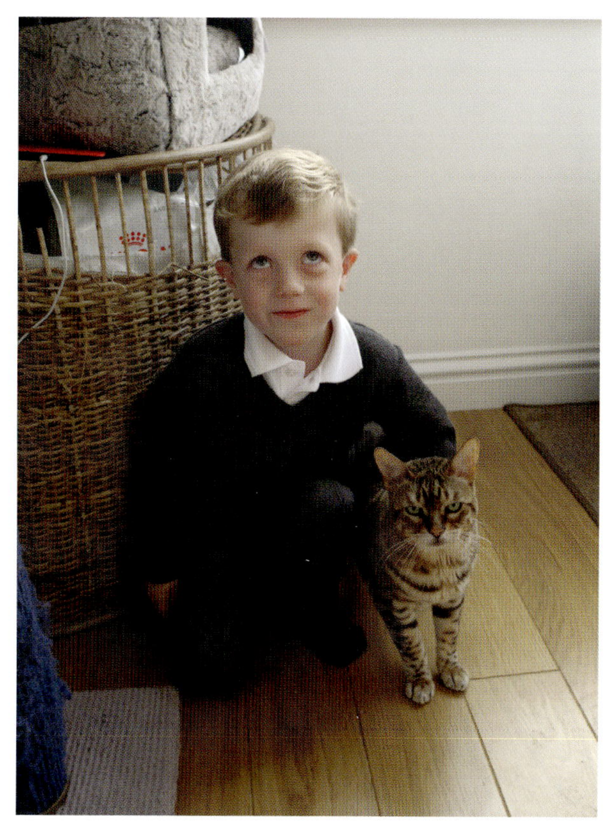

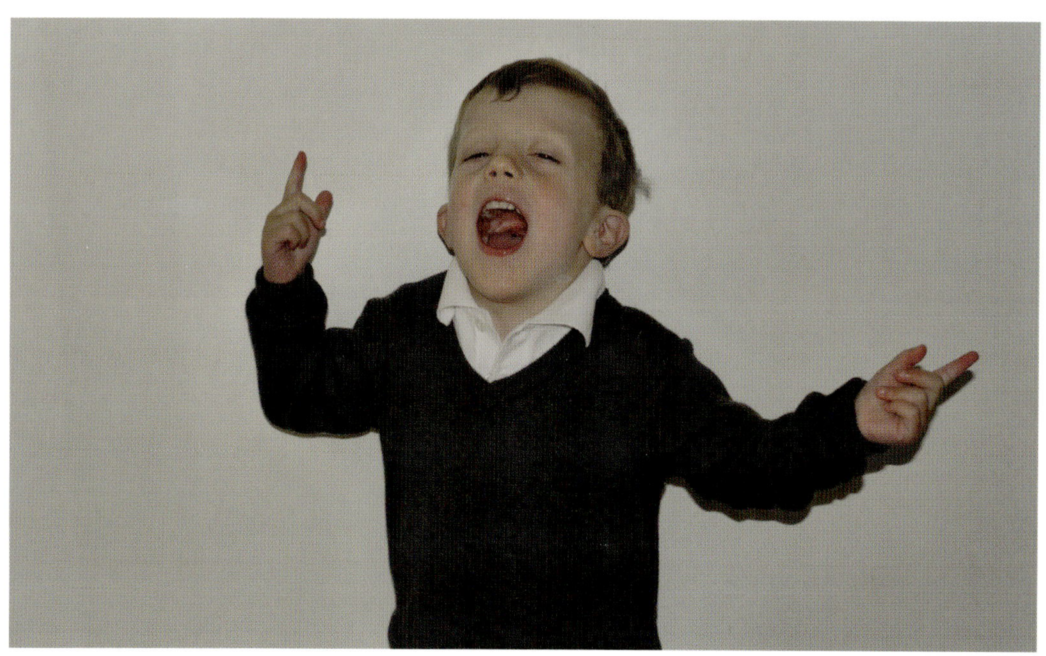

Here's Marco's first day in 2013.

kids, their first day at school and excited to be there. Signed in by parents to the same place we visit every day and that fact is not lost on us as we go through the same doors to the same place but separated by 100 years.

The records are so useful as they can show where a family came from or went without the ten-year gap of census. They can detail how many children were in a family.

Names that I found in the records included the first day at school for John Taylor Robertson and Freddie Beattie, both casualties of war; the bigamist's first wife, Roselina Will; Charles Duncan, who emigrated to Canada; his sister Jessie Duncan; Ida Robertson; and Elizabeth Duncan, who became James Coutts' second wife.

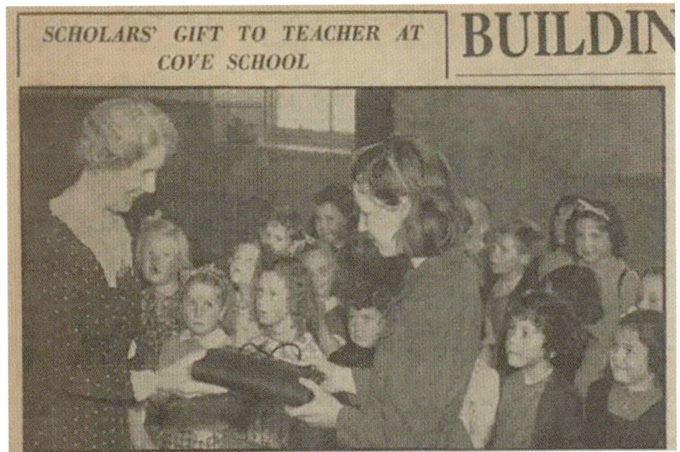

1 July 1944. Miss Mary Crombie, a teacher at Cove School for thirty-three years who was retiring, is presented with a handbag and cash gift by Helen Guyan, senior girl dux on behalf of the scholars. Former pupils and parents also recognised Miss Crombie's work with parting gifts of a wireless and a table. (Photograph from Aberdeen Journals Ltd. Used by kind permission of DC Thomson & Co. Ltd)

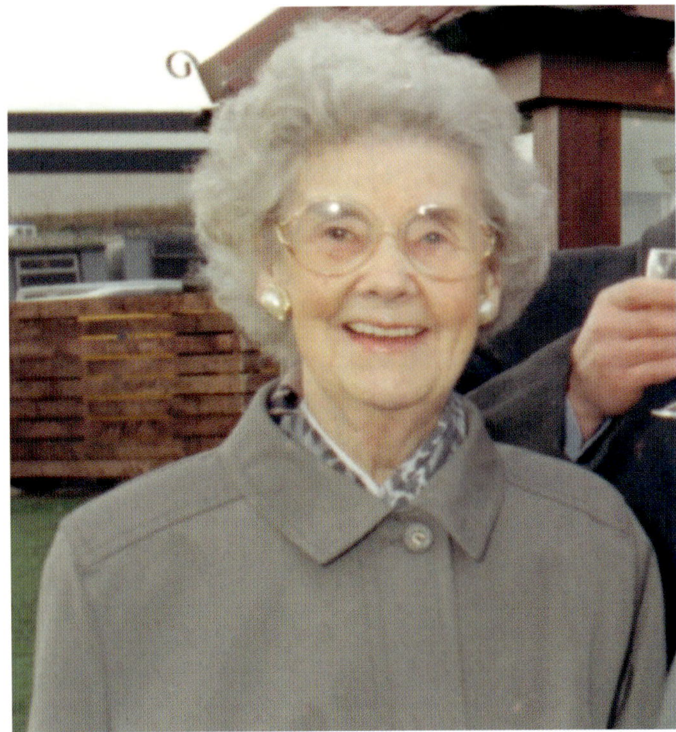

This is Ida Robertson, born in 1906. Her parents were Mitchell and Mary Robertson who lived in old No. 19 Burnbanks Village, modern No. 7. One of her brothers was John Taylor Robertson who died three weeks before the end of the First World War. Ida was one of the villagers who visited during the rebuild.

The Prisoner of War – Andrew Simpson Duncan, 1918–93

Every family suffers bereavement and heartache at some time but we all know families that seem to receive one cruel smack in the chops after another.

The Duncan family who lived in Burnbanks before the Second World War seemed to be suffering so much in a short period of time although I'm sure this wasn't an unusual occurrence during wartime.

In January 1939, Arthur Duncan married Jessie Bruce at the Nigg Kirk Manse. Only one week later Arthur's father, William Duncan, died in Aberdeen Royal Infirmary at the age of only fifty-eight. His wife, Janet Duncan (née Simpson), moved away from Burnbanks, a mile up the road to Cove to live with her daughter in Catto Crescent. Their son Andrew, who was born in Burnbanks, became a prisoner of war in 1940 when the Gordon Highlanders were forced to surrender at St Valéry-en-Caux when they became separated from the British Expeditionary Force during the retreat and evacuation at Dunkirk. Janet died suddenly a day before the surrender at only fifty-six years old, the cause of death is stated as simply 'Natural Causes'.

Andrew appeared in a photograph sent home along with other unidentified Prisoners of War.

The book by Stewart Mitchell, *St Valéry and Its Aftermath*, gives details of the Gordons capture, transportation to prisoner of war camps in Poland and Germany and covers the life of the POWs, their escapes and eventual release and return home. Andrew was incarcerated in the Lamsdorf camp, which is now called Łambinowice in Poland.

As the war was nearing an end in January 1945, Russian forces were advancing towards German-held territory. The Germans gathered prisoners of war in groups of 200–300 and marched west towards central Germany in what became known as the Long March. Several books have been published on this and give greater detail.

It is unclear which route Andrew took but he was back home and married Margaret Gill on 26 May 1945, very soon after VE Day. He died in Aberdeen in 1993.

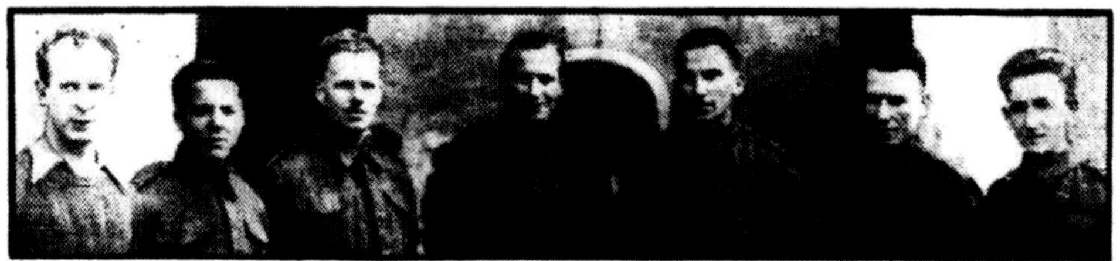

In this group of prisoners of war at Oflag VIIC is Private Andrew S. Duncan (third from left) whose parents, the late Mr and Mrs William Duncan, resided at Burnbank, Nigg. Shortly after he was reported a prisoner of war his mother died at 12 Catto Crescent, Cove Bay, where she went to live on the death of her husband. Readers will perhaps recognise Pte. Duncan's comrades.

(From Aberdeen Journals. Used by kind permission of DC Thomson & Co. Ltd)

The Last Wedding in the Village

This one came as a surprise but up to 2020, we were the last to be married from the village in 1999. There has been no one since.

Barry and Laura Craig were married overseas in April 2016 but we were the last to leave from here.

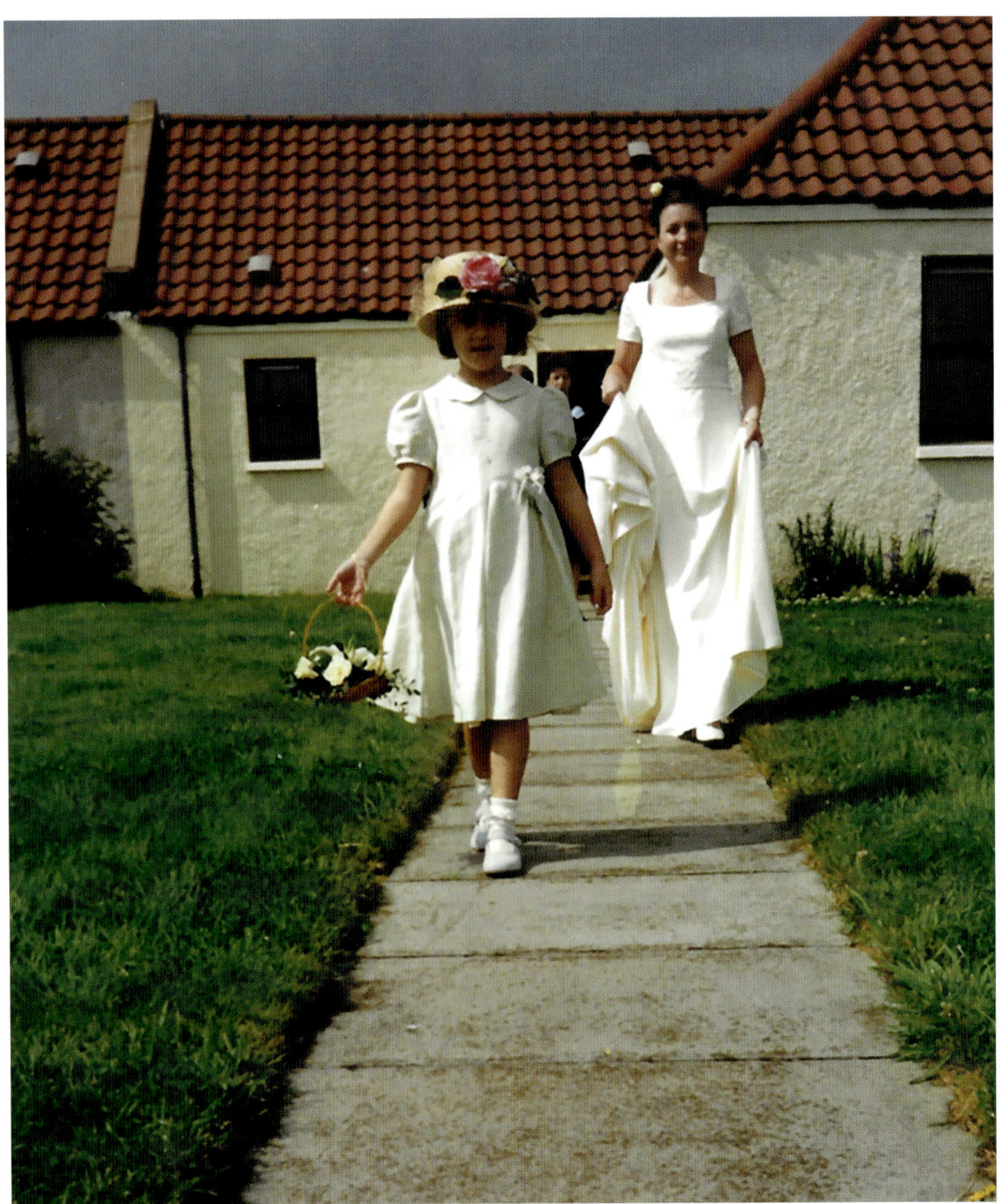

Our niece Brenda was our flower girl.

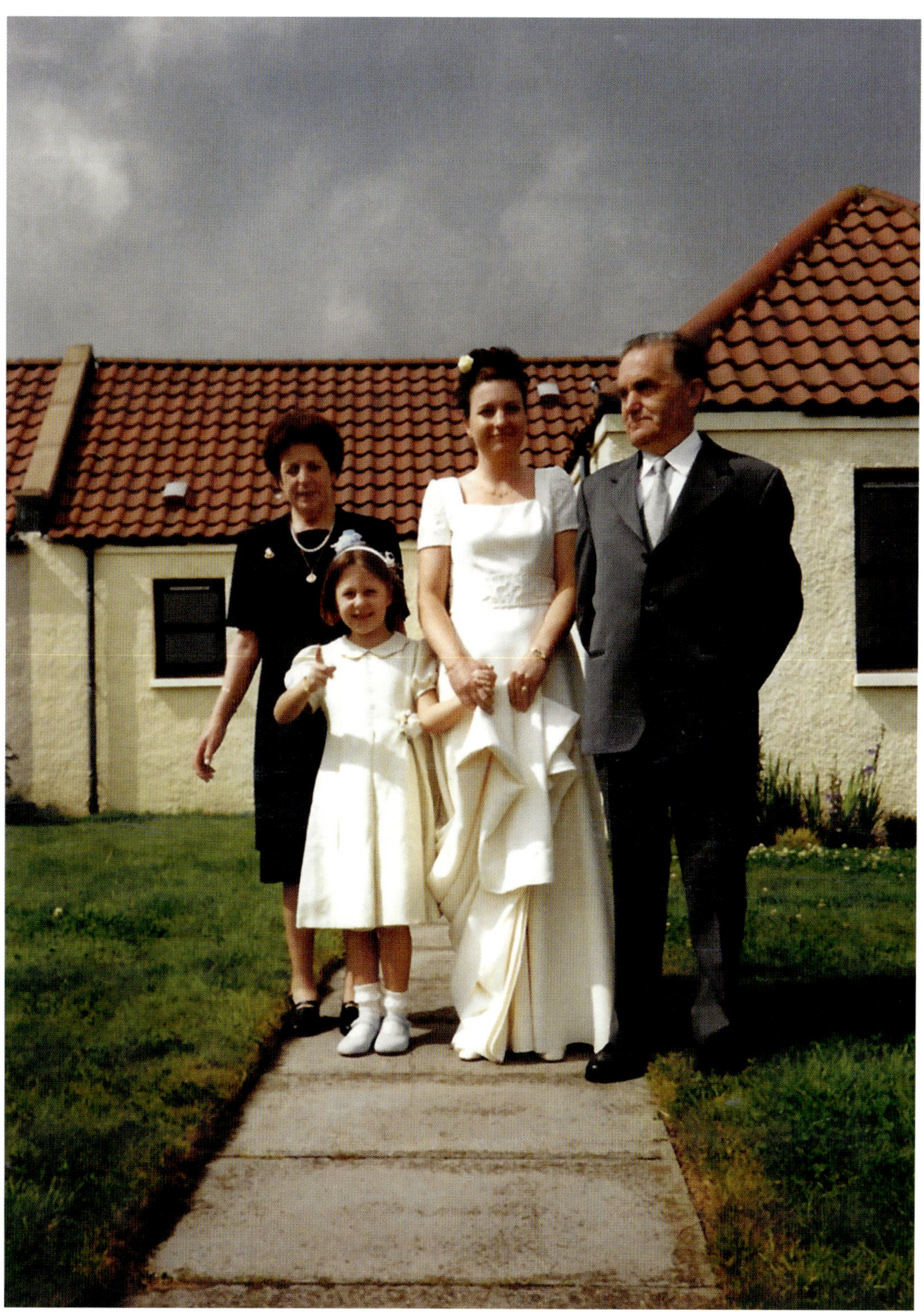

Rosa's Mum and Dad, Flora and Isidoro.

My Favourite Photograph

The photograph below is from Jake Beattie. The girl on the bike is his sister Dorothy and in my opinion it's the best one I have found with the entire project. To me it says so much about village life before the abandonment.

There are so many significant details: a derelict shell of a house in the background, thatched roofs replaced with corrugated iron, storm porches at the front of the houses and an external electric light on the extreme left.

The light can assist with dating the photograph from the early 1960s, as before then there was no electricity.

Our house is located in between the second and third chimney stacks from the left.

In the foreground is a cart with a barrel, hose and stainless-steel bucket. This was the village's water supply as it had no mains running water. Fresh water was drawn from a well in a field across the road and distributed amongst the villagers.

The ex-villagers I spoke to were very clear that conditions may seem basic to an outsider but they were happy and healthy and have very fond memories of their time in the village.

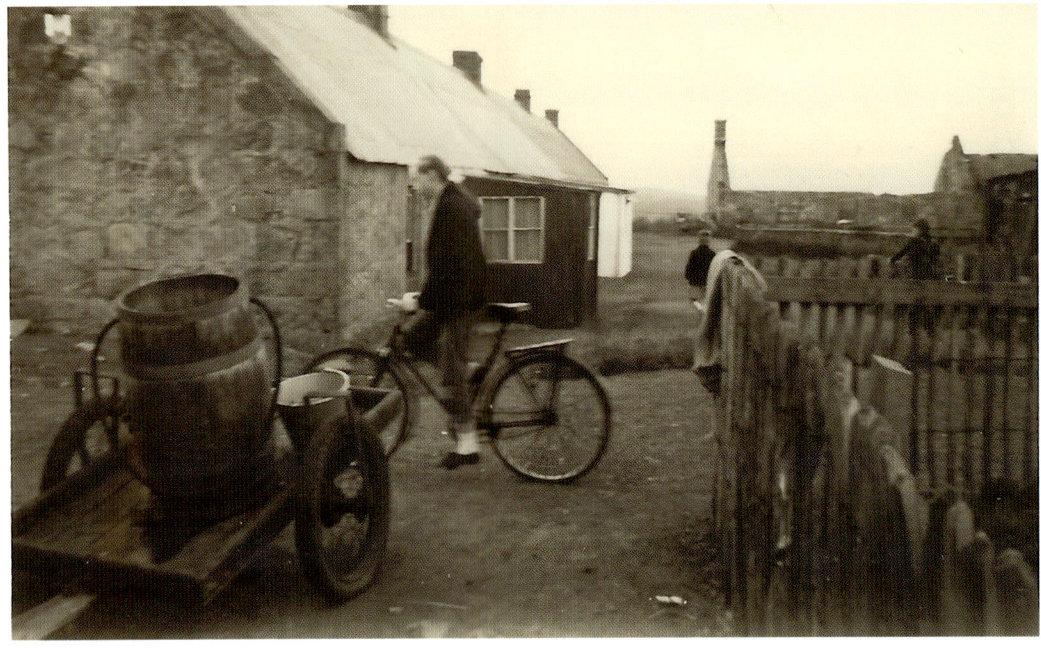

Sources and Acknowledgements

Where possible, I have listed ownership and credits for all photographs and maps. I apologise for any errors. Information sources are listed below.

People

Dorothy (Beattie) Kirton – the girl on the bike
Jake Beattie – the sodjer on the BSA Bantam
Moira (Riddler) Ritchie – last kid growing up in the village
Moira Beattie – Daughter of David Beattie and niece of Freddie
David Geddes – Champion of the SS *Norwood*
Gary Thomas – Aberdeen Journals archives
Anne Park – Local History legend
Vic Garioch
George Wood
Louisa Low
Douglas Gray – author of *Cove Bay: A History*

The current Burnbanks villagers. Always interested, always supportive.
So many other people.
My family, especially Rosa – proofreader and listening to all the stories and discussions.

Websites

www.britishnewspaperarchive.co.uk – An incredible resource. Impossible to do this project without it.
www.ancestry.co.uk – The best genealogy.
www.scotlandspeople.gov.uk – Birth, marriage and death certificates for Scotland, and valuation rolls.
www.deceasedonline.com – UK Burials and cremations.
https://billiongraves.com – Worldwide details of graves, pictures of headstones and a GPS locator to find the grave you're looking for.
www.aberdeenships.com
www.findmypast.co.uk
www.cwgc.org – The Commonwealth War Graves Commission.

Institutions

Aberdeen City Archives
Aberdeen Maritime Museum
University of Aberdeen Special Collections
Aberdeen City Libraries, especially David Oswald
The Deeside Field 1929 edition for the article by William Leiper – The Fishing Industry
  of Aberdeen Fifty Years ago
National Records of Scotland
National Archives
National Maritime museum
Royal Commission for Ancient and Historic Monuments Scotland
The Gordon Highlanders Museum, Aberdeen
The Highlanders' Museum at Fort George for First World War diaries
National Collection of Aerial Photography – NCAP
National Library of Scotland
Ebay

Other Writers

Casualty recovery online articles refer to www.1914-1918.net, or articles regarding
Battlefield Clearance by Terry Carter or the highly detailed writings of Peter Hodgkinson.

Stewart Mitchell, *St Valéry and Its Aftermath* – the story of the Gordon Highlanders'
capture in France in 1940.